PEERS IN PARLIAMENT REFORMED

PEERS IN PARLIAMENT REFORMED

William Wyndham

Quiller Press

For HP

First published 1998 by
Quiller Press Limited,
46 Lillie Road,
London SW6 1TN

Copyright © 1998 William Wyndham

ISBN 1 899163 43 3

Designed by Jo Lee
Printed by Biddles Ltd

CONTENTS

FOREWORD

William Wyndham's book on the future of the House of Lords could not be appearing at a more timely moment. A thoughtful and original contribution to the debate on the reform of Parliament, it must surely be heeded by all who feel that to keep the *status quo* is no longer possible. My own doubts about the present composition of the House of Lords were strengthened when I tried to explain the way it works to a group of refugees from what was then Communist East Germany in 1990; their astounded faces seemed to say that, if this is what the West is really like, we had better jump back over the Wall as quickly as possible. Reform of the Second Chamber is clearly a necessity but, as William Wyndham says, it must be reform that means more, not less, independence and democracy.

Egremont

Lord Egremont

PREFACE

This book was conceived on the night of May Day 1997 at the prospect of a New Labour government beginning with a huge majority, a full exchequer – and nowhere to go. For it had inherited also the Thatcher legacy of a Westminster Parliament which was both submerged by government systematically out of control and wholly unable to cope with globalisation in general and the European Union in particular.

Labour seemed then and has shown itself now obsessed by fripperies. Beyond the removal of the hereditary peers in the House of Lords from both sitting and the vote, it had no clear plans for the reform of Parliament. Devolution, in particular the creation of Scottish and Welsh Parliaments, was itself regarded as a side-show (now wall-papered) of Westminster, somewhere next door to parish councils. The restoration of Parliamentary government and the continuation of a United Kingdom in a setting that fulfils the aspirations of its constituent nations were concepts far beyond the new government's powers of perspective.

Round Big Ben's neck hangs a dome-shaped placard, 'in restauro' – but it is the restoration of the pick-axe.

This is a restoration programme of another sort. It looks at what the Lords do, could do and what without reform they cannot do, in order to restore Parliament to its rightful position balancing government and representing our varied people. It then proposes changes to integrate Parliament's influence on government into a single process from policy-making to implementation.

Constitutional reform can only be looked at in the round. That gives an unlimited choice of entry, provided that one never loses sight of the whole. Wanting a review of the whole machinery of British government, I chose the House of Lords. The initial reason was simply that whatever the new government had neither the will nor the vision to do, change to the House of Lords was both long overdue and inevitable. For that at least was thought easy by a government wedded to papering over cracks so as to avoid making the 'hard decisions' which serious reform requires.

But my inquiry has led me to believe my choice was serendipity. As I have gone along I found myself moving ever further from the conclusion in Ferdinand Mount's inspirational book, *The British Constitution Now* (Heinemann 1992). He thought, then at any rate, that rational reform of the Lords must come after reform of the Commons, which he and most political commentators (see eg Peter

Riddell's *Parliament Under Pressure* (Gollancz 1998) have long thought equally essential.

In seeking a scheme for reform of the Second Chamber which would both strengthen it and complement House of Commons, I have found that much of what goes with the one would sauce the other as well. Many of the changes needed to support and extend the House of Lords' present scope without even disturbing its structure could be as easily and profitably be introduced into the Commons, because they relate to the effective performance of Parliament as a whole. To some degree therefore what started out as a look at the Lords in isolation ends as a case study with ideas that others could apply to the Commons, for the purpose of encouraging the co-operation of the two Houses.

But this conclusion goes only in fact part of the way. It applies only to those changes which could be made without dramatic institutional reform. Here is another reason for starting with the Lords. Some of the ideas advocated here for the Lords are already being proposed in inchoate form by Ann Taylor, the Leader of the Commons, for the Commons; and, because they require no structural change, they could easily be extended in both Houses.

With a complementary Second Chamber, such as advocated here, those changes to the Commons for them might be enough, with minor titivations such as some decrease in the number of MPs and certainly of ministers in the Commons and other constitutional safeguards (which the Lords should have a part in) such as the regulation of referendums (their use and practice).

A complementary Second Chamber – this is the nub. A weak House of Lords has suited both governments and the House of Commons only too well. For there has been an assumed premise, all the more powerful for being unspoken, that any increase in the effectiveness of the Lords is *ipso facto* a weakening of government and/or the Commons. This premise is false. It depends on following a mistaken fashion: reformers have mistakenly concentrated on powers and membership of the Second Chamber, almost to the exclusion of a serious consideration of its functions.

This has been particularly unfortunate. Discussion of the Second Chamber's powers always puts the Commons on the defensive; discussion of its membership troubles the Lords. Meanwhile it had escaped everyone's attention that the solution to the need for two complementary Houses of Parliament was to hand. A vigorous and self-sown sapling was growing under the old tree. For the Lords were already beginning, quietly and without fuss, a gentle revolution.

Government is in truth a unitary and organic process from policy formation through legislation to executive and administrative action. Parliament as a whole has to be attuned to this whole process; but it is both illogical and divisive for both Houses to attempt all parts of it.

An extension of the Lords' current committee work, adequately supported by research and other staff and not hampered by Whitehall's self-serving grip on government information, could transform the Lords' effectiveness – provided it is seen what their function should be, what their effectiveness is for.

It is not suggested that their revising role of government legislation would much change. (No government seems to want that.) But if their main sphere of activity beyond that was seen to be limited to medium-term policy and to administration and not to include current government finance and policy, except insofar as necessitated by their broader perspective, the impasse with the Commons would, with good will on both sides, be overcome.

This approach dictated an investigation of Lords reform in two distinct steps. First what the Lords do, have done and could do, was considered in the light both of history and of current imperatives. Most of what is needed to put back Parliament into the centre of the picture, as the mediator between government and people, can be done by giving the Lords their heads (instead of striking them off), especially if the Commons in their sphere follow suit. The Lords have among their number, hereditaries, life peers and *ex officios*, a breadth and depth of expertise – and an independent-mindedness – that far exceeds the Commons. That is a resource not to be lost to the public by knee-jerk populism.

Simultaneously, the resulting increase in the Lords' workload made necessary a review of the practicalities of Parliamentarians' support. An extension of what is already in place requires a Parliamentary secretariat and a fair allocation of research assistance. The civil service is a government preserve. That makes fair Parliamentary scrutiny of government policy and administration an impossibility.

But what is left after a Lords' job-description of this kind is defined cannot be done without institutional reform. Regardless of their performance in the Chamber, the right of the hereditaries to take up their seat regardless of merit or election is unacceptable – has been, perhaps, for a full century. It is even, I think, unwise to allow such a large proportion, the life peers, to arrive by party-political and prime ministerial appointment. Both methods of filling the Upper Chamber ignore the public's new confidence instilled by the media (by TV above all). The people will no longer tolerate representation by a House made up of members in whose composition they have had no say, whatever their competence and good will.

This mental block, healthy in itself, has not only obscured the Lords' contribution and potential, it has precipitated the fall in public estimation of Parliament as a whole. And it has frustrated Parliament's natural powers of regeneration.

No fair appraisal of the Lords' performance or potential can be made without conceding at the outset that most peers, voting peers anyhow, whether hereditary or life peers, must submit to some kind of election. But once that concession is made, democratic dogma can sit back and relax. For the Lords' current type of casting can in fact be extended to fit the bill, for most of the play.

But not for devolution within the Union and continuing membership of the European Union. For both of these strategic issues Parliament as a whole, and its structures, are, so far, unprepared.

The Lords' theoretical claim to be the organ at Westminster that unifies the UK by taking account of national Parliaments and to be the Parliamentary channel of communication with the EU and beyond is guaranteed by logic and past performance – and by the implications of the very electoral reforms that the Lords' imbalance demands. By happy coincidence the political imperative of imposing an electoral mandate on the Lords has coincided with a constitutional imperative that Westminster should inter-relate with two new tiers of Parliamentary institutions at home and across the Channel.

The logic implied by this approach to reform – that you don't change until you know why and in favour of what – has dictated a book in three Parts.

Part I sketches in outline the House of Lords history in this century. The background to the Lords' imbalance with the Commons is put in historical context, with a view, then, to setting out the long string of abortive reform proposals made over the last three decades. Since many of these were so intelligent and democratically orientated, one is left at the end of Part I in bafflement as to why so little has been done. Such a long-drawn-out failure points to a cruel nexus of unsolved problems.

Part II accordingly analyses the obstacles to reform. They have been formidable and they remain.

Part III then reveals the heart of the book, which is a comprehensive programme of reforms for the House of Lords. This programme is structured to bring Parliament as a whole back to its rightful place as the people's scrutineer of government.

There is an attempt made to put together a scheme that may not suit altogether the initial predilections of any party but has within it something for everyone – and especially for the electorate, that silent majority that all politicians like to keep happily silent.

For any constitutional settlement must satisfy the minimum demands of all major groups but also have within it that unifying idea that builds to last. That idea must take account of all aspirations and can only come after a process of hard work building on patient and open debate. A settlement requires consensus, however hard won.

It is to such a settlement that this book is intended to contribute.

This is a long journey for a single book; and it will be helpful to set out a few guiding principles.

First: of the two options – between a new start and a rebuild of the old – the book goes firmly for the second option. That requires a search for the best of the past and its adaptation to a new age. So acceptability of its proposals will at least not depend upon too much untried academic theory, but more upon analysis of past performance and of modern conditions. These are issues in the mainstream of politics: they concern how the British people and their government interact.

Second: I assume that all Parliamentarians voting on legislation should, in the absence of overriding contrary reasons (which, however, I think there are), be in some way elected. Accordingly I oppose a mere replacement of hereditary peers with more Labour appointees, even as a stopgap measure. This is government feathering its nest in the guise of reform. Neither the public nor the hereditaries themselves want unelected peers to impede government legislation – except perhaps botched constitutional reform. Removing the hereditaries is a side-issue, however popular before the implications are thought about. Replacing them with government nominees would weaken yet further the Lords' authority in a 'reform' designed to increase the power of a government already outside Parliamentary control.

Third: though this is a study of Parliament's weakness in the face of government, the proposals are limited to the Lords and in no new way challenge the Commons' ultimate supremacy over the Lords. The balance between two chambers should, I think, be one of power versus influence. Otherwise some joint committee of both chambers has to be formed to try to mediate between irreconcilables – which is both untidy, inefficient and divisive. On the other hand, government is, almost by definition, in control of the Commons, and cannot safely be left in charge of the constitution too. Whether the reformed Second Chamber, as the residue of the ancient royal council, should retain some final say on constitutional matters is an issue not to be evaded.

This project has required huge reliance on the works and thoughts of many wise people, past and present.

I have tried, in the text and in the brief bibliography, to indicate those writers to whom I am particularly indebted.

But I am equally grateful to the Leaders in the Lords of the three principal parties, Lord Cranborne, Lord Richard and Lord Rodgers, who have been so generous with their time, to Lord Higgins who found time to talk even before he had a room in the Lords; to Professor Scruton, to Mr Ronald Butt and to Mr Ferdinand Mount, all of whom took time off from their own writings to give me advice; to old friends who have plied me with help of all kinds, especially to my one-time civil service colleagues, to Tom Lyon and to Lord Sudeley FSA, Parliamentary historian; to Mike Shaw of Curtis Brown, my agent and an untiring support; and to Lord Kingsland, the Shadow Lord Chancellor and Lord Egremont, my cousin, who have both stood behind me from the inception of a difficult project.

I should also like to tender my warm thanks to the staff of the House of Lords Records and Library who have supplied me, often at short notice, with necessary reading-matter.

I hope all they and others enjoy the results of their many kindnesses. But it is even more essential than usual for me to emphasise that the conclusions and all the mistakes are exclusively mine own.

HEADNOTES

FOR PARTS I AND II

PART I – 20TH CENTURY HOUSE OF LORDS

Chapter 1 – Introduction
1. Themes: Parliamentary reforms and family resemblances – fits of supremacy 1688 and 1911 – sovereignty (prime ministers or people?) – representation by media or Parliament – 2. Catching the drift of history – 3. New Labour's proposals – 4. meaning of consensus: victimising the hereditaries no substitute for a scheme of reform – 5. Ermined interests and balancing others: hereds and life peers don't represent – Tory hereds ready to make way for better – election of some active peers? -6. Interests of hereds – 7. Life peers – 8. Functions and powers versus composition – 9. Public and Parliament: keeping government honest – self-assertiveness of the silent centre – the information earthquake and government's Parliamentary bypass.

Chapter 2 – False Accommodations – a) Up to 1918; b) 1945-51
a) Parliament divided – cannot represent a united people – schisms and echoes – Salisbury's defence – and bowing to Gladstone (1868) – later lack of Tory restraint – Dizzy parties and 'irreparable blows' – Gladstone calls Salisbury's referendal bluff – Tory sledgehammers: Salisbury's denial of the mandate (1892-5) – and nemesis (1906) onwards – Dicey's challenge: 'turn UK federal and end Parliamentary government – Tories now to keep their heads – Asquith versus Lords' abuse of powers – Tories riding for a fall – Second Chambers and the 'mandate' – Lords unrepresentative, so reform or abolish! – 'Peers versus the People' – cynics on all sides – the King's Horses: the peers capitulate – 80 years of ordure – delaying powers and Money Bills – the new solution – the King's muddle – Home's warning.
b) Landslide 1945: Attlee and Addison – versus Salisbury *redivivus* – Lords' limbo – Addison' drops his mask: 'no question of mandate at all!' – 1949 Parliament Act a hammer without a nut – delaying powers and 4-year Parliaments?

Chapter 3 – An Age of Reform Proposals
A Second (weak) Chamber: Labour's two faces and Tory discomforts
– Labour's 1968 White Paper: consensus on abolishing hereditary voting rights – 1968-9: the best-debated reform package – hereditary Tory
majority – voting and non-voting peers? – contrast Labour abolitionists in '78 – quiet Lords in see-saw '70s – '72 Shepherd's criticism of
overmigty government – '76 Hailsham's 'elective dictatorship'- '78
Home report and Carrington *versus* extremist governments with small
majorities – Lomas:? selection of peers to ensure expertise – Butt *versus* giga-quangos – Winstanley: 'what's their job?' – '78 already
Liberals' federal aim – need for constitutional coordination –
Commons' failure to control – Chalfont *versus* Boyd-Carpenter: avoid-
ance of Commons' conflict or reserve powers against dictatorials – '78
Conservative Lawyers: elected senate, include Finance Bill in Lords
and joint procedure to resolve deadlock – Home report: emphasis on
HL composition, fears of upsetting Commons, HL abolition, written
constitution and constitutional court; ? hybrid House with Mediation
Committee to encourage 2 Houses' cooperation – Briginshaw: abolish
Lords and reform Commons! – summary: '68 Labour and '78 Tory –
Tory senatorials – Thatcher, but Tory stirrings and Constitutional
Committee – War Crimes Bill – Tory progressives *v* conservatives; but
no talk of functions – senatorials *v* traditionals – flaw in mandate theory – the Parliament-in-balance solution – Scottish YCs and Scarman
– senatorials and a 'broad church' – function: HL the core of government advisers – Leonard's Preleg Select Committees; Mitchell's paid
senators with constitutional, equality and human rights brief – Lords'
numbers – the traditionals – Cormack's compromise – Carnarvon's
demand for overall scheme – sovereign Blair and Selwyn Lloyd – consensual bottom-lines – prospects for consensus – backwoodsmen out
and life peers in – and more women – Blair's lecture (but debate later!)
– law lords, bishops *et al*: protectors of rights, minorities and multi-
culture? – *ex officios* and crossbench – MEPs and Westminster, regionalists and PR – wish-lists.

PART II – OBSTACLES TO REFORM

Introduction
Carrying our constitution on our back

Chapter 1 – Sovereignty, the Monarchy and the House of Lords
symbols of state and sentiment – the Queen in Parliament, but the people is sovereign – the Lord Chancellor, in principle, and other lords – the

Queen as head of state and of mystery – representing past and future generations – *ex officio*s and ancient government – rule of law – image-making and abuse of government power – Britannia and the lottery – symbolic fudge: are the people satisfied? – the Prime Minister; but the Queen can still be boss – elected Heads and weak Parliaments – Parliament is the prime obstacle to the reform of Parliament – Kafkan party machines – a people short-changed – two Houses at odds – EU the new Lords' territory – the people demand to be consulted: chat shows *versus* hard work – the Lord Chancellor in person and other lords in practice – LC out of parliament, unconstitutional discussions on the constitution – small 'c' conservatism: where do national referendums fit? – where are the English? – Europe in or out? – government fiddlers and outdated ceremonial – the Treaty of Rome, our Supreme Law – Europe and Westminster – summaries and symbols – but reform inescapable – the people could still wake up in time

Chapter 2 – Representation
Public doldrums are anti-democratic – a) government and the House of Commons – Parliament bowing to government – committees overborne by party – Commons bowing to the EU – unholy alliance: government and Commons
b) Mandates and Manifestos – government always has mandate of a sort – grandmother's footsteps: people power – the Salsbury Doctrine is no match for PM – presidential style but no president – US Congress versus spin – UK president needs a minder, Parliament – presidential elective dictatorship and buffoonery – New Labour headlong – strangulation by government: Parliament failing to ensure democracy – delaying powers and prevarication: what is settled by elections? – Parliament as arbiter has opted out.
c) Parliament, Europe and Referendums – the 1975 EU referendum – Finer's fine critique: legitimacy of referendums – refrerendums must supplement, not evade, Parliament – referendums in the constitutionalist's context – look out, Parliament: the world is coming! – and Europe is already here – though not many Tories know that – Euro-representation for UK?
d) Lords as constitution guardians? – only within a working Parliament – Parliament needs a Second Chamber for the purpose – for overmighty governments remain – our public indifference to our fate – indifference to be overcome by a unitary scheme for Parliament's control of government.

Part 1

20th Century House of Lords

INTRODUCTION

1. Themes

The themes at least write themselves. In setting out to write about the British Constitution now and how it might be bettered, you are at once encouraged. For you hope to hit on ideas that any reader may think worth considering; and you are finding we all breathe the same air – effortlessly. So, you think, it should not require a Solomon to come up with an analysis and proposals which can expect general acceptance.

You notice next, as you look through the Parliamentary reform proposals of a century past, their family resemblances that only the special circumstances of their generations seem to differentiate; and you wonder that there is anything left at all to say or do. So much to do.

This eerie deja vu does not apply to most historical subjects, particularly not to those which are alive right up into our fast-moving present. In fact the only parallel, even in Western history, that I can find, runs through the Roman Republic, where the same constitutional themes ran on, identified and unsolved, for centuries. Until two millennia ago, that is, a revolutionary genius, Julius Caesar with his genius of a grand-nephew and adopted son, Augustus, turned the Republic on its head. Those two, responding to the political imperatives of an unstable structure, created the Roman Empire which is still the foundation of our Western civilisation.

Two very different lessons drop out of this short story. The first is that a constitution can bump along indefinitely on old wheels without seeming to demand the maintenance which common sense repeatedly advises. The second is this: driving a banged-out car is dangerous. It always ends in tears.

There is one common factor in particular that brings the fate of the Old Romans poignantly close to home – the continuity of history through the continuity of the ruling families; and then the discontinuity that their very success in government brought when national prosperity outgrew even their tenacious control. For the British Empire was no less the bequest of the now defunct British landed aristocracy than the Roman Empire was of those Old Romans who littered Philippi Field.

What is more, the Caesars themselves were just one of those aristocratic families. They differed from their peers only in their determination to survive and in their insight into how to do it.But even so, the history is not theirs but Rome's. Had the Caesars fallen when the Republic disintegrated – which it would have done in any event – we should not be their heirs....

Our themes so readily present themselves, like actors. The Lords who with craft, hard work and public spirit stay on the field with the Commons long after losing to them the decisive battle. A family, the Salisburys, who for over a century keep the rearguard. And Prime Ministers with their retinues who stay in power at the expense of their rivals, Parliament and the people they lean on and affect to serve.

These three actors have been on stage a long time and there are some who like to leave them be. The structure may be rickety but the drama may still be in balance. If governments can put through their programmes and the people can get rid of them at election-time, why mess with our traditional pottage – especially with the Lords, who are peripheral to the action of the lead character, the Prime Minister in his train?

Two reasons, one historical and one right up to date. Our three actors correspond to the leads in three successive acts of our play. The decisive battle was not the 'Parliament Act 1911 but the Reform Act 1832 – which also begins the first Act of our interminable play, the modernising of the Lords.

After the Great Reform for eighty years the Lords kept going a dogged rearguard. The Settlement of 1688 settled the supremacy of Parliament over the monarchy. Despite fits of energetic resistance of monarchs by Britain's most able monarchs of the period, George III and Victoria, after 1688 the monarchy was progressively sidelined by Parliament. Hardening convention assigned to the monarch's ministers the realities of power; and it became ever surer that it was Parliament, not the monarch, to whom those ministers were answerable.

All the while the demography of Britain was irreversibly changing. An economy based on agriculture and landownership, on which the Lords' wealth and power depended, was being inexorably replaced by a country of industrial towns which inevitably the Commons better represented. Nevertheless, however concrete was the threat of the rising radicals – which some Tory Lords, such as Lord Lansdowne was more astute to evaluate than others, such as Salisbury himself – up to 1911 the constitutional relationship between Lords and Commons remained on paper (albeit under layers of dust, if not under dustsheets) undisturbed. In 1688 it was laid down that the two Houses were 'co-equal partners' and any Bill passing one House fell if it could not pass the other.

Even before 1688, in fact, the writing was burning into their Lordships' wall. For in 1678 it was laid down that initiation of money Bills was the exclusive prerogative of the Commons; and he who formulates policy, as any government knows, lays down nine-tenths of the law. So he who formulates policy on the national expenditure formulates at least seven-tenths of any policy that matters.

But when Lloyd-George brought in his critical 1909 budget with ninepence in the pound income-tax, there was no doubt that the Lords could throw it out if they dared. Which they did; and in so doing started the Second Act. We shall need to look later at the circumstances of the 1911 Act. Here we need but note that the Second Act has continued to this day – for another 80-odd years, in fact. But its final lines are at this moment at last being spoken.

In any good play the last Act is slowly prepared by all that has gone before;

but its action centres round some new circumstance – in this case, the audience has changed.

Parliament has never been sovereign except in so far as the government has been incorporated in it. Of course when they speak as one, whose voice is heard does not matter much. When they do differ, Parliament, it is true, has the last word. But the government has normally had some five years' uninterrupted spouting beforehand.

A clear idea of how sovereignty works in the state will be seen later as a prerequisite for proposals of constitutional change. What is needed here is the perception that the sovereignty of Parliament, even of the Queen in Parliament, is and always has been a myth, unless it is taken to mean the government in the context of the British Constitution. In that sense the great phrase of the textbooks that 'In Britain the monarch in Parliament is sovereign' has no more force than the unsurprising reflection that the government is the government.

So the pre-eminence of prime ministers is hardly new. Lord Home – Alec Douglas-Home – was the last to govern as head of a committee, was the last exponent of cabinet government as originally conceived. More is the pity, one might wish to think. But he didn't last; and durability is an essential for successful PMs, whose authority – though seldom their wisdom – grows with their time in office. Parliament without the Prime Minister is Hamlet without the prince.

What is new is the general perception that Hamlet will never be king. The people is king; in fact, is – and always has been – sovereign. And that general perception leaves Parliament almost out of a job. For when Ministers wanted to praise themselves (or even, when they could not avoid it, take the blame) they used to perform these rituals before their titular master, Parliament. Now Mr Blair sees his master as the people, and it is direct to them, on television, that he does obeisance.

It is not our wish to question the prudence of populist prime ministers, who answer in any case only to the ballot box – beyond the comment that such shows of humility will not long serve to keep them popular or respected. Any more than it served the British monarchy well to invite the public to peep first on to their lawns, then into their offices, then into their drawing-rooms, and finally upstairs....

The constitution, painstakingly grown, has at least amply prescribed appropriate times and places for rulers and governments to appear for public contact with the people. There was no need for the monarchy or ministers to take such thorny short-cuts, though once taken they are mistaken for highways and cannot be stopped up. Now we have the ultimate absurdity of a prime minister on TV in sanitised sackcloth and ashes 'apologising' for accepting huge and immoral party donations because a roast in Parliament can no longer be got hot enough. And meanwhile the just criticism of governments, that where they can they conceal under show and sauce their anti-democratic practices, has been left by the politicians to hard-nosed journalists....

What cannot be passed over by a constitutionalist is the effect on the people's representation. Government by media is no better, no more just or responsible than trial by television (which is in fact its precursor). For flattery of the people is neither governing nor listening. The proper place to govern and to listen is Parliament. And it is equally the fault of weak Parliamentarians, and of their parties and governments that like them weak, that Parliament is no longer the venue of government.

So we shall examine both how the House of Lords operates in government and how it might do so more effectively, but in the context of the people's interest in being responsibly governed. For government has outgrown Parliament and Parliamentarians also. A minister speaks – but on his own terms – direct to the people – hoping that the people, sure at last like teenagers they are grown up, will be conned into thinking this is a democratic practice which effectively serves their expressed wishes.

2. *The Drift of History*

The British are proud of their history; and because they like much of what they have, they prefer organic growth to revolution. When what is new comes from what was, it has roots and is likely to go on growing. When it comes from what is known, the future is more predictable, less likely to spoil what there is in pursuit of improvement.

But conservatism is often mistaken for complacency. We know that what we have is not ideal.We do want better, provided we do not end worse off from looking for it.Cautious but continual change is what we like. Hence the attachment of the British to their unwritten Constitution. It can be moulded insensibly to developing circumstances, just and only just so far as circumstances require.

But there is danger in pragmatic caution – the danger of drift. Currents can move fast:in this century the movement of events has been breathtaking. Our boat can stay comfortably afloat but we find ourselves suddenly far from where we want to be. Pragmatism requires more vigilance than any other -ism.

Our Constitution is of all things the easiest to change too late, because it is the very last thing we want to change by more than present circumstances clearly demand.

The most telling example of this is the 1911 Parliament Act itself. It was the high watershed in the long range of disagreements between a conservative House of Lords and a House of Commons ever more radical as patterns of representation changed in favour of a wider franchise.

But it was a change rammed through by the Commons with a view to getting a particular programme on to the Statute Book. In its preamble it stated the intention "to substitute for the House of Lords as it at present exists a Second Chamber constituted on a popular instead of a hereditary basis". It is characteristic of British politics that to this day no wholehearted attempt has been made to realise this intention.

3. *New Labour's Proposals.*

The Labour Government's August '97 proposals are no exception to the rule of constitutional creep. In 1991 Mr. Blair announced Labour's firm intention to eject from Parliament the hereditary Lords without proposing reasoned alternatives. This reappeared in Labour's spring '97 manifesto, 'Because You Deserve Better' as "Labour will open up our democracy and strengthen the rights of our citizens... Hereditary peers will no longer sit or vote in the House of Lords". On 24th August '97 the *Observer* leaked Labour's reassurance that though the hereditary peers would be stripped of their attendance and voting rights in this Parliament, "active peers would be safe from Labour's axe" in this Parliament pending more thorough reforms in the next Parliament.

This policy carries British caution to absurdity. It is neither a resource to ensure the government's legislative programme (which the Lords do not threaten) nor is it a programme of responsible constitutional reform. It is populist drift.

4. The Meaning of Consensus

Change has been on the agenda since before 1911. It is either long overdue or there is little to be done. Not many would want constitutional reform that did not answer – and answer definitively – a perceived and urgent need. Change otherwise will destabilise, without improving, democratic machinery in unforseeable ways.

Agreement that some aspect of that machinery is unsatisfactory is not enough to justify change. There must also be agreement on what it is unsatisfactory. Then the effects of change to it must be analysed and specific improvements agreed on simultaneously. When these essential steps have been gone through in the government, in the parties and the country, and general acquiescence reached on specific proposals, then and then only has consensus been reached that may lead to reform which may be confidently expected to improve the democratic machinery.

Labour's current proposals to remove the hereditary peers from the House of Lords, if looked at from this point of vantage, are not impressive. Heredity would rank in a large majority of minds below election (however conducted) or merit (however defined) as a qualification for the legislature. It was a justifiable qualification – perhaps – only when heredity in fact defined the passing on of the interests that provided people's livelihoods.

But to knock out the hereditary peers before you know why and with what to replace them is to amputate a sore thumb without knowing how to replace it, or indeed ensuring that it can be replaced at all.

Suppose for example that careful consideration led to the conclusion that the House of Lords should be abolished altogether – and there has been a body of opinion, especially among their younger brothers, the Commons, that so it should be. A temporary fudge with a bevy of new lifepeers and a quorum for 'active' peers selected by their political opponents would create new vested (and ermined) interests that would make the later radical reform all the harder to achieve.

Meanwhile a majority of hereditary peers would probably welcome a reform of their House that strengthened Parliament and our democracy, even if it led to their final departure; and being of that mind they would be in poor shape to oppose later, if undisturbed for the five years it might take Labour to make up its mind (and the country's) to abolish the House of Lords altogether. Not so if they were abolished now and their House as a whole were threatened later. Such a proceeding would be greeted by them and the majority with derision. In fact abolition of the hereditary peers now could foreclose the abolition of the House of Lords for a generation.

But assuming (though no attempt has been made to debate it) that the British would want a Second Chamber in some form to live on, it would still be irresponsible in principle unnecessarily to operate on the patient before diagnosis; and it would undermine public confidence in the process of reform.

5 – *Ermined and Other Interests.*

There are two kinds of interests at stake in any discussion of constitutional reform. There are those professionally interested in the *status quo*, and the public whom the professionals hope to serve. One might expect the former would be generally against and the latter in favour of change; but this is in fact seldom so – and not primarily for party political reasons. Politicians and civil servants have no doubt their roles to protect, but their day-to-day concerns keep them uncomfortably (if privately) aware of the faults of the system within which they have to work.

And the public is often against change. In a complicated world there is resistance to change which is not obviously necessary and no thanks for politicians who raise fundamental questions where there are not apparent answers.

It follows that for a package of reforms to get anywhere near general agreement it must satisfy two very different criteria. To meet with the approval of the professionals, it must oil political machinery while not disturbing too much the current political balance. To please the public, it must tend towards fair and transparent representation, preferably addressing by the way some maybe quite small issue of the moment which has caught the public eye. Often these two aims are in conflict – government power versus people power; and so for long periods, politicians like it better to stay quiet than to prick themselves on thorny issues.

The issue of the moment is the role of the hereditary peers. They are thought quaint but out of place in Parliament. Their situation was highlighted in Labour's manifesto before a huge and famous victory. By common consent hereditary is an anomalous qualification for public representation. But disinheriting the hereditary peers of their right to sit and vote is plainly no solution to reform of the Lords, even if it were agreed what the problem is; for unfortunately there are no elections for any member at all of the House of Lords.

Though lifepeers may in many cases represent parties and also governments, past and present, the public, by election, the lifepeers do not represent. On one view the parties and governments are a good part of the problem: they have too much power in the House of Commons already. Any change which accentuates that Parliamentary imbalance is not progress but retrograde. It is the public that is under-represented in Parliament.

Hereditary peers are easy meat for a Labour government with a strong majority. Their removal has caught the popular imagination for the moment; and it has a small political plus for Labour, since the vast amjority of them are Tory sympathisers. So does their replacement by yet more Labour sympathisers as lifepeers. These factors will simplify the passing of some Labour's less convincing legislation. But best of all for the government the hereditary peers can be cut off with little thought for the underlying issue – representation of the people – that their removal is meant to serve

The removal of the hereditary peers might be easy to carry through (or it might not) and for Labour even convenient and in the short term probably popular. But, in the absence of a well-debated scheme for their replacement and the reform of Parliament as a whole, it would not lead to the democratic stability of reforms sanctioned by consensus. It might (if carried through without serious opposition in the Lords) ease the passage of legislation for Labour by removing the Tory bias among hereditary peers. But in the context of constitutional reforms, even removing bias – desirable though it is – without replacing bias with stabilising reform upsets the party balance without increasing public confidence in the machinery of government. For public acceptance of constitutional change depends on a perception of improved democratic representation. Amputation is no ideal cure.

6. The Interest of the Hereditary Peers.
"This paper begins and ends with the stated conviction that hereditary members of the present House of Lords... would vote themselves into history with barely a backward glance in favour of a reformed House which was more effective, and whose composition commanded wider acceptance, than the present one" (Second Chamber – Earl Carnarvon and others, '95). The problem of reform is not peers' defensiveness but the lack of consensus on how to replace them.

For until the 1958 Life Peerages Act all peers were of first creation or hereditary. After 1911 this had been seen increasingly as an anomaly.

But being there to this day many hereditary peers have made a good job of it. Within its severe limitations the Lords has a fine reputation. There would even be some MPs who admit that the Lords have sometimes done their littler job better than MPs have done their big job.

The complaint against the hereditary peers is exclusively their preponderance of Tory sympathisers. If their sympathies were divided roughly in proportion to party strengths in the country the question of their removal might never arise. To quote 'Second Chamber again (this time summarising conclusions of Shell and Beamish):

"Analysis of voting patterns in the 1988-89 session has shown that, of the divisions where the Government formally took sides, there were 172 government victories and 12 defeats; but that if the peers by succession had been excluded from the House, there would have been 159 Government defeats, 21 Government victories and an equality in 4 instances. These figures are stark."

The interest of the hereditary peers is to ensure their demise to bring about (and sometime their resurrection into) a better House of Lords. But this does not mean they should have no part to play in a reformed House. A number of hereditary peers of established distinction would have no difficulty in getting themselves selected and/or elected under any credible regime that might now be set up. Labour now seem to wish to 'spare' at least 60 of them, pending serious reform in a later Parliament.

7. Life Peers

Few, perhaps negligibly few, would wish the hereditary peers' predicament set in stone: it impedes the Lords' effectiveness as a limb of Parliament and therefore of Parliament as a whole. But at least there is general agreement that it should be changed. In relation to the life peers there is no such agreement. But from one point of view their position is no less anomalous than the hereditaries'.

For lifepeers are not elected; and their elevation is the fruit of prime ministers', government and party interests, just those interests that it is Parliament's chief function to control. It is no answer to this remark that life peers, in pursuit of issues on which they may have outstanding special knowledge, frequently bite the hand of those very governments that elevated them. The hereditaries are frequently no less well-informed and recalcitrant. It is natural (and wholly proper) that Labour should object to the Tory preponderance of the hereditaries; but if that preponderance were rectified – for example by the creation of some Labour hereditaries and some limitation on the attendance of some Tory occasionals and some few others who might be agreed unsuitable – it would be difficult to deny that the very same objections apply to life peers as to hereditaries.

Life peers are not elected; and if the best way to ensure that those who sit in Parliament represent the British people is to have them elected by the British people, then lifepeers also should be elected. Is the present selection of lifepeers a satisfactory way of placing their contingent among the Lords? It is no great argument for those in favour to point to the excellent credentials and performances of Life peers (even is in many cases the credentials and performances of hereditaries did not match them). In politics, even more than in court, justice must be seen to be done. There are strong arguments in favour of a mixed Second Chamber, of a combination of election and selection. But I think that no combination of lifepeers and hereditaries, however well it reflected party and even other interests, would satisfy the deepest convictions of the public, unless at least a goodly proportion of its members were in some way elected by the public. That being so, any package of proposals for House of Lords reform that looks to increase the Lord's function in Parliament will not achieve the stability of consensus unless it provides for some public election of serving peers.

There will be a tendancy for those who favour a tinkering by numbers of the current composition to be also those who doubt the need for thorough going Parliamentary reform, especially the need for reform not just of the Lords but of the Commons also, and above all of the ways they complement each other (or not).

Life peers may well be more resistant than hereditaries to the notion that they (or some of them for some purposes) should be elected. They got there through hard work and effort. But many have never been politicians: therein lies part of their claim to leaven the lump – and not to be elected.

8. Functions and Powers versus Composition of the Lords.

However no route of life peers to the House of Lords is easy to trace out that could be expected to meet with general approval. The answers at the back of a maths book seldom make the problems look simpler to solve, even though mathematicians may hope, at the end of their search, for formulae of elegance and logic.

Our investigation will dance hither and thither over most current problems of government and state to show their interrelation, so as to locate at their centre the people, now self-aware and determined to take part in the formation and implementation of policy on every issue under the sun, and propose them a forum that might do it.

After a brief historical sketch, limited to showing how the Lords have come to operate as at present they do, and then an analysis in context of the recurring obstacles to reform, we shall review in more detail the main sets of Lords' reform proposals presented this century, before embarking on our own proposals which are intended to build for the future on the best of what has gone before.

In reviewing these earlier sets of proposals, whish bear clear and instructive interrelationships, one recurrent question will stand out, whether it is the composition of the Lords or their functions (from which their powers flow) that is in most need of attention.

Here there are few surprises. Lords' reforms from 1911 have been driven by Prime Ministers in the Commons anxious for any easy ride for their legislative programmes. Reforms that have affected the Lords' powers have always concentrated on reducing them, so as to ease legislation acceptable to the Commons painlessly through the Lords. Where changes to composition have also been attempted these have been application (the outstanding example being of course life peers) of the principle, going right back to Queen Anne in the early 1700s, that allows the sovereign to create peerages sufficient to ensure the passage of legislation crucial to his/her Ministers' programmes.

What is startling, however, is the case with which reforming governments have kidded Parliamentarians that composition and powers are the only two subject to consider. What matters most is what Parliament – and in particular, for this book, the House of Lords – is there to do. Until Parliament's job is defined and its performance assessed against that, reform proposals are beating hot air. Their shadowy forms without substance have condemned Parliamentarians into ever deeper limbo.

Not so Bryce in 1918. His critique on the Lords' functions is still quoted with general approval – which shows just how little action, how little progress, Prime Ministers with their retinues have permitted.

Governments have hogged the stage at the expense of Parliament and people. It is high time that the British constituional balance was redressed.

9. The Public and Parliament – Keeping Government Honest

Big changes come in two ways – in a rush or so gradually that they are hardly perceived. It happens that at the end of our century both kinds have come together. May Day 1997 will be remembered as the single day on which a realignment of the British political centre was accomplished. But over the past twenty years or more there has grown up a new political assertiveness. It was still true when I was young that the huge majority were content to grumble in the pub but to leave politics to the professionals except at election time. It is true no longer.

Availability of information and approachability of politicians has changed all that. The main agent of change has of course been television. The illusion of having the prime minister in my own living-room, of being one of a studio audience asking him questions direct, of being the interviewer who refuses to let him duck the question that is troubling me – all this apparent immediacy of contact has brought the voter on to the stage of day-to-day politics.

This new self-consciousness, self-confidence, is very healthy. Nothing better guarantees a democracy than its electorate vibrantly involved in it. But pride comes before a fall. Contact is not control. If we think that by asking Tony Blair an awkward question – supposing in fact this actually happened – we are influencing how we are governed, we are deceiving ourselves. What we are doing is giving him an opportunity to show how affably, approachably and altogether uncondescendingly he deals with us. The only hold we have on him remains our vote. And whatever he answers, we are much more likely to give him that than if we had had no opportunity to ask our question.

For a politician approachability is an essential of electoral management and has little or no effect on his policies. Alongside the mixing in by the media of people and politicians there has continued the dismantling brick by brick of Parliament's control of government.

Governments have become ever more sophisticated in manipulating electorates through the media, ever more ruthless in shepherding their MPs through the lobbies – on pain now not just of being 'disciplined' but of being deselected. At the very time when the public feels for the first time ready to be involved in the day-to-day business of government decision-making, the people's control of its government is weaker than ever it has been since the Reform Act.

In keeping a government honest there is no substitute for a vigilant and self-confident Parliament. By contrast nowadays so little is expected of Parliament, that its weakness and its inefficiencies are passed by without comment. But nowhere else can a government's performance be consistently monitored, its inadequacies and inconsistencies tracked, its priorities assessed.

Political landslides are like earthquakes – long-predicted and always a shock when they come. For they follow a perceived change of public attitude; but the significance of the change can only be assessed in the sequel.

Over the past twenty years there has been a vast and accelerating increase in the information available to the public about public affairs; and this has fed a demand to be more directly involved in the decisions of government. This demand both politicians and governments have been slow to react to. It is unwelcome news to them that their client public wishes to have a voice in their preserves of power. Politicians have accordingly made ever increasing palavers of their manifestos (which are set in stone by elections) and governments have sought to filter available news through their public relations agencies. First be a winner and then a spinner.

When ministers want to put a message across nowadays they put their heads not into Parliament but into the lions' dens of the Today Programme or Breakfast TV. The immediacy of such encounters is attractive to the public. Even Prime Minister's Question-time televised seems something of a private political game by contrast.

The direct result of this change in public consciousness has been a Parliamentary bypass. This is profoundly undemocratic, especially in view of the forces massed against constitutional change that matches the growth in public awareness. Governments have never relished being called to account for unpopular actions by MPs. Both Thatcher's and Blair's instincts are authoritarian. Governments and Oppositions are supported by parties who know that dissension in the ranks is an electoral disease. MPs themselves are never the first to draw attention to their general feebleness; nor is strategic complaint a profitable tactic for promotion.

Finally the third party is so mesmerised by the prospect of proportional representation in the Commons (which undoubtedly holds out a promise of many more seats for Liberal Democrats) that wider issues of public representation pass them by. Unfortunate: for sensitivity to fair political representation is at the heart of the liberal tradition.

What is worse – expectations of Parliament are so low that thoughts for its future are limited to who will be there. It no longer occurs even to commentators to question how Parliament works. Just one symptom of this is Labour's determination to eject the hereditary peers from the House of Lords without giving a thought to how the Lords could be made a more effective second chamber (or indeed what this would mean). The new government sees a populist move – nobody thinks the hereditary element should remain unchanged, least of all the hereditaries themselves – that eases its legislation through and increases the prime minister's patronage – and looks no further.

As if the world were not growing smaller, our people more engaged and better informed and the EU already over our threshold...

This is a book about making our democracy work – and using a reformed House of Lords as the primary instrument of improvement. There can be no question either in intent or in practical politics of returning the House of Lords to its (at least theoretical) equipollence with the House of Commons after 1688, to specify the date from which the history of the two Houses in recognisable form can be said to have begun. The guiding principle here has been to propose reforms which build on proven strengths, but without fear or favour towards those institutions in the British constitution that have outgrown their fair weight.

It is the theme of this book that the 'elected dictatorship' so eloquently foretold by Lord Hailsham in Opposition in the late '70s duly arrived under Mrs Thatcher after she won the 1979 general election, with Lord Hailsham himself her Lord Chancellor. But whether or not some written constitution or some new Bill of Rights might have forestalled this is highly dubious. The power of prime ministers has grown throughout this century and keeps on growing. Mrs Thatcher allowed the St John-Stevas House of Commons Select Committees, strongly favoured by Tories in Opposition, to get going. They constitute the single most effective Parliamentary check on government introduced this century. But the notion of a reformed House of Lords which might impede her grand design by asking too-good questions was altogether distasteful to Britain's longest-serving PM; and as her hold on power grew there were those in the Second Chamber who felt she treated it with contempt.

There were those among her supporters in the Commons who felt much the same. They got her in the end; and the dragon's teeth she sowed rose up on Mr Major.

The moral is not to criticise Mrs Thatcher. Her job was to rule as she thought fit; and she took what levers of power she was handed down, to do it in the most effective way she could find. More power to her.... The moral is that PMs are the last in the realm to whom deep constitutional reform should be delegated by the people. And this goes for all those others, their MPs, ministers, parties, hangers-on and Lord Chancellors (Lords Hailsham and Lairg) who are swept on in the PM's triumphal train. Parliament is not above the law because it makes it. And the two most basic rules of law are, first that nobody should be judge in his own cause and second that the judge should hear all those affected fairly and without fear or favour.

Great changes are brought about by spectral and tectonic shifts. At base there are two kinds of circumstance that politicians must respond to – changes of opinion and changes of underlying reality. The Blair government has shown a wonderful flair in managing the first, so that it appears blinded to the second at its feet. News management above all won the shift in perceived power. But how to cope with an electorate come of age and with a new world rising up within Westminster's closed doors, New Labour has just no idea of. We have Toryism without commitment softened by a few concessions to old Labour ideals (with equal lack of commitment).

1. FALSE ACCOMMODATIONS

A) UP TO 1911; B) 1945-51

a) Up to 1911

The House of Lords has never truly had a golden age; and since the Civil War it has been in interminably slow decline. In theory after 1688 the two Houses were equipollent – of equal strength; and it was at least true that unless an Act passed both Houses in those days it could not become law. But already (in 1671 and 1678) the Commons was claiming the monopoly of initiating some kinds of appropriation Bills. And early in the 18th century the Lords' consent to the Treaty of Utrecht was procured by the threat of creating a dozen peers to force it through. This may indeed have had more to do with the government's persuasiveness and the sympathies of Queen Anne than with the influence of the Commons; but it showed already the Lords' weakness as an offshoot of the royal prerogative without a clear constituency and identity of its own.

The 18th century was however the golden age of the landed aristocracy. Not till near its end did the loss of the American Colonies followed by the threats external and internal flowing from Revolutionary France mobilise the forces that carried through the 1832 Reform Act, in the teeth of dedicated opposition from the House of Lords. From then on the Commons' claim to represent the new expanding industrial Britain could not be gainsaid.

That in no way checked the rivalry between the two Houses whose interests were in truth irreconcilably opposed except when a Tory government happened to be in power – which thanks to Mr Disraeli's cleverness happened more often than either Mr Gladstone or a historian in retrospect would have thought probable.

But Gladstone knew the force was with him; and it was his spiritual descendants, Lloyd-George and Asquith, who in 1911 broke the unrepresentative power of the aristocracy and set the Commons over them. In so doing they left an ugly breach in our constitution that is unplugged to this day.

But the conclusion was not obvious to 19th-century Britain; and there were other issues of abiding interest entangled with it – the Union, public representation, the growth of prime ministerial and party government. Moreover it was fairly early in this century that the first serious reform proposals for the House of Lords were put forward by Lord Bryce. Since 1919 the Lords' wings have been further clipped; but in Lords reform nothing substantial or beneficial has been achieved.

It has been thought above all that any great improvement to the Lords' position could only be at the expense of either government or the Commons, if not both. In the short-term this is always likely to be true. But that is a short-sighted view from all points. Especially as the government and the Commons are where they are supposedly to serve and unite the people, rather than to protect their power-base. In fact governments could be both better and more secure, and the Commons could exercise their powers more effectively, if the Lords were suitably reformed.

There is a marked chain of events from the Irish Church Disestablishment issue of 1868. Disestablishment of the Irish Anglican Church was seen by many English as a threat to the integrity of the United Kingdom, as indeed subsequent events showed it to be.

Passions already ran high. Disraeli, suddenly Prime Minister of a Tory minority administration, found Gladstone ramming through a series of Commons motions in favour and following this up with the introduction of a Bill. Disraeli claimed that the issue should be reserved to the forthcoming Parliament; and in this he was supported by his Lord Chancellor who denied the Bill had any popular mandate. Nevertheless the Bill passed the Commons on 16th June and moved to the Lords.

There the third Marquess of Salisbury was waiting for it. He began here a championship of the Tory Upper House against the (generally more) Liberal Commons that outlasted his retirement as Prime Minister in 1902 after the death of Queen Victoria.

Wellington, himself deeply impressed by the French Revolution and the saviour of the Kingdom afterwards, saw things differently. For Wellington the Lords were bound to follow the Commons, with whatever distaste, on pain of civil disorder if not of revolution. "The Queen's Government must be supported," said he.

This Salisbury saw as relegation of the House of Lords to nothing more than the Commons' 'echo'. His disquiet was understandable. Since 1688 – and before that more so – the Lords had been the Commons' 'coequal' partner; and this balanced structure had been only undermined, not pulled down, by the Reform Acts. As the tide swept deep out, nobody could tell where it would end or what it would leave.

Salisbury resolved to take the people as his master and not the Commons, to claim, where with the barest credibility he ever could, that the Tory Lords represented the firm and settled intention – "the cool and deliberate judgment of the generality of the nation".

At the start there was much in favour of this doctrine and with variations it has been the leitmotif of the Tory majority in the House of Lords ever since. In the thick of defending the Union, as Salisbury (and many others) saw themselves doing, it became twisted out of all proportion. But its original foundation is well worth a moment's examination, if only to point up how attitudes have changed so as to invalidate it before deciding whether any modification of it might retain some vitality even now.

Salisbury, aware of the general caution and patience of the the nation, pointed to two facts about his age which have been dramatically turned upside down in ours by the information revolution. He drew attention to the obvious fact that scare stories and provocation could and did call up then much unbalanced fear in an underinformed electorate; so they had delegated politics between elections to the politicians.

At the time Salisbury's defence of the Lords had much persuasive power. How greatly things have changed. The public now is snowed under with undigested information and wishes to be engaged in public debate to the point where Parliament is being pushed into the sidelines. The modern equivalents of his points might be that the public is confused by a surfeit of information and opinions from a multitude of sources and needs a Parliament that can sift and research them in a reasonably non-partisan spirit and thereby both lead and respond to the public debate upon them.

But to have proposed such a relationship between the public and Parliament in the second half of the last century would have been absurd. The public's access to information since then has had a profound effect on the Parliamentarian's role that has not, perhaps, been as yet well responded to.

In the particular circumstances of 1868 the Tory attitude to the electorate was reinforced by the undoubted fact that Irish Church Disestablishment had not been on the political scene at the time of the previous general election. Not only did the electorate of the day require time to settle its opinions, but its opinions on this issue had not even been canvassed.

But in the forthcoming general election it was; and Gladstone's Liberals were returned with a thumping majority of over a hundred. Not for the last time the Tories' claim to empathise in some special way with the British electorate was falsified. But Salisbury now acted with great wisdom and prevailed upon an unwilling House of Lords to let Gladstone's Bill through.

> … when once we have come to the conclusion from all the circumstances of the case that the House of Commons is at one with the nation, it appears to me that save in some very exceptional cases, save in the highest case of morality – in cases in which a man would not set his hand to a certain proposition, though revolution should follow from his refusal – it appears to me that the vocation of this House has passed away, that it must devolve the responsibility upon the nation, and may fairly accept the conclusion at which the nation has arrived.

(Parliamentary Debates 3rd Ser 17vi1869, vol 197, cols 83-4)

One may be sure if the Tory Lords had always shown this restraint towards the end of the century and later in the lead up to the Parliament Act of 1911, the history of their House would have been very different. In 1869, in any case, the Lords emerged from their defeat smelling of roses and with a new sword fashioned for use. The House of Lords could now claim to be the arbiter between the people and the House of Commons when (the House of Lords considered that) the Commons had over-extended their mandate from the people in a general election. It is unfortunate for the history of Parliament and the Lords in particular that they overused their weapon in the struggles to come. We are still paying for their overtaxed inheritance.

For a while the Tories did not much need their weapon; for soon they were in power. In February 1874 Disraeli won a Commons majority and stayed in office until 1880. Then however Gladstone was again returned with a strong majority.

By 1882 Gladstone was being hampered by the obstructionist tactics of the Irish Nationalist MPs led by Parnell and introduced the cloture and the guillotine as a means of ending the interminable and forcing through legislation. These measures must have seemed justified by good sense. But from them have grown governments' control of Parliamentary time – one of two main factors combining over this last century to whittle away the independence and significance of the private member. The other is, of course, the individual member's overdependence on his party. Salisbury was not slow to fasten upon both of them and to claim the House of Lords as a counterweight:

A House of Commons, enslaved by the caucus, and muzzled by the cloture, would be a very different body from that which has hitherto been the glory of English history.

A House of Commons, weakened so, puts the Lords on their mettle – though it must sometimes invite obloquy also:

The cause of the animosity with which the House of Lords is occasionally pursued is because it is occasionally thought it may perform its primary duty... When people have got together a scratch and accidental majority... an intense desire is nourished... [to] deal some crushing, some irreparable blow, that no future Conservative government can undo; and it is greatly feared that, when this proposal is made, the House of Lords may possibly say: 'No, this was not the ground on which this last election was conducted; we will not allow this thing to be done until the nation has been allowed to speak.'

(F S Pulling, *The Life and Speeches of the Marquis of Salisbury* (1885) vol II p117)

Lord Salisbury did not have long to wait before the Tories were confronted with just such a proposal – now known as the Third Reform Act. This enfranchised householders and lodgers in the counties and introduced a standard voting qualification, so as to establish a uniform franchise throughout the country. The Tories were of course fundamentally opposed to the extension of the franchise, despite its obvious moral justification. But they had a genuine complaint against the Bill; for it extended the franchise without redistributing seats, which they rightly saw would give their opponents an unfair electoral advantage especially in Ireland, itself the fundamental *casus belli*. He demanded that the Bill be put before the people:

In the presence of such vast proposals we appeal to the people... If it is their judgment that there should be enfranchisement without redistribution, I should be very much surprised: but I should not attempt to dispute their decision. (Parliamentary Debates, 8th July 1884)

Gladstone called his bluff. He remarked to the Queen that the Commons had never been dissolved at the call of the Lords. Such a principle would subjugate the Commons to the Lords; and, he added: "the attempt to establish it would certainly end in organic change detrimental to the dignity and authority of the House of Lords."Gladstone was plainly right; and one of Salisbury's great strengths as a statesman was to know when he was beat. As a result he was able to gain a point of lasting significance that today remains unresolved.

Salisbury responded in a public speech:

...there is the question, how far it is legitimate for the House of Lords to press for a dissolution. Well, I think that any such claim on the part of the House of Lords would not be justified by the Constitution. But the House of Lords has the right to say this: 'We do not approve of the measure you bring before us. If you like to accept its rejection, well and good; if you object to its rejection, your remedy is to appeal to the people.'

All fair enough. But by reason of his reasonable stance he was able to point to the true hole in the constitution. For he drew the distinction, still alive today, between pressing for a dissolution on matters of general government policy and on tampering with the constitution. Ministers, he said, all spoke under a 'fundamental fallacy': "... they ignore the fact that this is not a common question of legislation. It is a vital question: it is a question of the revision of the Constitution."

Salisbury won his point. A compromise was reached whereby the Lords passed the Reform Bill after a Redistribution Bill had been introduced into the Commons. Moreover Gladstone was soon forced to resign after a Commons defeat and Salisbury himself formed (in June 1885) a minority government. But Gladstone won the ensuing general election at the end of the year – only to lose office again seven months later after Irish Home Rule split the Liberals. Salisbury became prime minister with a large majority until 1892.

From Gladstone's return in 1892, with a majority of only 40 seats including the Irish Nationalists, the clarity of Salisbury's thinking suffered in the melée. From 1868 we have seen a referendal theory of the House of Lords. As an unelected House it would always bow to the nation, but it would also hold in check the tendency of the nation's elected representatives to profit from their election to go on frolics of their own. The permanent Tory bias of the House of Lords, even in those days, always gave a hollow ring in some ears to their high-sounding claim; but in a period of unusually swift constitutional development, a stabilising force in British politics may well have been salutary. From now on however the Lords sought to apply tests of Liberal mandates which could not even in principle be satisfied; so that the Lords' opposition became undisguisably partisan. Said Lord Salisbury: "No human being can tell on what question...the present Government was returned."

This comment was made in the context of of Irish Home Rule. He added to it the notion that for the mandate to hold in that case it would not only need to be clearly referable to Irish Home Rule, but it would need to show a majority for the measure in both England and Scotland – or as it was put a 'majority of the nation in all its main divisions' – which Salisbury of course knew Gladstone had no hope of doing. Such an attack on a Liberal mandate immediately after a general election struck at the root of Salisbury's own strategy. It contrasts uncomfortably with his statesmanlike reaction to losing the 1869 general election. For the sole justification he had claimed for the Lords' opposition to unpalatable Commons legislation had been its being out of tune with the nation's settled wish.

In 1884, as we have seen, he had come within an ace of claiming a right for the Lords to demand a general election in such circumstances. Now on the contrary he was saying that a general election would resolve nothing unless it was called (at least primarily) on a single issue. Where, as in 1892, the Liberals brought in a wide reform programme, it became impossible, according to Lord Salisbury, to determine what the people had voted for at all. Accordingly the Lords were free to oppose whatever they disliked from the Commons; and none could say the House of Lords were flying in the face of the people's will.

Having resolved on demolition, the Lords attacked the Liberal edifice from 1892-1895 with sledge-hammers. Their main target was the Government of Ireland Bill, which differed from the Home Rule Bill of 1886 in providing for Ireland to elect Westminster MPs to vote on Irish matters (excluding as before defence, trade and foreign relations). But they wrecked the Liberals' local government reform, and Asquith's Employers' Liability Bill also, by inserting a contracting-out clause.

Irish Home Rule divided Britain in extremes of political passion and leaves even today its legacy of dragon's teeth. The Lords might have been wiser to stick to Salisbury's earlier distinction, in 1884, between revisions of the constitution and other kinds of government legislation. His true state of mind may well have been closer to his caveat way back in 1869 that there could be cases where the Lords should oppose 'in the highest case of morality – in those cases in which a man would not set his hand to a certain proposition, though a revolution should follow from his refusal....' Either of these approaches might suggest modern conclusions from an unresolved gap in our constitution. Instead one can only point to events. Rosebery succeeded Gladstone as Prime Minister in March 1894. Salisbury won the next two general elections and resigned in 1902. From 1906 the pendulum knocked the Tories and the House of Lords like ninepins further and further down the hill; and a legacy of bitterness made constructive compromise impossible. In politics honesty may not be the best policy – but cynicism always brings its own nemesis.

It is instructive to track the writings of A V Dicey, the famous constitutional lawyer, against these events. He figures in Mr Mount's book (The British Constitution Now) as one of the 'Three Simplifiers' – the other two being Walter Bagehot and the later Fabian Sir Ivor Jennings. In fact he was much in Bagehot's tradition. He concentrated on the supremacy of Parliament as the engine of government.

The driving force in Dicey's thought was, anyway, undoubtedly to maintain the integrity of the Union. All his thinking was governed by the threat of Irish secession, to which he opposed an idiosyncratic idea of Parliamentary sovereignty. In 1886 – *England's Case Against Home Rule* – his was a simple, if unbalanced, proposition: "Turn the UK into a federal state, and parliamentary government as we know it is at an end."

By the Government of Ireland Bill of 1893, in *A Leap In The Dark*, he had introduced the novel idea of a referendum if the Lords were forced to cave in, to secure the approval of a majority of the UK electors to the principle of Irish Home Rule. Here he refers to this proposal as unconstitutional – though in his zealotry he brushes this aside. Elsewhere he comments that in 1890 the very idea of referendums in British politics was virtually unknown, but by 1894 it was all the rage. The change of course was engendered by Tories looking for a majority, no matter how or where, against Irish Home Rule – a final example if proof were needed of the truth that constitutional theory is stifled in the heat of political battle.

Finally when the House of Lords had sunk against the iceberg of the Parliament Act, in *A Fool's Paradise*, Dicey was, mealy-mouthed, preaching revolution, should the Parliament Act be used to force through the 1912 Home Rule Bill. "What are the limits within which the tyranny either of a king or of a democracy justifies civil war is not an inquiry on which I will enter." Here Dicey was intending his readers to recall the view of Bracton, who died in 1268, that the king – and by extrapolation any government – is subject to God and law which put him on his throne. "The right to restrain an erring king… is rather a right of revolution, a right to defy a faithless lord and make war upon him, than a right that can be enforced in form of law."

Mr Mount must be justified in condemning such incendiary sentiments from a respected constitutionalist, whose trade is to hold the ring for fair and civilised political debate. But the rising Tory gorge of desperation and unreason in the two decades leading up to the Parliament Act is well illustrated by this morose champion. No rational policy of compromise could be expected from a party so discouraged and out of sorts. It takes cold courage to make the best of a bad job. Such in fact was the temper of Lord Salisbury's calm approach to irresistible change in the period from 1868 to 1885. His policy then suggests lessons still alive today – and musings how history might have gone had he and others kept their powder dry.

Nevertheless when by the 1906 general election Asquith was returned with the Liberals in a large majority, the stage was set for revenge. In 1906 things were already moving fast. In fact the Lords succeeded in blocking the Liberals' Education Bill, when their Unionist amendments demanding denominational teaching were both unacceptable to the Liberals and not insisted against.

Conversely, with the 1906 Trade Disputes Bill, which gave trades unions valuable legal immunities, the Lords let it through without substantive amendment. For, said Lord Lansdowne, the Leader of the Unionist peers: "I believe the juncture is one when, even if we were to win for the moment, our victory would be fruitless in the end. I shall not vote against this Bill."

These two skirmishes – one in favour of the Liberal government, and one in favour of the Lords – might be thought to be indicating a chance of a workable compromise; but any such hope would have been illusory. Godfrey Le May in *The Victorian Constitution: Conventions, Usages and Contingencies* (1979), at p191: "…The Unionists were prepared to ignore their doctrine of the mandate when an insistence upon it might bring them into direct conflict with organised Labour. In other matters, however, they resorted to challenging the Government to put their measures, one by one, to the judgement of a General Election."

This version of the mandate to which the House of Lords adhered from 1906 was an adoption of Lord Salisbury's tactics that hamstrung the last Liberal Government of 1892-5, mitigated only by Wellington's advice of old that no successful opposition was worth a resulting revolution. It was a doctrine designed to limit to vanishing-point the Lords' recognition of any Commons' policy they disliked as sanctioned by the result of a general election. As Balfour put it: "The power which the House of Lords has, and which it undoubtedly ought to exercise, is... to see that ...laws are not... the hasty and ill-considered offspring of one passionate election."

For the constitutionalist looking for lessons to be learned, it matters now not at all that there was no public outcry at the Lords' mutilation of Liberal Bills on a whole range of matters. Such a strategy of Opposition was plainly a cynical abuse of the Lords' constitutional powers. The corollary of Salisbury's own deformation in the later 1890s of his own original mandate theory of 1868-9, which was now the cornerstone of Tory Opposition again a decade later was this: that no general election, however fought, necessarily resolved any issue in advance, since in any one election inevitably more than one issue might arise. Consequently any measure that the Lords did not like (and that meant any measure that was not a Tory measure) must be either dropped by the government in the Commons or put again to the people either in a further general election or – and here appeared again Dicey's 'unconstitutional' innovation which he as a constitutionalist was happy to approve when it suited him – in a referendum. Seldom has pride shouted out so for a fall.

Nor was the fall long delayed. Our sadness must be that genuine problems of both democratic theory and practice were masked by the partisan squabble, none of them resolved and some hardly canvassed to this day. The Tory Lords cynically abused their power: so far as they claimed that their policies represented the public will, their claim forfeited all credence when they systematically flouted the policies of elected governments.

Not however that the Tories had even then a monopoly of democratic unrectitude: Lansdowne's proposals for a more representative Second Chamber were turned down out of hand by Asquith who had no ambition to see a more legitimate and responsible opponent of his policies. Patience has its human limits; and he had suffered as Liberal Home Secretary in the 1890s...

But the heat and dust of old battles need not blind us now. Before turning to the final pitiful scene these problems should be identified.

Central was the question how a bicameral system should operate. No perfect solution has been found, though the US Congressional system is the nearest to a workable model. Where the two House have different constituencies, functions or times of election, conflict, occasional and sometimes prolonged, is inevitable but never in the limit unresolvable, if not by joint committee or ad hoc, then by the ballot-box. What made the struggle early this century between the House of Commons and the House of Lords unresolvable was the position of the Lords beyond the reach either of the elected government or the ballot-box.

No less significant was the question of the mandate. It is the nub of democracy; for the mandate is supposed to be – by all governments is claimed to be – the people's wishes that they carry in their dispatch-boxes. Before the public became seduced by the tabloids into an insatiable and almost exclusive diet of sleaze, it was politicians' habit of evading fair accountability that placed them low in the public's rating of the professional classes. It was plainly unfair for the unelected inbuilt Tory majority in the Lords to claim the exclusive right to speak for the public. But the doubt remains of the public will that is always claimed to be behind individual measures of a government normally elected as a choice of evils. The doubt can only be sharpened as parties seek ever stronger moral suasion over their members, especially when it is carried to the borders of tyranny by governments over their MPs in the Commons.

Lastly there lurked the doubt about the need for a Second Chamber at all. Those who now oppose a Second Chamber which can within at least prescribed circumstances box with the House of Commons are crypto-unicameralists. Many of the most influential are MPs who know that an obedient and weak House of Lords lessens their work-load. But at the beginning of the century obedience was beyond what the Commons could expect of the House of Lords. The Lords instead just forfeited their claim to represent the nation in any unbiassed way. They never recovered it.

Since the Lords are not representative their House cannot stand without reconstruction; and these three questions resolve to two. They become, first: how should the House of Lords be reformed to complement the House of Commons? and, second: how should this reform improve the representative function of Parliament? For if these two questions cannot be answered positively, they resolve yet further into the single question: how can the House of Lords be most quickly and painlessly abolished? This simple cascade of questions is already in the air; and it will haunt every page of this book.

The Liberal lead-in to the Parliament Bill was a walk over huffings and puffings. The delusory success of Lord Salisbury's last years, first in frustrating the Liberal government from 1892-5, and then in winning two elections on the back of tactics which sinned against his best principles, had embittered party relations beyond hope of compromise. A clash of powers between the two Houses could not be avoided.

After the second Liberal election win of 1910, when at last Lord Lansdowne conceded that Asquith's government had the people's authority to legislate on the House of Lords, Lansdowne put forward proposals for changing the composition rather than the powers of the Lords. Asquith turned down the proposals out of hand. He was already confident of the King's willingness to create enough Liberal Lords to swamp even that Tory preserve. He had no wish for a Second Chamber whose irreproachable membership might develop legitimate opposition to his policies.

Lansdowne was by nature a moderate and a statesman; but his proposals came of course far too late. Taking up the baton from his old friend the Third Marquess of Salisbury cannot have easy, either, when the Fourth was by now ably supporting his predecessor's later intransigence.

Said the fourth Marquess on 23rd May 1911 (HL *Hansard* vol 8, cols 710-1):

It is admitted on all hands that a House of Commons is elected without, as the phrase is, any mandate for particular measures, and yet is entitled to deal with them... But you must not say that the House of Commons in these respects represents the exact opinion of the people. It does not follow. It may be so; it may not be so. And according to our ancient Constitution the only means of preventing a miscarriage of justice in consequence of the possibility of the House of Commons legislating in conflict with the wishes of the people lay in the power of your Lordships' House to refer such Bills to the people.

We saw how under pressure the third Marquess denied any claim by the Lords to force a dissolution on Gladstone. Salisbury referred instead to a dilemma which might at any moment be presented to the government in the Commons by the Lords – either to accept a Commons' rejection of a Bill or to call an election to sanction it. But when it became clear that, in Tory eyes, not even a general election need settle any particular issue, all government policy was permanently at risk. Intolerable!

Nevertheless there were huge democratic gulfs close under the stormy political surface. The Liberal band-wagon could fairly be accused of careering in several directions at once, towards some kind of independence for Ireland, towards the new empowerment of organised Labour, towards major changes in education and taxation. It was far from clear how all these huge issues could fairly be said to be irreversibly resolved, in terms of a manifestation of the people's will, by a general election.

And when in fact in 1910 there was not just one general election but two (of the 'Peers versus the People') the Liberals had their majority drastically cut and won both in similar results with the support only of the Irish Nationals and Labour. That there was a lawful government that could do what it liked was clear; but what its mandate was from the people was a philosophical question which bore no resemblance to political reality. To this day we await a theory of the mandate which is more than a licence for politicians to do what they hope they were elected for.

It is the common feature of tragedies good and bad that the end seems inevitable and resolves nothing. With tempers already high, David Lloyd George, as Chancellor, brought in his revolutionary budget of 1909 introducing taxes both on high incomes and on land sales. The Lords threw it out at second reading. The first general election of 1910 (January). Despite their suspect Commons support, the Liberal government were set on introducing a Parliament Bill to restrict the Lords' rights on money Bills and to redefine their powers versus the Commons. But a conference of the two main parties, the Liberals and the Unionists, could find no basis of agreement. The Liberals took their Parliament Bill through the Commons, which was duly stalled at second reading in the Lords.

Lansdowne came up with serious counter-proposals that in less inflamed times would have merited serious consideration. A joint committee presided over by the Speaker was to determine whether a Bill was a Money Bill; and if it did so determine, the Lords would agree to forgo any right of amendment. For other Bills a joint sitting of both Houses would be called to settle disputes between the Houses lasting over a year. Finally when such a dispute was a 'matter of great gravity ... not adequately submitted to... the people' it could be settled by a referendum.

The Liberals' refusal to take these proposals seriously led to the second general election of the year, in December. The following May the Parliament Bill practically in its present form passed the Commons; and this time it received an unopposed second reading in the Lords. But this was no kind of concession by the Lords, who strengthened the earlier Lansdowne proposals by excepting the Crown and devolution from the Bill's limitations. But the time for compromise was past. In August the King's agreement to create up to 500 new peers was made known. The peers capitulated.

The result was a huge mess which is a Herculean task to clear out. All Parliament is an Augean Stables caked up to the windows with over 80 years of unfinished business. The Lords are hamstrung and their running-mate, the Commons, over-confident and out of training in consequence. The 1911 Parliament Act was never intended even by the Liberal Government to be any-thing but a stopgap measure pending the replacement of the hereditary Second Chamber by a 'popular' one. The very word in that context at that time shows the fighting spirit and the absence of thinking-through with which their momen-tous Parliamentary change was carried through.

So there is no way that a look at delaying powers as an expedient can be avoided, so long as this is not thought more than just one piece in the puzzle. For most of those who advocate an increase of the powers of the Lords, after or in conjunction with reform of their composition, normally propose a return from the current delaying power brought in by the 1949 Parliament Act to the longer delay sanctioned by the 1911 Act itself. Those, however, uneasy about having a Second Chamber but who stop short of outright abolition propose cutting the delaying power yet further (even after amending the composition).

One might conclude that once the Lords' composition – and even their func-tions (which as we shall see in Part III is the real issue) – are agreed, the main out-standing matter is the length of the delaying power to be agreed upon. This should mean that the *principle* of a delaying power is agreed upon for generally understood reasons. But this is not at all the case.

Under the constitutional settlement of 1688 a veto of a Bill by either House defeated it. This balance was encapsulated in the formula of a "coequal partner-ship". The effect of it was, with the Monarch, the indivisibility of Parliament and the government. Unless they spoke as one there was no new legislation. The King it was himself that broke this unity and balance by agreeing to overbear the unfair and unelected Tory majority by swamping the the chamber with Asquith's nominees.

One may regret that the Tories caved in (perhaps, partly at least, in defence of the Monarchy itself) and did not leave the King and Asquith to carry out their threat. If heredity is as certain a determinant of political orientation as some think the effect must have been to eradicate for good the hereditary Tory major-ity. In any case the absurdity of such a method of constitutional change would certainly have brought other adjustments in its wake, so that we should not be left an inheritance of nearly a century's constitutional stagnation and mess, which it is now almost impossible to convert back into a running stream of sweet water.

In any case the delaying power of the House of Lords was brought in as a transitional measure and Britain is still in that transition, though whither is anyone's guess. The delaying power is the fruit of patched-up crisis, not a consensual solution to a recognised problem generally debated either at the time or since.

What then was the constitutional justification in 1911 for the delaying power – and is it the same today? Its scope was to allow the House of Lords to delay legislation, other than 'Money Bills', from the Commons for up to at least two years spread over three sessions between its second reading in the Commons and its final passing in the Commons. The result was to allow the Lords to frustrate Commons legislation in the last two years of a Parliament. The 1949 Parliament Act simply cut the delay from two years to at least one year over two successive sessions. The rationale of both provisions is accordingly the same and they can be discussed together.

Money Bills were outwith the delaying powers of both Acts. So the casus belli of the 1909-11 dispute between the two Houses – the 1909 Lloyd George budget, which the Lords threw out – was decided wholly in favour of the Commons. The principle of the delaying power has nothing to do with the Commons' traditional area of superiority over the Lords, which arose from the people's insistence on never being taxed by the government without representation. The substitution by the 1911 Act of the Lords' veto of legislation *other than* Money Bills was therefore a naked assertion of the Commons' claim to represent people *to the exclusion of the Lords* after the Lords' delay had given time for debate.

This observation leads straight back to the doctrine of the mandate already discussed. The doctrine is full of holes on both sides of the argument. Those whose claim is that any policy or provision mentioned in a party manifesto gets the people's imprimatur when that party wins a general election because the people have spoken, have to face the objection that people vote for a party on balance and often as a choice of evils – and anyway the acceptability of a particular policy cannot fairly be judged until it is first set out in full in black and white (as almost never in a manifesto) – and then tested by debate against alternatives. Those however who object to mandate-by-manifesto have to explain why they profess to know the people's mind better than the people themselves as expressed in a general election – and/or to propose a better way of finding out the people's will. The only obvious candidate is the referendum (already on the political tapis, as we have seen, since the latter 1890s). But the referendum is open to all kinds of abuse by government; for the people's answer depends too much on the phrasing of the question and the confusion of foreshortened and unstructured debate.

The untried candidate is provision for full, informed and structured debate led by Parliament and taken to the country – not necessarily at all by general election. For public debate to be led by Parliament, however, Parliament has to earn the respect of the public by the depth of its understanding and expression of it, by the authority and power given by the structuring of its institutions and by the calibre of its membership – by its functions, powers, and membership.

It is to such a system of government scrutiny by Parliament, seen as an organic process from policy-making through prelegislative debate right through to the executive's use of its powers and administration – and to the Upper Chamber's crucial contribution to that process – that this book is dedicated.

Meanwhile it is clear that a delaying power on its own does not amount to the constitutional safeguard it was intended for. Delay on its own does not spawn debate but rancour and confusion. Furthermore its advocacy under fire looks more like Micawberesque opportunism – desperation waiting on events to change the political balance – than respect for democracy.

There is a most interesting footnote on the muddle of the 1911 Parliament Act. What swung the Lords' defeat was George V's pact with Asquith to swamp the House with Asquith's sympathisers if Asquith won the general election called to decide the matter. But Asquith didn't. It was a tie. Liberals and Tories won 272 seats each. It was the support of over a hundred Irish Nationalists and Labour that Asquith relied on for his majority. Asquith's 'mandate' for the 1911 Act was doubtful indeed. But in the end-game the king-moves are often decisive. The King was afraid of Asquith's cabinet resignation. Later in 1913 he recorded with implied regret that he was not advised that in those circumstances he could have avoided the chaos of yet another general election, by instead calling on Balfour to form a government. Balfour, though without a majority, could then decently have bided his time before yet again going to the country. None can say what the agenda and what the result of an election say a year later might have been. Nor what might have been the effect on the British 'constitutional' monarchy...

Moreover neither general election nor referendum as an alternative or supplement to the delaying power necessarily fills the lacuna or resolves an impasse that anyone can see is once again a possibility. For a general election, as in 1911, may not be decisive; and a referendum may be misleading. But the search for a solution is imperative if the House of Lords is to regain a firm place on the scene. None can put the result of failure than this comment, in bold type, in Lord Home's report in March 1978: "The natural consequence for our institutions of the crude equation of parliamentary government with the right of a party majority in the House of Commons to authorise a government to do anything for which it claims a mandate must be eventually a unicameral Parliament."

It is hard to think of a worse outcome of the current outbreak of constitution fever for public representation than the fratricidal abolition of the Lords by the Commons without a complete overhaul of the chamber that is left. A single House of Parliament that combined the functions envisaged in this book for both Houses is however theoretically possible, but not in this author's view a political practicality. For the House of Commons has for many years shown itself so much more aware of the Lords' failings than of any conceivable shortcomings of its own. Nevertheless many of the ideas recommended here could easily be adapted to the unicameral system that Labour has frequently advocated. It is to the next sustained squabble after 1911 – from 1945-51 – that we now come.

b) 1945-51.

The Labour landslide of the 1945 general election took the Tories and Winston Churchill by surprise. Nothing remotely like a Labour overall majority of 156 had been expected by anyone. The scenery hurriedly reverted to the political discomfort of 1911. The triumphant Labour government with a large Commons majority were faced with a House of Lords solidly hostile to what to them seemed a programme as revolutionary as Asquith's. The crucial difference was Attlee's unassailable Commons majority which made futile any claim by the hereditary Lords to represent popular feeling more truly than the elected Commons.

In the Lords Labour were led by Lord Addison, a formidable reformer. The Tories were led by the fifth Marquis of Salisbury, the grandson of the Tory doyen up to the turn of the century. It was as if the Fates had redealt a hand of bridge which all the players could recognise, so that unfinished business could be concluded. The two leaders came to a working relationship that protected the House of Lords' precarious position for half a century, though in terms of the politics of the day it was a relationship of Aesopian inequalities. Not only was Addison firm in the seat of power, but he was older and more politically experienced. Addison needed to shepherd a revolutionary programme through a pack of chained wolves. This he did with great skill. "In the face of an overwhelming Conservative majority, he was responsible for the safe passage of a large and far-reaching, even revolutionary, legislative programme." (K and J Morgan, *Portrait of a Progressive* (1980))

Viscount Cranborne (as he then was) set out during the debate on the King's Speech the Tory response to to their predicament. It was an adroit application of his grandfather's mandate doctrine, the Salisbury Convention.

"Whatever our personal views, we should frankly recognise that these proposals were put before the country at the recent general election and that the people of this country, with full knowledge of these proposals returned the Labour party to power. The Government may, therefore, I think, fairly claim that they have a mandate to introduce these proposals. I believe it would be constitutionally wrong, when the country has so recently expressed its view, for this House to oppose proposals which have been definitely put before the electorate." (HL *Hansard*, 16th August 1945, vol.137, col. 47)

In retrospect he embroidered his view:

"Because of the large Labour majority in the Commons in 1945...[we made] it our broad guiding rule that what had been on the Labour Party programme at the preceding general election should be regarded as having been approved by the British people. Therefore... we passed all the nationalisation Bills... on the second reading and did our best to improve them... at committee stage. Where, however, measures were introduced which had not been in the Labour Party Manifesto at the preceding election, we reserved full liberty of action." (HL *Hansard*, 4th November 1964, vol 261, col. 66)

Nothing better could be made of the Lords' limbo. To this day it remains the 'broad guiding rule' of the Tories in the House of Lords, which to their credit they have on occasion applied against proposals from their Tory friends. Lord Carrington (in *"Reflect on Things Past"* 1988, pp 77-8) encapsulates both Lord Salisbury's view and his own:

Cranborne reckoned that it was not the duty of the House of Lords to make our system of government inoperable... This meant that the Lords should, if they saw fit, amend, but should not destroy or alter beyond recognition any Bill on which the country had, by implication, given its verdict. The Lords... should not frustrate the will of the people... by and large the Salisbury convention – of no wrecking amendments – was observed. To this day the convention continues... Later in life I applied the same convention myself.

Despite this continuing Tory unanimity on the duty of restraint, and observance of it 'by and large' the principles implicit in it were not accepted by Labour when it did not suit them to do so. What point there was in the two-year delaying power left with the House of Lords by the 1911 Act lay in the Lords' ability to block unpalatable legislation during the last two years of a Parliament. By that time in the life of a Parliament it could be claimed that an electoral mandate grows a little thin.

This of course in no way presupposes that the people is no longer behind the government; but by now another general election is in the offing. As Lord Cranborne said, "If the government are hampered in their work, they can always go back to the sovereign people of this country from which Parliament gets its authority." (HL *Hansard,* 31st October 1945, vol 137, col.163) The House of Lords cannot force an election; but the House could hold off legislation towards the end of a Parliament until the Prime Minister called for a dissolution.

This arrangement did not suit Attlee. For the Iron and Steel Bill might run out of time as a result of the Lords' delays. Faced with political reality Lord Addison accordingly tore away the figleaf of entente in the House of Lords. After two happy years of symbiosis with the Salisbury convention, in early 1948 Lord Addison dropped his mask. The Labour Government had no intention of going to the hazard of a general election to get their Bill on the statute book. They preferred instead to fix the constitution to make an election unnecessary. A new Parliament Bill was brought in. Said Lord Addison at second reading:

The claim to decide whether a subject is or is not in accordance with the mandate of the people contains this implication that, if this House is of opinion that it is not in the mandate, this House is at liberty to reject it. We challenge that implication from the very start...

(But this was 1948, not 1945!)

...We claim that it is for the elected representatives of the people to decide whether an issue is or is not the subject of Parliamentary activity... We do not accept... that this House, entirely unrepresentative, shall be the final arbiter as to what is and what is not the opinion of the people. (HL Hansard vol 153, col 634)

Lord Addison's salvo blew the Salisbury convention out of the water. For its intention was to find a *modus vivendi* of the Upper House with the Commons which recognised the rights of both Houses. Where the main parties were divided and Labour was the government, the sole prerequisite for an understanding between the Houses was agreement to it between the parties. There was no such agreement, nor, according to Lord Addison in 1948, had there ever been. Not many were truly surprised at this. But Labour's 1948 Parliament Bill left no doubt of the fact.

Lord Addison maintained, "There is no question of mandate at all." He adduced the fair point that: "Of necessity in the life of a Parliament, a large number of issues which were not foreseen at the time of the election…Take the [India] Independence Act. None of us had foreseen … the circumstances… at the passing of that Act… It was not a subject of mandate." Lord Salisbury was however justified in believing he had the better of the argument while being overwhelmed in the battle. For there was clearly a huge difference between a government's response to an international crisis (however much brought on by Labour's own bungling) and a constitutional Bill of the first importance brought in *ad hoc* to get the government out of time trouble. The working of British Parliamentary democracy was clearly a matter of even more importance than Labour's Iron and Steel Bill.

Lord Salisbury moved an amendment declining second reading to the Parliament Bill to 'for which the nation has expressed no desire'. Lord Addison adjourned the Bill to give time for consultations and the preparation of the White Paper, *Parliament Bill 1947: Agreed Statement* (Cmnd 7380). The Paper called itself an *Agreed Statement on Conclusion of Conference of Party Leaders*. But it was an agreement to differ. The government vouchsafed a 'Second Chamber possessed of proper facilities for debating public affairs and for revising legislation.' But it represented the Tory objection to the Bill as an attempt to 'force the Government to seek a General Election against its own inclination and that of the Commons'. This was plainly misrepresentation. What was truly at issue was the proper length of a Parliament. There were (and are) strong arguments for shortening the length of a Parliament from five years to four. There was no justification for the government's changing the constitution on the hoof. Once the constitution becomes a football, Parliamentary democracy is itself at risk. In this case the Tories were unquestionably correct that the whole intention of the 1911 Act was being frustrated by the Bill.

But the 1911 Act itself was used to force through the new Bill without the Lords' consent. It became law (very possibly unconstitutionally) in December 1949. By that time the government had already accepted (on 24th November) the substance of Lord Salisbury's point on the Iron and Steel Bill by agreeing not to appoint any member of the new corporation till after the 1950 election. So the 1949 Parliament Act was not even used for the shaky purpose for which it was constructed!

The 1949 Parliament Act was the repudiation by Labour of the Salisbury mandate doctrine, to which the Tories in fact still cling. "We do not accept… that this House, entirely unrepresentative, shall be the final arbiter as to what is and what is not the opinion of the people." Thus spoke Lord Addison. He was not of course trying to be fair. At no time could it ever have been said fairly of the Tories that they thought any but the people themselves the 'arbiters' of their own opinion. Moreover no one has made a better practical defence of the House of Lords anomalous position, 'entirely unrepresentative', than the third and fifth Marquises of Salisbury and their successor Lord Cranborne.

But the fact remains that the Salisbury Convention has never been fully accepted by the Labour party. Its corollary, the Lords delaying power, has been seen by Labour as no more than a right to have enough time to consider and

(occasionally) revise Commons legislation. This does not square with the trenchant statement by Lord Cranborne in his *Politeia Anniversary Lecture* of 4th
December 1996 that 'the Salisbury/Addison doctrine... accepted in constitutional circles [and] known as the Salisbury Convention... is definitely part of our
constitution'. But a convention requires all party agreement or at least all party
practice. Whether or not Labour should have accepted the doctrine as the only
basis upon which the House of Lords can currently operate, it is hard to convince
that Labour in fact ever did accept it.

Lord Addison's repudiation of the doctrine depended on the House of Lords
being 'unrepresentative'. The Life Peerages Act 1958 (extended to women in
1963) did nothing but exacerbate this yawning gap in the House's foundations.
Selection of peers has done nothing for representative democracy. It has
increased only the power of the parties and the patronage of the prime minister
at a time when their stranglehold over the Commons has grown ever more suf-
focating.

The 'mandate' theory depended on the unassailable point that the later a government gets into a Parliament the further in time and events it gets from the verdict of the people. Moreover since it was first propounded, the succession of
notable events and their communication has accelerated to a bewildering degree;
and the people are demanding an ever greater share of the action. These are
arguments for shorter Parliaments, perhaps of four years and on a regular cycle.

Now the Lords' exercise of a delaying power does not at present favour rational debate outside Parliament – debate in the country, where it belongs when
Parliament is in disarray. For in the Lords' current anomalous position the merits and demerits of exercise of their power on any Bill would be lost in the smoke-
screen of Labour acrimony about the Lords using their power for any purpose
whatever. However such prejudice would evaporate after reform acceptable to
Labour of the House's functions and composition. To more recent proposals for
such reform we now turn.

2. AN AGE OF REFORM PROPOSALS
1966-79

Labour's General Election win of 1966 marked another turn of the slow tide in House of Lords affairs. For Labour's manifesto promised to prevent frustration of House of Commons' measures by delay or defeat in the Lords. This was followed up in the Queen's Speech of October 1967 by an invitation to interparty consultations. Whether or not these took place, however, or arrived at agreement, the government pledged change by legislation in the coming session.

The history of actual relations between the two Houses, however, as sketched in the previous chapter, shows the credibility gap between Labour fears of frustration and delay and any likely sequence of events. That gap in turn shows Labour's idealogical rather than practical motivation then for change – much as now. A striking conclusion from any analysis of reform proposals over this last thirty years is the persistence of attitudes little disguised by changes in political language.

But the paradox of Labour's continued hostility to a House of Lords which remains (neither obstinately nor triumphantly) unchanged is at once dispelled by the irreconcilable conflict in what might be called Labour's public and private face. In public Labour makes much – and with evident justification – of the House of Lords' unrepresentative membership. But in private this weakness is cherished by Labour: better by far a Second Chamber permanently under the sword of Damocles than one which might from some base of electoral respectability (and independence) put government legislation under uncomfortable scrutiny.

This conflict is more acute in Labour circles than among Tories, but only because no Tory Prime Minister this century could have abolished the Lords' hereditary voting rights even if he (or she) had wanted to. *All* recent PMs have preferred an obedient to an effective House of Lords. The difference has been the two kinds of offence which disobedience has occasioned. Among Tories it was hurt family feelings; among Labour supporters, a delicious affront to their public conscience.

There have been many *ad hoc* complaints from all points of the compass about the membership of the Lords, that it is undemocratic (but never, to its credit, anti-democratic), unrepresentative, unpredictable, ill-informed, 'backwoods' or backward-looking. And all these complaints have at one time or another been justified – and on occasion rebutted, with equal justification, as the inevitable price of independence. But *all* these complaints systematically evade the point at issue, which is not the Lords' membership but their *function*. Tory leaders, from embarrassment over membership, have been debarred from proposing reforms, even in government, let alone in Opposition; and this to them has been a relief. They wanted no more than Labour did a Second Chamber with a function that might challenge their monopoly of power. Otherwise their attitude is no different to Labour's. Obedience before effectiveness; and that is anti-democratic!

This preamble underlines how up to date is the story (see Michael Wheeler-Booth, "The Attempted Reform of the House of Lords 1964-69", Table 38, 1969) of the Parliament (No. 2) Bill of 1968/9. Before the end of June '68 the Inter-Party Conference on House of Lords Reform had drawn up proposals, leading towards an uncomfortable consensus. The main bone of contention remaining was whether the proposals would be implemented at the end of the session or at the end of the Parliament.

But on 18th June 1968 the House of Lords threw out the Southern Rhodesia (United Nations Sanctions) Order allowing Mr Wilson as PM to cut the Gordian knot. The Lords' action was declared (rightly) as against the spirit of a consensual approach to House of Lords reform. The government would press ahead with radical reform legislation. In November accordingly the White Paper on *House of Lords Reform* (Cmnd 3799) was published.

The White Paper in its rationale for its proposals made no attempt to balance change of membership against change of function. On one hand the right to vote from hereditary succession and a permanent majority of one party were declared, very fairly, inappropriate. But on the other the composition and powers of the House of Lords were declared to impede its carrying out its role as a Second Chamber as effectively as it should: and such a statement unexplained was Wilsonian gobbledygook. It screams for the response: "How not and why not?"

Accordingly we are not to be surprised that the proposals themselves signal the irreconcilables in Labour's thinking on House of Lords reform – between the demand for formal representational rectitude on one hand and for obedience on the other. For once the first is achieved there can be no escape from prescribing the Second Chamber's functions and then giving it the appropriate powers. What cannot be reasonable is to make sensible proposals on membership and then without explanation of its functions to cut the chamber's powers; and that is just what the White Paper proposed. Labour's failure to come to grips with the function and powers of the reformed chamber was as glaring then as now. But nobody should be surprised at that: it is a subject as difficult as it is controversial. What was silly was to propose simultaneously a strengthening of Lords' membership and an unexplained diminishing of their powers. That is like promoting an executive and cutting his authority at the same time.

Nevertheless the justification for abolishing hereditary voting rights was generally agreed even in 1968; and since then general agreement has become almost unanimous. So Labour's White Paper proposals on this deserve careful study. It may be possible to build out of them a scheme of membership close enough to consensual politics to make way for debate on the genuine issues of government – which are the Second Chamber's functions and the powers required to meet them.

The White Paper on *House of Lords Reform* was, as we have seen, a more substantial document on membership and voting rights than when when it skated over functions and powers. These are its salient points:

a) the Prime Minister would continue to recommend new peers to the Queen for creation by her: this would confirm (and on balance increase) the PMs powers of patronage;

b) the hereditary system would be phased out but remain in place for current peers: future hereditaries would not have a seat in the Lords;

c) the quota of bishops would be reduced by degrees from 26 to 16 (as later accepted by the 1970 Archbishops' Commission Report);

d) the House of Lords would become a two-tier chamber with both voting and non-voting members; apart from the vote, non-voting peers would have undiminished rights to speak, ask questions, move motions and amendments and sit on committees;

e) all life peers and peers of first creation could apply for the vote, subject to attendance of a third of sittings and retirement (for most) after the Parliament in which one reached 72;

f) current hereditaries would be non-voting members, save for those created also life peers; at that time added life peers would make up a voting House of around 230, in which the government would have a 10% majority over those with party affiliations – but crossbenchers would hold the balance.

g) on functions and powers, the only proposals were to cut yet further to six months the Lords' power of delay to legislation and to abolish their right to reject a statutory instrument.

There was much sense in a) to f) – though little sense in g), especially when Labour were claiming to make the Lords more 'effective' – and the White Paper got heavy endorsement in debates in both Houses.

In the Bill that followed there were modifications on remuneration; and the Prime Minister restated the wish to implement the Bill at the end of the session. Such insistence was not helpful. It was not intended to be. The Bill had its Commons second reading in February 1969 and was duly referred to Committee of the Whole House as a constitutional Bill – but in effect it ran out of time. Over about ten weeks it consumed over 80 hours of Commons time on the Preamble and only the first five clauses of the twenty in the Bill.

On 17th April 1969 the government admitted defeat "in order to ensure that the necessary Parliamentary time is available for priority legislation." (HC *Hansard*, vol 781, col 1338.)

No better package of Lords' reform has been proposed from that day to this, if the standard is defined by one well-canvassed and likely to command all party support. For if the prevailing view is right that no constitutional settlement can ever be beyond the reach of later Parliaments, consensus is a prerequisite for stability.

The White Paper dealt neatly and fairly with the two generally perceived defects in the composition of the House of Lords – the inbuilt Tory majority and hereditary voting rights. By the new distinction between voting and non-voting peers the proposals allowed for the continuing and varied expertise of peers to be brought to bear in debate – where more is always achieved by a strong speech than a vote. They also envisaged the continuance, for a while at least, of the most effective hereditaries in their positions unimpaired. The government's modesty in not demanding an overall majority was generous to cross-benchers.

The political defects however were equally obvious. It was not just that the White Paper ignored function and cut powers without reason. But the phasing out of hereditaries and replacement with further prime ministerial nominees could do nothing for the redress of the balance of Parliament and government. It could only increase the Prime Minister's powers of patronage, exercised in the name of the Crown. Even at that time the PM's power was of concern to constitutionalists – and since then we have had Mrs Thatcher and Mr Blair, and the advent of Europe.

But the hereditary feuds of Lords and Commons are never far below the surface and still obscure, with rivalry between the Houses, Parliament's serious weakening in the face of the ever-encroaching power of government and *vis-à-vis* the demands of international relations – especially of course from the European Union. If these serious systematic weaknesses are not cured, Britain as a whole will suffer. It is to be hoped that MPs will look a little more outside the closed circuit of Westminster.

Well – the proposals fell. In the short run there were two sets of consequences.

The first was a long Labour backlash against the Lords. Bills were introduced hostile to the powers of the House of Lords, by Robert Sheldon MP (twice) and Dennis Skinner MP in his House of Lords (Abolition) Bill 1975-76; and also by Lord Alport and Lord Mitchison. These Bills made no progress, but they signalled unfinished business loud and clear.

This trend was encapsulated by the 1978 Labour Party Statement by the National Executive Committee (as approved by the previous annual party conference). The House of Lords was declared to be "an outdated institution, completely inappropriate to a modern democratic system of government". Since the House of Lords, in the NEC's opinion, had no longer limited itself to the role of a revising chamber accepting the government's mandate, their preferred solution was House of Lords abolition. Failing this, the Statement advocated the end of the Lords' delaying powers and right of rejection of subordinate legislation. But even this was seen as an interim measure since an elected House might challenge the Commons and replacement of hereditaries by life peers would simply increase government's powers of patronage. The only problem foreseen after abolition was the Lords' veto on the prorogation of Parliament beyond five years – to be handled instead by referendum.

The Labour backlash was more than counterbalanced by the quiet effectiveness of the Lords' performance during the see-saw 'seventies. Nobody now could advocate simple abolition of the House of Lords without acknowledging the heavy extra strain that the Lords' absence would throw on the Commons already hanging by only a thread or two after the exponential increase in government legislation over the past thirty years. Abolitionists nowadays have also to acknowledge the increase in government power and control of the Commons which abolition of the Lords could only accentuate. Both points were ably made by Labour peers already in the early seventies.

In early 1972 Lord Shepherd, who was then deputy Opposition leader in the Lords noted the increasing concentration of power and influence within the government and executive, and the increase in delegated and subsidiary legislation – 'Parliamentary control and scrutiny have been weakened'. To put the Lords in order it would not be enough to remove the hereditary succession to vote in the Lords and the permanent Tory majority. It was necessary to consider how the function of the House of Lords might be developed to help the Commons and to provide Parliamentary control and scrutiny.

It is of course easier in Opposition to make cross-bench remarks. Lord Shepherd could hardly have made similar remarks after his party won the February general election two years later, since he would have been criticising his own government. The bug-bear of constitutional change has been the exaggerated interdependence of government and government majorities in the Commons which has made impossible the impartial separation of Parliamentary weakness from government's excessive strength. But Lord Shepherd's comments have been as apposite under every government since as when he made them in the *Parliamentarian* 53 in January 1972.

Lord Willis's unstarred question of 20th June 1974 (HL *Hansard* vol 352, col 1073) accordingly gains in emphasis when it is noted that Labour were by then back in power. He prodded the government for plans for House of Lords reform. Despite anachronism the House was working well but against the odds. Only reform could remove the Commons' persistent distrust of the Lords and allow the Second Chamber to bear a greater share of the Parliamentary burden. It would be difficult to find a shrewder critique of the House of Lords and the need for reform than that offered by these two Labour peers. The slightly later comments of two equally distinguished Tory peers take these lines of thought each a step further. The Hailsham Dimbleby Lecture of 14th October 1976 defined as 'elective dictatorship' a British constitution under which the government is uncontrolled by Parliament. Then in March 1977 Lord Carrington (in the *Illustrated London News*) commented on the difficulties the Lords were having in applying the Salisbury Convention (so-called) and argued for an elected Second Chamber as a counterweight to an unrepresentative government.

There were in fact many highly intelligent ideas for Parliamentary reform floating around in the late seventies. Many of them came from reform-minded Tories, culminating in Lord Home's Report of March 1978 (*The House of Lords: Report of the Conservative Review Committee*). Lord Hailsham's lecture and Lord Carrington's article are best seen as luminaries in a star-cluster, analysis of which spotlights the whole range of issues underlying the need for reform.

Lord Hailsham, no doubt prudently, concentrated on the weakness of the House of Lords without dwelling on the compounding corresponding weakness of the Commons that sticks Parliament under the PM's (like the Roman Emperor's) thumb. He commented however that the House of Lords must ultimately be abolished or, preferably, replaced. For the Lords is not effective in controlling the advancing powers of the executive. It is "arguably less persuasive than a powerful leading article in *The Times,* or even a good edition of *Panorama"*. He accordingly argued for a Second Chamber elected by proportional representation to represent whole regions. Finance and the political colour of the executive would remain the province of the House of Commons.

Implied by the suggestion of regional and proportional representation was the Tory fear of the day (shared for example by Lord Carrington) of extremist government elected by a comparatively small proportion of the electorate. The unpredictabilities of first-past-the-post Parliamentary elections combined with the threatenings and slaughter of the Labour NEC of the day made such fears far from unreasonable. If Labour had won the 1979 general election by however small a Parliamentary majority and by whatever small proportion of the British electorate, it is highly unlikely that the constitutional problems the British would now be facing would include the future of the House of Lords. But they *would* include Parliamentary weakness in the face of a prime minister with a working majority in the House of Commons.

Lord Carrington's proposals six months later arose directly out of his current experience as Leader of the Opposition in the Lords. The Aircraft and Shipbuilding Industries Bill originally published in May 1975 had caused much ill-feeling and was ultimately defeated as to the most controversial section (on ship-repairing companies) on a Parliamentary technicality. This was a most instructive episode that laid bare the underlying anomalies of manifesto mandates on one side and the Salisbury Doctrine on the other.

Lord Carrington argued for a stronger Second Chamber with more power and a politically credible composition elected on some different basis and cycle from the Commons. The House of Commons would remain ultimately supreme but the Lords' delaying powers (restored to those of 1911) would compel an extremist government to gauge public opinion before implementation.

So he proposed, as had Lord Hailsham, a Second Chamber elected regionally by proportional representation. A third of the members would retire every two years; and continual elections would keep the chamber in touch with the public. A Second Chamber given authority and electoral credibility in this way could, he thought, expect its delaying powers to be restored to those of 1911.

The Hailsham and the Carrington proposals taken together with the aborted changes in 1968-69 raised between them almost all the Parliamentary issues visible up to the advent of Mrs Thatcher. But a brief review of the flush of proposals brought around the late 'seventies will bring the agenda of unsolved problems (all still unsolved, together by now with others) into sharper focus.

It is not possible to deduce an underlying consensus from them except at a superficial level, that is a Second Chamber was necessary but the House of Lords as constituted was not it.

Some such as Kenneth Lomas MP (who introduced his House of Lords Reform Bill in January 1976) settled for selection of peers in order to ensure the greatest expertise of members. His solution was exclusion of the hereditaries from the vote and their replacement by prime ministerial selection in consultation with the political parties and a House of Commons Select Committee, who would sift annual nominations from industry, science, the arts, commerce, political parties and trade unions.

The categories from whom nominations would *not* in this scheme be considered looks in retrospect as striking as those who were to be considered. Nevertheless the requirement for representative specialists in Parliament as legislation becomes ever more complex, technical and all-embracing is undoubtedly something that constituency selection has never even tried to cope with. And it is strongly arguable that particular expertise is a matter for a Second Chamber, part of whose job should be revision and perhaps the continuing scrutiny of policy.

But the arguments against such a scheme, especially in retrospect, are no less clear. For the Lomas scheme would make the House of Lords a giga-quango. The point was put forcefully at the time by Ronald Butt in *People and Parliament* (Hansard Society, 1978). The Lords had lost, in public perception, prestige and effectiveness finally by the gradual replacement already of hereditaries by life peers. For the new dispensation, via prime ministerial patronage, could not be considered any more democratic than the old via the accident of birth. The need for membership mainly by election was clear. However, so also was the requirement that the Lords could not rival the Commons. Ronald Butt favoured a local authority basis of election, or failing that a return to the 1918 Bryce proposal of election (of the majority) by the Commons in regional groupings.

The schemes of the period, bright and varied, can be seen as a patchwork quilt. One issue so far left out was covered by Lord Winstanley (*The Times*, 10viii77) in *"The House of Lords needs reform but first we must decide what its job is"*.

In common with many at the time Lord Winstanley's first concern was possible domination by an extremist group in a unicameral system; and others of his recommendations had much in common with other schemes we have mentioned. But it seems now that there are other reasons for a Second Chamber at least as strong as the need to counter the extremist threat. Indeed for our quilt Lord Winstanley emphasised one such himself: the need for a Second Chamber that is more than 'a mere brake on the system', with a positive value of its own. Why should the Lords be restricted to slowing down and placing restrictions on the Commons?

It is a fair criticism of almost all schemes of all periods (with the distinguished exception of Lord Bryce's all of eighty years ago) that they concentrate too much on composition at the expense of function. There are two equally strong sets of reasons for this. The first is Tory embarrassment at hereditary membership resulting in a permanent Tory majority in the House of Lords. If there is anything about reform on which every serious politician and political thinker could be persuaded to agree it is, I think, that this is constitutionally indefensible.

But the second is fundamental. Any critique of powers of the Lords makes inevitable an examination of the performance of the Commons in their control of government. Three things are sure: the Commons are not doing this adequately; governments are only too content with the fact; and the Commons do not want the Lords to step in and do it for them. And this is no party political point; for it was as true under Thatcher as it is true under Blair. It has accordingly been considered politic, if not statesmanlike, to skate around the Second Chamber's functions in every serious scheme within living memory, while the government's grip of Parliament has become progressively crippling. The first requirement of reform is to ease this stranglehold over Parliament in the interest of public representation and debate.

A further big issue, already implied by Hailsham and Carrington, was brought centre-stage by the Interim Report of the Liberal Party Working Group in 1978, *Reform of the House of Lords*. The Liberals were batting for some kind of a federal system of government. Their ideas then look now prophetic of the British movement towards decentralisation, regionalism and the Welsh, Scottish and perhaps other Parliaments. Their conclusion was that any federal settlement would increase the need for an effective Second Chamber, which should be elected (mainly) by proportional representation on a regional basis. We should perhaps now see this last suggestion growing into a chorus. For if the Union is to survive it must, to meet the public's expectations of involvement in their own affairs, be combined with stronger elements of local, regional and national control.

Before looking in some detail at the Home Report of March '78, there are two further items of the period to consider – the public debate between Lord Chalfont and Lord Boyd-Carpenter in successive issues of *Parliamentarian* (58 and 59, 1978), and the very different scheme proposed, also in 1978, by the majority of the Society of Conservative Lawyers chaired by Lord Campbell of Alloway (as he now is).

Lord Chalfont started from the Commons' complaints the previous autumn over delays in the Lords from Lords' amendments to government legislation and the belief that an elected Second Chamber would come into conflict with the House of Commons as its rival. But he was also clear that the House of Lords should have some independence to make its distinctive contribution to democratic government.

The corollary of his concerns was to put avoidance of conflict with the Commons above the authority which an elected Second Chamber would acquire. He returned accordingly to Labour's two-tier plan of the failed Parliament (No 2) Bill of 1968/9. Interestingly, however, he also foresaw that the movement towards national and regional devolution might necessitate considerable modifications to the government's earlier scheme.

By contrast, Lord Boyd-Carpenter objected to the 1968/9 Bill on the ground of the powers of patronage that appointment of peers gave to party machines. Accordingly he leant against the abolition of the hereditaries' rights. He pointed to the high average age of appointees (who tend to have been elsewhere long established before achieving the accolade of appointment). As against this, hereditaries often succeeded earlier and picked up the Lords' workload with energy and ability as an obligation inherited along with their title.

Lord Boyd-Carpenter raised two other points of interest. He discounted the danger of Tory "backwoodsmen" skewing legislation off target. He believed: first, that their power would only be kept in reserve against a dictatorial government; and, second, that a Second Chamber filled with the appointees would lose the control over governments seeking to delay a general election beyond five years. Theoretically he should be right on both counts; but in practice his conclusions are not so certain. As to the first, the "backwoodsmen" should never have been called in to overbear the "active" Lords objections to the poll-tax. But they were. As to the second one may imagine that the electoral backlash of such a procedure would make such an abuse politically suicidal – and reversible by any subsequent Parliament.

The debate between these last two peers was not in the mainstream. It makes refreshing reading to turn to *House of Lords Reform*? Report by the Constitutional Committee of the Society of Conservative Lawyers, 1978 – the majority report.

Before examining it, however, we should mention the Group's minority report, if only because of its unyielding nature. The main report being intelligent heresy, it called upon those unsympathetic to it to voice conservative feelings. Attractive as *jeux d'esprit* can be, they do not naturally commend themselves in discussions of constitutional reform where the goal is stability through consensus. In the face of the imaginative main report, the minority accordingly stated that the Lords should remain as is with appointees and the hereditary system undisturbed and no retirement age. The minority however doffed a cap to modernity by suggesting that appointees should include some by virtue of their positions in the professions and academe, in the unions and industry.

Such proposals had and have little to commend them as a reform programme because they address none of the constitutional ills generally perceived. They amount to a denial that reform is needed at all. If the minority is right we live in a greater blessedness than most of us perceive. But then the British are famous pessimists and traditional self-denigrators – and constitutionally averse to change unless clearly necessary and leading to a known result.

The majority report makes very different reading. It is a plea for an elected senate as Second Chamber. One may wonder whether this proposal was in part, as was perhaps the minority report, prompted by the very same panic in the face of Labour's then declared unicameral policy. But the report deserves examination in its own terms. For if a Second Chamber is an agreed requirement and if serious Parliamentary reform is unstoppably under way, then an elected senate is a clear option. It may help to have it more favourably considered if one scrubs the name with its republican gloss. In fact all the practical provisions of a "senate" are as referable to a constitutional monarchy as to an elected head of state (especially if the elected head performs the same function as the monarch anyway – which is the model generally proffered by anti-monarchists). But the word "senate" is still so redolent of the old Roman hatred of kingship that it clouds discussion of the option.

The Conservative Lawyers envisaged a Second Chamber of some 300 members to be elected from not more than 100 multi-member regional constituencies for a six-year term with biennial elections of a third of the membership. If, as the stage Irishman might say, we were not 'starting from here' with a millennium of constitutional history not only behind us but all around us, such a prescription might well look very attractive, especially because as we shall see it is the only scheme of the time which even by implication tackled the question of the Second Chamber's *functions*. But to fit it out for the British electorate it needs British clothes.

The majority report advocated a more emphatic role for the senate than the House of Lords at present plays; and to this end sacrificed the whole current peerage system of hereditaries and life peers alike. But this role was not restricted to defence against some anticipated tyranny. An attempt was being made to give a new Second Chamber the electoral authority required to scrutinise government legislation and policy across the board. Even Finance Bills were included though high percentage majorities were required to force the Commons to think again. The procedure generally envisaged was this. A Bill as rejected or amended, if by the required senatorial majority, would be referred back to the House of Commons. If the Commons were not content, the senate would vote again. If the result of the earlier vote was repeated, then the deadlock would be broken by a Joint Vote procedure. Under this the question would be resolved by a simple vote of both Houses voting together.

Since under the Conservative Lawyers' scheme there was no suggestion of limiting the number of MPs (as under some other radical proposals for Parliament), the effect of this procedure would be to give a weighting of more than two to one in favour of the Commons. But this advantage would not disarm those concerned for the supremacy of the Commons, especially in financial affairs. The House of Commons has fought successfully for centuries for the last word on Money Bills. Overwhelming reasons would have to be adduced before this right was taken away; and those reasons would need to accompany proposals to do so if there was to be any realistic hope of their being accepted.

For such a radical increase, then, of powers in the British Second Chamber a powerful argument is needed: with this the report was not forthcoming. But one may try to read between the lines. The majority were plainly discontented with the performance of the Commons as government scrutineers. One reason must have been the natural discontents of a party out of office. But another can only have been a feeling, echoed in this book, that MPs under party pressure are becoming increasingly ineffective in controlling government excesses in the interests of their wider public. Nevertheless erecting a rival to the House of Commons was no substitute for taking the bull by the horns in the interest of public representation and debate. A further reason for the minority report could have been a very natural feeling that the present House of Lords was being wished away without the presentation of a politically practicable replacement.

No such criticism can apply to *The House of Lords: Report of the Conservative Review Committee* under the chairmanship of Lord Home of the Hirsel, of March '78. For it was at once less radical and less imaginative. This report however sets the standard, even today, of Tory thinking on House of Lords reform, just as the 1968 White Paper represents the best of Labour's proposals on the subject.

The Committee was appointed by Mrs Thatcher early in 1977 to consider the future of the House of Lords. One is bound to say that Tories of that era did much better in constitutional affairs when out of office than, after the first fine flush, in office afterwards. For the St John-Stevas proposals for House of Commons

Committee reform date from the same period and he was able to introduce them as Leader of the House soon after Mrs Thatcher's victory of 1979. A cynic might say there is nothing like being simultaneously out of office and under attack to disabuse Tories of their dislike of overt thought. This was very much the frame of mind displayed in the report which noted Labour's hostility to the Lords' use of their revising powers and the Hailsham drift towards elective dictatorship.

The fundamental defect of the report has already been noted – its unbalanced concentration on composition at the expense of a coherent view of the functions of the House of Lords. At first sight the Committee saw the Second Chamber as little more than a constitutional long stop (Lord Home was a distinguished cricketer as was Mr Major, in enthusiasm anyhow, after him). If the Opposition could not stop a fast ball, the Lords on the boundary might – if their unacceptable composition was traded for a return to the delaying period provided by the 1911 Parliament Act and cut by Labour's successor Act in 1949.

Such an unthinking acceptance of the Lords' functions – apparent only, because its underlying motive was to avoid upsetting too much the Commons' pretensions to infallibility – limits the democratic usefulness of a Second Chamber almost out of sight. Worse, it invites the question, well, if the Lords is only a constitutional safeguard, could not *that* be provided, and better, by a constitutional court applying maybe a written constitution? Huge and hideous issues come here to the surface which will be considered later. Suffice it here to say that to make the best case for extending the Lords' powers it is quite essential to make clear what those powers are *for*. This even applies to reinstating the Lords' delaying powers to those under the 1911 Parliament Act, as the Home Committee in common with others, proposed.

That said, despite the limitations of the report, there is much in it alive today. Beginning from the unsurprising premise that the present composition of the Lords is wholly indefensible, the report concluded that the House is too lacking in authority to act as a constitutional watchdog. A change in composition would be needed to justify an increase of powers to that end. After a review of some alternatives the Committee ended up with a hybrid House. Two-thirds of the 430 members would be elected for a nine-year term (with triennial elections of a third of these). The remaining third would be prime ministerial appointees in consultation with a small committee of Privy Counsellors. A transitional complement would include all current life peers and 50 selected hereditaries who would however have no right of succession for their heirs. Some bishops and law lords would remain.

The notion of a hybrid House smells of untidy compromise; but compromise is an essential for any scheme that seeks to build anew out of old stone. The criticism that cannot be avoided is that nobody could test the scheme against criteria of success. There would be a Second Chamber that acts as a constitutional safeguard – but even this is hardly unpacked as a concept. For – against what and how? How is the evil elective dictatorship defined and how would the amended House guard against it? It is not suggested that the Committee would not have had convincing answers to these questions; only that stable agreement to a scheme – let alone the best available solution – can only arise out of a compromise based on explicit premises which define the objects of the exercise.

Two intriguing footnotes to the report. First, the new Second Chamber would (somehow) be guaranteed a right to veto any proposed change to its powers. There are two presuppositions here: that the House would always vote to perpetuate itself; and that such a right could be infallibly granted – beyond the power of the House of Commons, for example, to remove it. Second, the report recommended the creation of a Mediation Committee composed of members of both Houses. Its function would be to try to defuse argument and ease relations between the two Houses. Any attempt to foster liaison between the Houses must be advantageous especially after reforms which initiate a new balance of power within Parliament.

With the Home Report we have arrived at the lead-in to the 1979 election campaign which resulted in the advent of the Thatcher era and not of the Labour elective dictatorship which many in all parties had anticipated. The period between 1967-79 embraced most of the constructive thinking about reform of the Lords since Lord Bryce in 1918 and indeed up to date. Reform was left in suspension during the long Tory years that succeeded it.

But eruptions are the more catastrophic for being suppressed. Lord Briginshaw deserves the last word: *"Abolish the House of Lords!"* (1979). For abolition will be their fate, whether at a stroke or by a thousand cuts, if no package is now proposed which is worthy of the people's respect, which enhances the people's control of government. As Lord Briginshaw pointed out (in theory at least), a reformed House of Commons could do all the work of the House of Lords if revising machinery was set up in the Commons, and in his view should do so.

He added a very practical suggestion that the Commons committee work could be strengthened by an electoral college to ensure selection of the best minds for particular jobs. No doubt the motive of his pronouncements was to consign the Lords to oblivion, not to open up debate on improving the performance of the House of Commons. But this he also did and it should not be forgotten. Reformers should have as their aim first and foremost the most effective public representation in Parliament and then and only then decide whether two Houses or one would do it.

Time for a thumb-nail summary of the period 1967-79, fruitful but only in ideas...

The Labour White Paper of November '68 *House of Lords Reform* stands up well by comparison with the Home Report of March '78. The first is notable first because it was almost agreed – and second for its distinction between voting and non-voting peers. This proposal many peers dislike; but it is doubtful whether any have come up with a better proposal. From the viewpoint of public representation the major failing is the scheme's reliance on prime ministerial appointments to supplement the lost hereditaries; and that is a counter-democratic change, especially if this book's diagnosis is correct that the chief present defect in the British constitution is the dangerous monopoly of power by government.

The Home Report of '78 (perhaps for purpose of summary to be conflated with the Carrington and Hailsham ideas) counters this defect by proposing a mainly elected Second Chamber and by offering to trade off the hereditaries' voting rights by a return to the delaying powers of 1911 – though the effectiveness of these is never demonstrated. But the Report suffers from an almost universal malaise of all thinking then and since, from ducking the question of what the Second Chamber is *for*.

The reason for this pussy-footing, which has in fact frustrated intelligent debate then and ever since on Parliamentary reform, is deference to the Commons' toes. Any effective chamber supplements the Commons, with the implication that the Parliamentary performance of the Commons may not be perfect and complete in every particular. In some circles this is not thought a nice thing even to hint at, regardless of the representation of the electorate that the Commons is proud to serve. Naturally, the deeper the inadequacies secretly acknowledged, the higher the challenge from even modest powers of the Second Chamber.

No such deference was shown by the Conservative lawyers whose 'senate' would have directly challenged the Commons even in financial affairs – which is generally thought neither desirable nor politically a starter. Nor by most Liberals whose federal blue-print may turn out the guiding star of the Blair administration. Those devoted to the Union may well however see in a regional function and in representation in the Second Chamber a force for unity through open debate.

We are left with a number of highly intelligent commentators. Pride of place among these goes to Lord Winstanley for daring to ask what the Second Chamber is for and for suggesting a more positive – even perhaps proactive? – role for it; and then maybe to Mr Lomas for proposing a mixed *compote* of the great and the good (though not dissimilar to what has developed since) to carry out by implication greater functions than the Lords have ever been encouraged to undertake. Out of all these an eclectic solution is to be sought. Only one element is missing – the European Union which the Lords have since tackled as no other – the element which makes reform now unavoidable.

3. THE HOUSE OF LORDS TO DATE
1979-97

The advent of Mrs Thatcher in 1979 consigned House of Lords reform to outer darkness. She was not known for her enthusiasm for a second chamber to balance the House of Commons, nor for her welcome of sturdy debate on her policies whether in Parliament or outside it. Arguments with her, of all post-war prime ministers and beyond, were the least likely to favour prospects of advancement. But what was bad, as time went on, for her understanding with the people and for the authority of Parliament was good for Tory discipline – so effective indeed that for some Tory MPs it became necessity. Chaos was Mr Major's reward for attempting to treat all his supporters as grown-ups.

But while reform in the Lords was stalled, the St John-Stevas reform of House of Commons Committees – itself a development of Richard Crossman's reformist enthusiasms – was allowed by Mrs Thatcher when she came in to proceed. His 14 Select Committees which shadow departmental expenditure and policy were adopted with modifications by the Lords to very good effect, especially with respect to Science and Technology – where heavyweight minds in the Lords were brought to bear – and to European Union legislation, which the Tory majority in the Commons found distasteful and had left low down on their agenda. Otherwise the House of Lords in 1997 is much the same as the House of 1949 with the crucial exception of the life peers, men and women. The life peers have progressively taken up more than their fair share of the burden of the functions of the House, and contributed much to the wide spectrum of views and expertise for which it is famous.

What the life peers have not done, however, except as a side-wind of party patronage, is to increase the democratic respectability of the House of Lords. Lord Addison's criticism is as apposite now as it was in 1949. The Lords is unrepresentative. If there is to be a Second Chamber in our Parliament some kind of election of a preponderance of its members is mandatory if it is to have the authority to carry out whatever its functions are decided to be. So it was, to be democratically respectable, Mr Benn and to be Prime Minister, Sir Alec Douglas-Home, gave up their peerages to enter the Commons, both under the 1963 Peerages Act. Without the legitimacy of election of most of their membership, the Lords will remain for ever second-class Parliamentarians.

While the Tories are in a majority in the Commons, the Tory majority in the Lords causes only occasional embarrassment to government. The Lords certainly do not support Tory governments as unthinkingly as Tory Prime Ministers would wish (see eg the Lords' treatment of the War Crimes Bill in Part III below). But from 1979 to the advent of the Blair government in 1997 reform was not a government priority. This was Tory shortsightedness – better always to repair your own defences than leave it to your enemies – but a fact that ushered in the very elective dictatorship that Lord Hailsham prophesied against.

During the Tory years 1979-97 reform was stalled. But governments are nobody's ideal as initiators of constitutional change; they have too sharp an axe of their own to grind, and it is their own governmental power, not their electorate's interest that they look to. For Mrs Thatcher, so far as she foresaw at any rate, the permanent Tory majority in the Lords was no threat to her government or her party; and certainly Lords reform ranked after many other legislative priorities. But the insouciance of her government did not stop even Tories thinking.

Her own Conservative Parliamentary Constitutional Committee set up in July '79 continued to sit into her premiership. The two papers it produced in February 1980 were in fact a fair indicator of the trends of reformist thought over the period. Their two trends might be characterised as the senatorial and the traditional.

The nub of the first is the need for a Second Chamber with the full authority that election would give to act as a counterweight to the House of Commons which is seen frequently as too much a creature of the government and the ruling party. The second's is the advisability to keep healthy the living parts of the old British tree.

The first paper was much influenced by the fears of the day of an extreme government elected on a minority vote. The Second Chamber would need the confidence of being mostly democratically elected to combat anti-democratic antics of such a government. Accordingly at least two-thirds of its members were to be elected by proportional representation. Of these *either* all would be elected on a Euro-constituency basis *or* about 200 on that basis and another 100 on a county and metropolitan authority basis. The non-elected component could be prime ministerial appointees or elected from among the peers by themselves. The members of the Second Chamber would be called Lords of Parliament.

The second paper looked to the split that radical change would do to the Tory party. Removal of the inbuilt Tory majority was unavoidable; but the House should remain non-elected, perhaps of around 400 members. Of these 100 would be elected by the hereditary peers from among their number at the start of each Parliament, 150 would be chosen from the great and the good for a fixed but renewable term and the remaining would sit *ex officio* during their terms of office as Law Lords, bishops, TUC representatives, Council Chairpersons and so forth.

Setting the two papers side by side like this, one sees the senatorials as primarily concerned with democratic weight and the traditionals as concerned with political practicalities – of which the most stringent is always in fact what governments and their posses of MPs will tolerate. That is a false antithesis. Both groups want changes to the Second Chamber that will allow it to work as an effective democratic organ within an organic constitutional whole. Meanwhile one cannot avoid noticing that as usual the *functions* of the Second Chamber are not discussed, as if everyone knows them or is content with what the Lords in fact do and how.

We will follow first the senatorials. For their ideas do have one function, however vague, in mind – that the the Second Chamber should act as some kind of constitutional safeguard. The only admitted fear however is of an extreme government in a minority; and one can think of other resources than a Second Chamber, against that eventuality. Notably, from the same period, come the twin recommendations of Vernon Bogdanor (see especially his book, *The People and the Party System* CUP 1981) – general elections by proportional representation, combined with referendums on Bills that would alter the constitution.

But these solutions ignore the underlying weakness of Parliament – and Parliament is the problem. That is shown by the narrowness of the target that the Bogdanor recommendations (in common with many proposals of the time) were aimed at – the 'elective dictatorship' *under a minority government*. The failing that concerned him occurs where a revolutionary government that has been elected on a minority vote – say of not much more than 40% of the population – railroads legislation through the Commons, perhaps with a tiny majority depending on very minor parties. This is indeed a serious and easily conceivable injustice, if the Commons were more even than usually supine, that might be forestalled by a referendum *if it was managed fairly* and might be made impossible by PR. But it is not the only possible injustice. What of bad government by a government with an unassailable majority? To remove the question from the clouds of today's politics: how might a more representative and better organised Second Chamber have improved government between 1945-51 or between 1979-92?

As usual we are skating round the 'mandate' theory. The flaw in the theory is now becoming plain. Its genesis was adversarial. The underlying issue which it addressed, the scrutiny of government by Parliament, was genuine enough. But the form the theory took was dictated by controversy. The distortion brought about by a newly representative House of Commons, controlled by one party, in conflict with the House of Lords, as ever unreformed, forced the Lords to find some plausible justification for their continuing role. This, in a famous letter to Lord Carnarvon of 20th February, 1872, is how Lord Salisbury put it:

> The plan which I prefer is frankly to acknowledge that the nation is Master, though the House of Commons is not, and to yield our own opinion only when the judgment of the nation has been challenged at the polls and decidedly expressed. This Doctrine... has the advantage of being: 1) theoretically sound, 2) popular, 3) safe against agitation, and 4) so rarely applicable as practically to place little fetter upon our independence. (*Life of Robert, Marquess of Salisbury*, G Cecil, H and S 1921)

One has to go back to the letters of Cicero to find so trenchant an expression of conservative principle subjugated to controversial expediency. It is not surprising that the nugget of Lord Salisbury's theory is concealed in a bed of fool's gold.

For the government while it is the government has always a mandate to govern; but how it governs is subject to Parliamentary scrutiny and control; and Parliament is in no way relieved of its duty by any party manifesto. For once in government, a party represents the nation, as an MP, once elected, represents all those in his constituency, not just partisans. If Parliament fails to scrutinise government policy responding to the nation as a whole, then it must be given the powers to do so and its obligation firmly thrust back upon it. Therefore as the Commons becomes ever more under the sway of one party or the other, the Lords must have the function of restoring a democratic balance.

But at this point in his logic Lord Salisbury ran out of options. Even had he wished it, there was no way he could then have proposed a structure for the Second Chamber that could have restrained a Tory government as firmly as he, through it, sought to restrain the Liberals. It is to our generation that he finally bequeathed his (then) insoluble problem – the problem that the senatorials are chiefly concerned with.

The two most thoughtful contributions to the reform debate of the 1980's came from two startlingly different sources, from the Scottish Young Conservatives – 'where are the snows of yester-year?' (see *House of Lords Reform*, 1981), and from Lord Scarman, (*'Power House'*, the *Guardian*, 6th June 1988.)

The Scottish YC's began from the likelihood (then) that Labour would abolish the House of Lords altogether on the pretext of making Parliament more democratic, thereby removing the Lords as a constitutional safeguard. Their report accordingly proposed a House of 400 members, two-thirds elected, one third nominated. The larger component would be elected by PR geographically, one third of them biennially at the time of local elections. The nominated third would initially be elected by the peers from among their own number. After a transition period however they would be appointed for a 12-year term by the prime minister on the advice of a Committee of Privy Counsellors. Meanwhile all present members would be allowed to attend but without voting rights, rights of succession or salary. Law Lords and bishops would remain (though the establishment of the Church of England would be reviewed – they were, for all that, Scots).

Most intelligent of all were the Scottish YC's proposals on the Second Chamber's powers. The House of Lords would henceforth have a right to delay legislation for a single session only; but they would continue to have their veto over extensions of Parliament, to which would be added a new right to require a referendum on other constitutional questions.

It is hard to believe that a more viable package at that time could have been devised. But as senatorials perhaps they could have listened a little more to the traditionals; and their plan now would need to take account of recent developments.

Equally constructive and, by reason of his eminence more authoritative, was Lord Scarman's *Guardian* contribution seven years later. He saw a democratically elected House of Lords as a prerequisite to a modern definition of the powers of government. More liberal (at least with a small 'l') than Lord Hailsham, he had nevertheless, in Mrs Thatcher's ninth year in government, taken up his colleague's cry against 'elective dictatorship'; and he manifestly took the danger of it very seriously. For he recommended that at once, before any detailed scheme of reform was drawn up, a new Parliament Act should be enacted to ensure that constitutional amendments could not be passed without the assent of both Houses.

This recommendation is as alive now as it could have been then, if only to prevent an indisciplined government from rash, inchoate and ill-thought-through reform. The present Leader of the Lords, Lord Richard, was asked on the Today programme, on the day that Labour's Cabinet Committee on Lords reform was set up, January 13th 1998, whether or not the Labour government would proceed with reform before they had a viable overall scheme. He responded that such a scheme would be an 'invention', not what he had, which was a policy. All Labour's varied and radical reform programmes would accordingly go ahead independently of each other. It is hard to think of a better prescription for muddle and chaos, where options will be closed by lack of liaison, or a stronger justification for an effective Second Chamber.

What was most striking in Lord Scarman's prescription, however, was his concept of the 'democratic' method he thought appropriate to election to a Second Chamber. For his 'constituencies' would be based on churches, business, professions, industry, trade unions, social workers, ethnic groups and others besides regional representation. That would indeed be a Second Chamber of all the talents. That his daring *ballon d'essai* was not set in stone is shown, however, by his proposal that a joint Parliamentary Committee be established to review House of Lords membership and review Lords reform. His method of inspiring thought is refreshingly Socratic.

What comes from it into this mind is the implication for the functions of the Lords. Throughout the eighty years since Bryce reformers have been mesmerised by the undemocratic composition of the Lords' House. When they have dragged their gaze from this Gorgon, they have looked no further than to the Lords as a constitutional safeguard. The thought they might have other functions is limited to faint praise of an obedient revising role, and, occasionally, of their wise debates. Lord Scarman by implication takes these subsidiary functions a whole chapter further – and also on a leap back to the House's origins as the government's core of Parliamentary advisers. For it is the corporate wisdom of the Lords, including that of many hereditaries, that the Commons cannot and has not matched. This in turn has implications for a public policy-making role for the Lords, carried out in public – as a counterweight not to the Commons but to the government's monopolistic Whitehall machine.

Among the senatorials, next in line for review, to maintain a political balance is the article of Dick Leonard MP, "Replacing the Lords" in the *Political Quarterly* of October '95.

Many themes are echoed here from a Labour standpoint that show the measure of underlying consensus between the two main parties. Add to the cauldron, first, the regionalist bias, with PR, of the Liberal Democrats which appears here as among members of all parties elsewhere. Add, second, the general agreement that heredity, at least on its own should not give the right of a vote in the Lords. (That sometimes appears to be the *only* official Labour view on the subject: see Lord Richard's comments in *The House Magazine* for 7th March '94. For minimalist caution has led most unfortunately to Labour's piecemeal approach to reform.) Add finally, as below, the very British wish to keep what is best of what we already have. Then, perhaps, one gets a sniff of the all-party agreement that could lead to stable reform.

Dick Leonard takes the argument far beyond Lord Richard's stake in the ground. He proposes a Senate of Senators, with five-sixths of a body 360 strong to be elected by PR from regional constituencies, concurrently with the quinquennial Euro-elections. The remaining sixth should be co-optees to supplement the elected members with specific qualifications, interests and cultural (preferably *not political*) affiliations, particularly for under-represented minorities.

There are other points of interest in his scheme. Besides a veto on extending a Parliament beyond five years and a general three month delaying power on non-money Bills (unusually measly) – but delay to the next Parliament for Bills diminishing the rights of individuals (what doesn't?) – he proposed the establishment of Pre-legislative Select Committees. Their extended use could, in both Houses much improve the standards of knowledge and debate among Parliamentarians, and would be akin to the Special Select Committees recommended, as developed, elsewhere in this book.

Two points stand out: Dick Leonard's insistence that the Lords, to be effective in whatever functions, must be predominantly elected, and his understanding that election cannot on its own guarantee specialist and high-calibre membership. One begins to deduce from his proposed co-optees (as in Lord Scarman's suggestions) the senatorial functions which he has at the back of his mind – in his case mainly the protection against the 'elective dictatorship' of social minorities and the underprivileged. It is striking both that he does not consider the Commons can be relied on for this function and that as an MP he does not see fit to say so.

Other senatorial schemes follow strands of alternatives discussed. The most complete is 'Reforming the Lords' by Jeremy Mitchell and Anne Davies of June '93. Their 300-member Senate would be paid in line with MPs. Thirty of them would be prime ministerial appointees as recommended by a Committee of both Houses to be chaired by the Senate Speaker. Their appointment would be for a non-renewable 9-year period on a triennial one-third rota. The remaining 270 would be elected from 15 regions each electing 18 members by PR.

The Senate would have equality with the Commons on constitutional matters and a special responsibility for human rights. Most interesting of all (this an American sort of a Senate) the Senate's committee work would be much expanded with new structures; and committees could summon Ministers and co-opt outsiders. The Senate would also monitor and approve public appointments.

One issue so far not touched on directly is numbers in the Second Chamber. Generally senatorial prescriptions tend to be slightly smaller. Dick Leonard's 360 voting members is in the middle cluster of 350-450. So is Peter Hain's 450 (he is another senatorial: see his Second Chamber (Reform) Bill 1992. A Labour Committee of May 1980 suggested a selected body of 250; and in June '93 Mitchell and Davies proposed, as we have seen, 300. At the other end of the spectrum in *The House of Lords: Into the 21st Century* of July '93, 'Commoners' suggested a chamber of 500. So did Conservative Action for Electoral for Electoral

Reform in *Reform of the House of Lords* of April '83. But in *The House of Lords* in the House Magazine of Feb '95 Austin Mitchell MP suggested 600. However the current record belongs to Patrick Cormack MP who also participated in the Feb '95 article but earlier, in October 1990 proposed in *The House of Lords – A Parliamentary Symposium* suggested 650, to match the Commons. But Patrick Cormack is a traditional; we meet him again later.

Numbers depend on too many factors to admit of easy comparison. The final number is in fact a resolution of disparate decisions going together to make an overall scheme. Function and variety of expertise, corporate spirit and cohesion, who is to be selected or elected representing whom, what constitutes a good debate in a half-empty chamber and emphatically cost – if members are to be salaried and properly supported: all are factors weighted differently in different opinions. But one thought that leaps from this preliminary look is: are all members to be treated the same, especially as professionals with regard to the vote and salary and other support?

Most would say that the influence of a strong speech much outweighs a vote. Some would say the vote is essential for participation. All that needs be said now is: *if* it was possible to have a well-knit core of properly paid and supported pros, supplemented by a wise throng of varied specialists and part-timers, one might keep costs down and standards of contribution up. That way one might select a number from the left of the spectrum for the core and a total from the right to allow for dedicated occasionals.

But here we trespass on the ground of the traditionals – unless we decide senatorials are concerned with the core and traditionals with not losing the supplementals.

So we come to the traditionals. On the whole they do not come up with self-standing schemes, as the senatorials do. For their point of view is defined by a wish to retain in any shake-up specific features which they see as valuable in the *status quo*. In that sense all those who want the Lords to retain their role as a constitutional safeguard (even if this means only their power to veto an extension of a Parliament), even those who want the Lords as a debating and revising chamber – and that includes the vast majority both of the electorate and of Parliamentarians: in short most of us are traditionals.

But the kernel of the traditionals want to change only that part of the set-up that no longer works. The hereditary 'backwoodsman', for one example, however rarely he is in fact seen. The sniping at the Lords' electoral illegitimacy from the Commons, for another example, whenever the Lords do anything inconvenient to the government majority. Traditionals see how the Lords perform with one hand bound behind their backs and forgive their limitations for the sake of what they do actually achieve. Consequently their proposals in general have a bitty look.

The exception is Patrick Cormack MP who must therefore represent them here. His prime concern recently has been to find a compromise that might attract all-party support, while preserving the House's best features and leaving its current powers unchanged (as shown in his comments in *"The House of Lords" – The House Magazine of February '95*). At that time he proposed that the hereditaries should from among themselves select a maximum of 150 for each Parliament. Appointee peers should not just be politicians; but MEPs might be members *ex officio*.

However five years earlier in T*he House of Lords – A Parliamentary Symposium*, chaired by Lord Hailsham (*The House Magazine* of October 1990) Patrick Cormack came up with an overall scheme by "careful pruning and skilful grafting" to make the House of Lords more efficient and representative. Here the traditional was disguised as the senatorial: his revised Second Chamber voting peers were indeed to be called Senators.

As we have seen there would be 650 of them, to match the Commons and be nominated at the start of each Parliament. 400 would be chosen from life peers (150 from the Cross-benches and 250 by the parties in proportion to general election seats). 100 chosen from among their own number by the hereditaries. The remainder (apart from a maximum of 25 new life peers for each Parliament) would be *ex officio* appointments to broaden the representative catchment of the House.

His list is of *ex officios* is imaginative; and as with all imaginative proposals, he carries in by side-wind implications for the functions of the House. He would include chairs of statutory bodies, local government, various religious leaders and others as determined by a joint Lord Chancellor's and Speaker's Conference. Here is a compromise scheme worthy in its day to stand alongside the best.

Patrick Cormack's scheme shows that his heart is with the traditionals. But his head is with the senatorials. The result is an ambitious scheme. More modest but also perhaps more politically aware is the paper of August '95 *Second Chamber: Some remarks on reforming the House of Lords* by Lord Carnarvon, Douglas Slater and others. Its theme is deceptively simple: responsible Lords reform cannot be carried out piecemeal, as proposed by New Labour. For any change upsets the present Parliamentary balance and forecloses possible options. This even applies to doing away with the hereditaries' rights in one simplist stage and leaving the rest to future consultations.

We shall return to these implications at the end of this chapter when we bring the political scenario into the New Labour era. Here it is important only to note the authors' firm *dementi* that they and the majority of their hereditary colleagues would gladly bow out to a better second chamber, if such were devised. But they cannot willingly assent to change not encapsulated in a scheme which is properly thought through. Their heart is in keeping the best of what is, if possible. But their head is in methodology. You do not start decapitation surgery with neither diagnosis nor a full scheme of treatment. It is hard for any democrat to dissent from this plea.

But it is not easy to put such a point over to a government with a huge majority because it is natural for a strong government to want Parliament to stay weak. It is also natural for a weak Commons not to want to see a Second Chamber growing in authority. Elective dictatorship is with us. It has been for years. Said Ian Harden and Norman Lewis in *The Noble Lie* (Hutchinson 1988): 'Parliament does not govern… neither does it fulfil the constitutional promise of accountability implicit in the notion that authority to govern flows through Parliament.'

Trenchant and incontrovertible. There is not enough information public, not enough government scrutiny, not enough policy debate. The 14 select committees set up in the Commons in 1979 'to examine the expenditure, administration and policy of government departments and their associated bodies' are indeed the strongest pro-democratic force to emerge since World War Two. 'But the committees do not make policy or take decisions; they may bear the tokens but do not wield the instruments of power.' (*British Government and the Constitution* Colin Turpin, 2nd Ed'n '90)

Faced with the colossus that is modern British government, the traditionals feel we need all the help we can get, including what we already have, and the senatorials feel we need a whole new Second Chamber. Perhaps both are right.

All see the problem as the control of government by Parliament. The mandate theory, forged in the heat of battle to plug a wall, lasted over a century – not bad for a plug. But the castle now is crumbling. The weakening transformation in 1911 of the Lords' veto into a delaying power was in the end fatal, though not unjust. As an alternative a power to force a referendum is no encouraging thought – at any rate as a solution on its own, rather than in combination. Are we stuck?

An analysis shows a gradual convergence of views over the last thirty years which might, with reasonable compromise, lead to constitutional change by consensus if only an even stronger counter-current, that of prime ministerial power based on party domination in the Commons, can be diverted into a more democratic direction. On the resolution of these opposing forces depends the outcome of the Parliamentary reform that is now inevitable. On the one hand Labour's antipathy to an elected Second Chamber has been opposed – in Opposition – by Mr Blair. On the other, as Professor Max Beloff has explained (quoted in F W Benemy, *The Elected Monarch*, Harrap 1965 at page 235). 'Ever since... Lloyd George the prevailing tendency has been towards the exaltation of the Prime Minister at the expense of his colleagues and the House of Commons'. So, says Benemy (at page 245), 'the Prime Minister is sovereign'. For a French observer who saw way back in 1955 the British shape of things (M. Duverger in *Political Parties*, Methuen): 'Officially Great Britain has a parliamentary system... in reality the party alone exercises power.'

The observation of modern prime ministerial power is nothing new, though commentators of equal shrewdness have tended to concentrate on either one essential component at the expense of the other. Few however would, I think, espouse as dominant today either of the two alternative models, supremacy either of the House of Commons (Bagehot) or of the Cabinet (Jennings). For Parliament 'does not govern' – that is the Noble Lie – and the Prime Minister rules the cabinet or not at all.

Most telling here are the comments of Selwyn Lloyd (himself once thought a possible Prime Minister) on Macmillan's 'night of the long knives' of which Selwyn Lloyd was himself the prime victim: 'The Prime Minister carries great burdens and I did not dispute his right to change his team.' He was quite clear that his sacking was neither unconstitutional or without precedent. Its justice was a different issue altogether. But he accepted he should be sacrificed to the fortunes of his party and accepted from Macmillan a commission to improve the Conservative Party's organisation.

So a scheme can reasonably be put together for Lords reform that may hope for political consensus – with the permanent proviso that it is government's and the Commons anti-democratic interest to oppose (in however clandestine a fashion) an effective Second Chamber. With this aim in mind, it is worth summarising an all-party wish-list that can be regarded as a list of ingredients for the pie. No ingenuity will be enough to ensure they are all included, without spoiling the flavour; nor will the result be to everyone's taste. But this attempt may inspire others to do better.

We may begin by stating requirements without which no consensual solution will be possible:

a) no abolition of the Second Chamber altogether. *Pace* eg Lord Briginshaw in *"Abolish the House of Lords!"* (1979), the House of Commons has shown itself to be grossly overloaded already, as well as inefective in controlling the government;

b) no general control of Money Bills to be given back to the Lords: commentators are unanimous on this, and anyhow the Commons would rightly regard Money Bills as the last dividing line between the two Houses. This need not however prevent the renewed chamber from discussing finance to the extent necessary for its functions;

c) heredity no longer to be, at least on its own, a justification for a vote in the Second Chamber. Other hereditary rights are not necessarily affected.

We may not agree, theoretically, with any or all of these exclusions. It is just this writer's judgment that the weight of general feeling in favour of them is so overwhelming that to stand out against any of them would defeat any all-party solution that might otherwise be attainable.

Once these stakes are firmly in the ground, however, it is surprising how many open questions remain. This is reflected in New Labour's current intention to bring in a Bill around the end of 1998 to abolish the hereditaries' rights in the Lords and to plug the gaps with extra life peers (including some current hereditaries), pending the recommendations of some kind of constitutional conference to settle everything that truly matters about the reformed Second Chamber. This irresponsibly piecemeal approach to reform has already been adopted for the Scottish and Welsh Assemblies. Since the Labour government has no overall scheme for reform but only, according to Lord Richards, Leader of the Lords (on the Today Programme) 'a policy', it is likely to continue eating the constitution alive until the public loudly complains. But public outcry is unlikely until Parliament itself is strong enough to come up with a more responsible way of proceeding. Which is unlikely before Parliament is reformed. That is why at the moment we *are* stuck – in a vicious circle.

It is nevertheless possible to conceive a better way forward. The many intelligent proposals made over the years testify to a general recognition of this.

So now for our wish-list. Having ruled against the abolitionists, one finds that a combination of the senatorials with the traditionals in the present fluid political flow allows for the inclusion of a surprising number of apparently antitheti-cal views.

We want a Second Chamber. It is to supplement and so far as possible not to challenge the House of Commons. In return the Commons is to work more will-ingly and harmoniously with the renewed Upper House. In return for that, the Commons (and the government) is to respect the Lords' constitutional role (whatever that is to be). The Lords are to include all the talents for additional functions so far unspecified, except that they will include the Lords' current functions of legislation and debate.

If we now turn to the minimum demands of the three national parties, there is nothing inconsistent with this little summary. Labour are determined to dis-miss the hereditaries' voting rights from the chamber but anxious for continuity and to respect the careers of those hereditaries already established. The Tories are prepared to agree, always provided that Labour's treatment of the hereditaries is part of an agreed overall scheme which retains what is best in the House of Lords and strengthens its constitutional role. The Liberal Democrats want this scheme to include PR and national/regional features in election for at least the majority of the new Second Chamber's membership. Such elections it seems that both Labour and Tories would consider favourably, since devolution of some kind is irreversible and the main parties' chief concern seems to be that what Labour has impetuously begun will not result in the break-up of the Union, that is, Britain as a unity.

Thus far the prospects of some reform package being generally acceptable seem open. Such an outcome is well worth striving for. We need not stay stuck.

A flashpoint is however foreseeable soon if Labour's penchant for acting first and thinking afterwards (already shown in the Scottish and Welsh referendums) is repeated by ruling the hereditaries out of the Chamber before the government has worked out what to do and consulted the other parties and the country about what to do generally about the Lords. The Blair government is bound to expect serious opposition to its tampering with the constitution so as to go off at half-cock. For it could by so doing ruin the consultation process and the hope of ulti-mate consensus and the stability it would bring. The chief defect of 'elective dic-tatorship', even as benign in intent as Thatcher's and Blair's, is the misuse of overriding power to stifle serious debate and consensual policy-making.

It is to be hoped that vociferous concentration on this already notorious fea-ture of the new populism will forestall such bungling this time. But a more seri-ous venomous snake lurks in the long green grass. That snake is Established Power. The power of a popular government basking in the applause of an omnipotent majority in the Commons. A Second Chamber which can temper such a dangerous if smiling beast is a threat that the beast is in a position to crush before it grows into a nuisance. The temptations are obvious. But so is the right of the public to a Parliament that does its job.

Luckily no-one thinks the Commons, already overstretched, could do the Lords' job as well as its own. And the current leading to responsible and open government is as unstoppable as devolution. The public will get bored soon enough of the cry (of whatever government) 'what is in our manifesto is carved in stone'. Signs are everywhere that the people demands to be consulted on policy and how it is being implemented. That requires a working Parliament. It is high time to move towards it.

For our wish-list, the framework is set by the three exclusions on page 53 – no abolition, no money Bills, no votes by heredity – together with the guidelines of the three main parties. Within the framework, however, the permutations are endless. Choices are reserved for Part III when specific proposals are considered. Here it will be enough to list in summary the main ideas with some idea of where they come from – and in no special order except that, in deference to the heavy majority of commentators, membership is treated before functions and powers. Since this listing is illogical, it will be reversed when we build up our own scheme.

1) Hereditaries in or out?
Labour opinion is hardest against the continued voting rights of 'backwoodsmen' – who in fact rarely attend, but did so, to the Tories' lasting harm, for the poll-tax. Backwoodsmen are those peers, overwhelmingly Tory, who, for a variety of reasons, are not regularly engaged in the affairs of the House. This lack of commitment (though often inspired by the House's low public esteem) is seen as compounding their non-elected status as a disqualification.

At the other end of the scale are those established hereditaries of distinction and regular contribution whom even Labour would like to treat as diligent life peers, at least during transition to the new Second Chamber.

In between are the largest body of hereditaries who, like many life peers, make occasional distinguished contributions on issues that interest them. Also like many life peers, some are cross-benchers – peers who accept no party whip and apply their intelligence and experience freely, and without fear or favour of party, to issues as they arise. Their combined wisdom is impossible to quantify and finds supporters in all parties. But on balance, in the interests of representative government, both Labour and Liberal Democrats would like to see them out.

By contrast Lib-Lab (with more emotion than logic) would probably mostly prefer to see life peers of equal contribution and attendance staying in. It does not sway them that life peers are no more democratically representative than hereditaries. For life peers have at least been appointed for some contribution of their own, even if, in some cases, only to party. But, predictably, there are Tories who support continuing hereditary rights; for, however deplorable in theory, the fact is that some have fathers who die a little early so that their heirs arrive younger at the House than most life peers. It is indeed from these that many established peers of distinction come. Age of members is often seen as a structural weakness of the Lords.

Some of those who support a continuing hereditary contingent think, with Lord Diamond (see his Hereditary Peerages Bill [HL] 1993), that the male domination of the House – another historical injustice – could be softened by female succession, especially when there is no male heir of equal proximity.

Some have proposed that a contingent of the best hereditaries should be chosen by election by themselves out of their own number.

2) *Life Peers (plus First Creation Peers)*
The general wish is that some at least (probably most) were elected and more were younger.

Labour, especially when in office, has a tradition of preferring an appointed Second Chamber to an elected one. Why upset the Commons with what they want to see as competition? And why run the hazard of some extra election, when one can control by appointing one's faithful? (These, like all good carica-tures, are not supposed to indicate more than underlying attitudes. Nor do they suggest that the party faithful, after 'being there' a little time, do always toe the line!) Full appointment was the chief weakness of their otherwise admirable plan in the late 'sixties. Its unavoidable consequence is an increase in the patronage of the Prime Minister. But Labour's knee-jerk reaction to entrenched privilege – the hereditary peerage above all – is to create a privileged corpus of their own.

In Opposition this temptation is less strong. So it was that in July 1994, in Cardiff, Mr Blair advocated an elected Second Chamber. Two years or so later, by contrast (in *The John Smith Memorial Lecture* of February 1996) with the prospect of office invitingly closer, he restricted himself a) to lambasting the Tories in the Lords – with obvious justification – for the manner of their passing of the poll-tax legislation; b) to restricting hereditaries' rights in short order to those of already established contributors, who in the interim would be metamorphosed into appointee life peers; and c) to debating democratic accountability later.

Therefore 'later' is where the 'democratic and representative Second Chamber' of the Lib-Lab pre-election joint declaration of March 1997 now lan-guishes – with the Liberal Democrats now – January 1998 – excluded from the Lord Chancellor's think-tank on constitutional reform. Labour opts for the easy meat of excluding the hereditaries and replacing most of them, until something better turns up in some consultation process of Labour's choosing and under their firm control, with a posse of yet more appointees. An elected Second Chamber is kicked into the blue yonder.

So constitutional reform goes with parties in power: they are deflected from their virtuous resolutions in opposition by the roller-coaster of the government machine and by their institutionalised terror, whatever their majority and popu-larity, of easing the reins of their control of Parliament.

The Tories, by contrast, are free to be virtuous. They can point to the high standard of contributions of many life peers from all walks of life, of many hereditaries too of varied experience. They can demand a continuation of cross-bench and specialist restraint on ill-thought through policy and legislation. Some (of all parties) would like this principle extended to a broadening of *ex officio* rep-resentation, if some part of the Second Chamber is to filled by continuing appointments.

Above all Tories can show the irresponsibility of half-cock reform of Lords membership, in the name of their House's traditional duty to guard the consti-tution.

3) Law Lords, Bishops and other ex officios.

The appellate jurisdiction of the House of Lords derives in history from the monarch as the fount of justice and his court. Though technically run as committees of the House it is simply and no more than the highest court in the lands it covers. In particular it has no special constitutional role beyond the workings of the general law. So it is readily detachable from the Lords' main function as an integral part of Parliament.

The House of Lords as the highest court of law has retained universal respect amid the criticisms that have been directed at the Monarchy, Parliament, government and all their works. Part of their esteem nowadays derives from the law lords' control (in company with the other judges) of government administration through their powerful development recently of administrative law which has replaced much of Parliament's traditional function as the organ for the airing of grievances.

Another achievement over the past half century has been the enormous development of the law of negligence that has gone far to compensate the public for the jarrings that living in ever closer proximity with neighbours brings upon every citizen. The *de facto* increase of the judiciary that has fitted them largely into the vacuum left by Parliament in the protection of the individual both from his neighbours and against the encroachment of government sits oddly with the protestations of law lords that they leave Parliament to make new laws and themselves do nothing but interpret what law there already is.

But the value of the judges' contribution as 'check and balance' against government's and other attacks on individuals' rights is generally recognised. No commentators that I have found wish to change the law lords' judicial function, save that some would want it extended to the function of a Supreme Constitutional Court, generally under some new written constitution.

But the law lords have frequently shown themselves formidable and influential debaters on the floor of the House, often on not strictly legal issues. Frequently they have acted as cross-bench opposition to government excesses. (This contribution has been quite separate from the Lord Chancellor's special functions as Speaker of the Upper House and *de facto* minister of justice.) There is a strong majority among commentators in favour of law lords remaining *ex officio* as members of any reconstituted Second Chamber. The few dissenting voices have generally seemed moved by a wish that all its members should be elected and to have thought little further ahead than that. The only live issue is the law lords' numbers as members. The Home report, for example, in 1978, suggested 12. Most now might favour a fuller complement. Any decision depends on the balance of the chamber as a whole.

For those who see Parliament's failure to control the executive as the chief wrong to be righted in coming reforms, the law lords' continued membership is beyond question. For the judges have been awake while Parliament as a whole has slept.

The judges indeed are the modern example of working constitutional development in line with social change – of that practical flexibility which our vaunted 'unwritten constitution' has been thought throughout this century to give.

Otherwise the century's history is of government abhorring the vacuum, and accordingly marching in, by *anschluss*, to possess it. Constitutional creep can only be directed, given purpose, if the public is vigilant for its liberties and Parliament is as jealous of its duties as of its privileges. Which they have not been.

The bishops, regrettably especially for them, are in almost the opposite case from the judges'. In earlier decades their 'relevance' was frequently questioned, as church attendance declined and more and more professing Christians (Anglicans especially) became armchair attendees. In this they are hardly talked of.

Here neither the decline of the Anglican Church nor its disestablishment need be discussed; for its position seems one of the few constitutional issues not on the tapis. Nor is either the aim or effect of establishment any longer the exclusion of other faiths.

Senatorials and liberals both like the idea of a Second Chamber representative of Britain's multicultural society. As long ago as 1970, the Archbishops Commission Report, *Church and State*, under the distinguished church historian Owen Chadwick, accepted the Labour's 1968 White Paper proposals that the Anglican bishops should be reduced from 26 to 16, as did later the 1978 Home Report. The archbishops recommended that this reduction should be made in favour of other religious leaders. Their Report does not seem to recognise, at least explicitly, the need for non-Christian leaders to be among them. But probably such an extension would now be taken for granted. In any case the Chief Rabbi is already a life peer. This indicates the appropriateness of Islamic and other representatives. There is a strong movement to invite the cardinal Archbishop of Westminster to be ennobled, if papal dispensation for his taking part in secular government can be, as expected, obtained.

Ex officio nominations, especially if they go beyond law lords and Anglican bishops, tend towards a leavening of an elected membership by a nominated contingent. This is thought by many to strengthen the crossbench tradition of the House and to be extendable towards its specialist expertise, for particular functions and areas of policy. To make sense of this we need to know what the House is there to do, and we return to this later. Here note that where experts or cognoscenti are nominated there is *somewhat* less scope for prime ministerial and party patronage, which could be limited even more by cross-party selection committees. Note also that, however unsystematically, some such policy has been implied by the appointment of many life peers since 1958. Traditionals will lean towards perpetuating a practice that has been seen often to work well.

One candidate class of *ex officios*, however, cannot be omitted – Members of the European Parliament. Since the House of Lords Communities Committee was set up in 1974, the contribution of the Lords in the wasteland of European legislation has been diligent and immense. They took up a burden that the Commons had neither the time nor the taste for.

There has been a persistent undercurrent of cross-party dislike of the EU, except among Lib Dems, and especially in the Commons. Many MPs see the whole panjandrum of European institutions as an encroachment on the authority of the Mother of Parliaments, which to them means them. This has led to the childish ostracism of MEPs from Westminster. Their position is made worse – and MPs' defensive impotence more tetchy – by the whole EU structure which at once bypasses Parliament through the Council of Ministers and superimposes EU law over the law of member states. One might have expected that the Commons would have welcomed the slow increase in the powers of the European Parliament, in order to slot into it and offset the increase of unscrutinised executive power that the EU system has conferred on government. In practice the Commons have preferred to ignore the Euro-Parliament altogether, probably in the hope of keeping it (like the House of Lords!) weak, even though they have found no other way to influence EU policy.

Meanwhile the Lords have patiently shown the way in their scrutiny of EU documents. Naturally many of them are anxious to carry over this contribution into the new Second Chamber. One way of expanding the Lords' European role would of course be to make MEPs *ex officio* members of the chamber. But MEPs have a busy life across the water and would not be able to attend with the regularity that the senatorials, especially, would wish of their senators. In practice this would be likely also to apply to other *ex officios*, not just lawlords and bishops, much of whose usefulness as members would depend on their remaining at the top of their professions. A main cause of the Lords' being seen as a refuge of gerontocrats is the need at least for partial retirement before full participation in Parliament.

Accordingly a way is needed to find a provision for part-time contributions by *ex officios* – and we shall suggest by others too. In a pluralistic society variety of contribution is generally sought.

So far the wish-list has looked at the aspirations of the forward-thinking in the two main parties, whom we have been finding correspond broadly to senatorials among Labour and traditionals among Tories. There is a third category, the regionalists who generally also espouse PR. They belong in the tradition of the 19th-century constitutional reformers. They are to be expected among the Liberal Democrats. But they appear to have a surprising following in the New Labour government, though one may doubt whether their espousal goes much further than an overriding desire to keep out the Tories at one end and the Scottish and Welsh Nationalists at the other.

A wish-list should include a picture showing how in principle these three traditions – the senatorial, the traditional and the regional – might be combined. For any consensus must be founded on features of all three. An example of an attempt to move towards such a consensus is to be found in the Liberal Democrats' Torquay Conference paper of September 1993, *Here We Stand – Proposals for Modernising Britain's Democracy*.

We look in vain in such documents, coming from whatever party, for in-depth consideration of a new Second Chamber's functions and powers. These difficult questions are virtually ignored. The emphasis, as always, is upon membership, which depends logically upon them. That said, the paper shows how debate on such a combination must go. For it contains two options, one senatorial and regional and the other the same with a traditional dash added 'to retain a measure of continuity and the expertise available to the current House of Lords'.

Option I envisages a chamber wholly elected from fifteen regions one each from Scotland, Wales and Northern Ireland and from 12 English Regions, each with 15 members elected by STV. Elections would be for 6-year terms. A third of members would come up for election every 2 years. Scotland, Wales and Northern Ireland would each have their own Parliaments.

Option II however throws a sop to tradition (without enthusiasm and in brackets) by allowing for 60 non-voting members selected by a senatorial committee to join them. These selected members would be appointed to offer 'a broad range of experience in matters likely to come before Parliament'. Here as so often underlying themes beside Lib Dems' central preoccupation of regional decentralisation (and elsewhere in the document, EU participation and PR) are hinted at, not explored. For Option II is meaningless without the unspoken aims of complementing the Commons, better preparation for legislative and other debate, continuity with hard achievement in the Lords and their working tradition.

It should now go without saying that if such functions (and others) are seriously contemplated for our Second Chamber, the balance of membership would need consideration *ab ovo* – not to mention an overhaul of the Second Chamber's functions and powers and of the interplay between the two Houses. But the Liberal Democrats deserve credit for attempting to bring together in one document thoughts on most of the areas of public concern about the workings of our democracy.

Above all they do not aim at a 'policy' of flinging all the balls up in the air and catching them, if they can, one by one or seeing, when they drop them, where they fall. I do not think that an unfair characterisation of Labour's approach to constitutional change *so far*. But eager beavers, however inexperienced, are capable of learning – if and only if they are are prepared to engage in a searching debate that teases out and carefully informs public opinion. We wait and prod and hope.

For a wish-list for functions and powers for a renewed Second Chamber that is to be based exclusively on earlier party proposals can only be unsatisfactory and remarkably short. The very attempt shows the paucity of available ideas. Probably the concentration on membership reflects the depth of public helplessness in the face of a government grown insensibly into disproportionate power at the expense of Parliament, its powers and prestige. Obstacles to reform is the subject of the next Part of this book. Meanwhile here goes...

The Second Chamber, as regards its functions, should:

a) as now, revise and improve legislation, however controversial, sent up from the House of Commons (which will not include Money Bills) – but without any in-built party bias;

b) as now, supplement Commons debate on all public issues – but with the greater authority that public election of at least most of its members would give. It sems to be generally assumed that, whatever kind of election is decided upon, the Second Chamber will legislate and debate with greater wisdom, or at least more democratically and representatively;

c) as now, supplement the Commons on EU legislation, but preferably without any increase, and probably a diminution, of powers (for Labour objects to the Lords' veto on subsidiary legislation) and certainly with a minimum of increased expenditure, whether on salaries or on secretarial and research help;

d) carry out a), b) and c) with more regard both to national/regional aspirations and to considered continuity of policy;

e) as now (?), act as guardian of the British Constitution (whatever that may be);

f) somehow, do all of a) to e) without antagonising either the House of Commons by apparent rivalry or the government of the day (and preferably without criticising either) – regardless of the issues involved and even if they include constitutional issues.

The Second Chamber, as regards its powers, should:

a) carry out its functions with the minimum of powers – probably little greater than its powers as at present (Labour would like less; and traditionals might favour a return to 1911 from 1949);

b) retain its veto on the prolonging of a Parliament beyond five years.

If that were all that is possible, one could well wonder: "Why change at all?"

The rest of the book will be dedicated first to investigating the contradictions underlying current aspirations on the functions and powers of the Second Chamber, and then on cobbling together proposals both on functions and powers and, in consequence of those, on its membership.

Part II

Obstacles to Reform

INTRODUCTION

The foregoing historical sketch, Part I, was limited, as promised in its Introduction, to showing how the House of Lords has come to operate as it does. This succeeding Part is limited to explaining how its reform, evidently demanded by its history, has become stalled for, now, nearly a century.

The title, Obstacles to Reform, suggests a misleading neatness to this endeavour, as if the notion, 'obstacles', defined a category of homogeneous but resolvable difficulties thrown in the way of effective democracy by a conspiracy of governments, parties and Parliamentarians. On the contrary 'obstacles' is a ragbag of constitutional and historical anomalies – a sort of Lord High Everything Else's dispatch-box – so heavy as to outweigh and obscure the reforming efforts of conscientious and fair-minded governments.

There are two general ways to approach a pile such as this. The first way is the easier, the more elegant and dramatic – and suits the tidy-minded. It is the way of abolition, the Herculean cleaning out, that wipes off the past back to a *tabula rasa*, so as to write a new beginning. That is not the British way, not the way sought in this book – and not a way recommended by any overwhelming human happinesses brought about by those 20th-century dictatorships who demolished in order to rebuild.

The other approach is the cautious trail of the snail carrying its baggage on its back and trying to make the best of it. It allows no insouciance about the destination (quite the contrary); but it requires a thorough understanding of what we begin with (and without), that can indicate what we can make of it.

So the list of 'obstacles', which begins with the Monarchy and the House of Lords as they now are, is no hit-list for destruction but a muddle to disentangle. It resembles a tell in the desert, with a village on top and the leavings of generations underneath, which we now set out to make more habitable.

Chapter-headings of this Part II:
1. *The Monarchy and the House of Lords*, especially in their ceremonial functions, and, generally, the paraphernalia of government. Here also include Parliament's ineffectualness and the interrelations of the two Houses.
2. *Representation*. Here include the Salisbury Doctrine, the Mandate, Referendums, the European Union – and current popular attitudes to government.

1. THE MONARCHY AND THE HOUSE OF LORDS

Much of the British Constitution embodies, like a coral reef, British history, its unfinished business, its awkward compromises. What is visible and living bears no satisfactory relation to present or foreseen needs. But we are reluctant to throw it out, provided only that it is not 'too' expensive (whatever criterion we should attach to that), for fear of losing something whose importance we do not understand.

Accordingly of all our institutions the Monarchy is the hardest to justify *in terms generally agreed*. For a determined majority of the British demand its survival; but the Monarchy is above all a symbol of uncrystallised and inarticulate aspirations, and not only of ours but of later generations of Britishers. To make clear consensus yet more of a will-o'-the-wisp, the Monarch's role is now at least almost *wholly* symbolic.

For the Monarch now, at least in theory, has no direct political influence, whether in the redress of grievances, in debate or in legislation. The Queen does no more than, in prescribed circumstances, to hold the government's pen. Only when the government is inoperative, for example on the fall of the government, does the Monarch's role come alive – and even then within prescribed limits. True, it is still vigorously debated what those limits might be. But not that there *are* limits. Outside those, even in matters once exclusively ascribed to the Prerogative, the Monarch has no powers that are not those of the government (the GCHQ case).

It remains to be seen how the judges would treat a Monarch that refused to give the Royal Assent to a Bill that had passed all its Parliamentary stages, including a Bill to abolish the Monarchy itself. Constitutionalists would fervently hope that issue would never arise. But the logic of some recent cases suggests the Monarch has no such power of refusal. The reversal of roles is complete. Parliament started out as the recalcitrant puppet of the Monarch; now the Monarch is not even entitled to kick against Parliament's pricks. One may be right to doubt whether the judges would ever in fact come to that conclusion (whether indeed they would be right to do so, but the decision is undeniably theirs). For the Queen in Parliament is a unitary if abstract sovereign of monarch, Lords and Commons: a statute to be binding should in theory receive the assent of all three, as a trinity. But, anyway, one cannot doubt that the Monarch's role is wholly symbolic, if that means it is exercised wholly on behalf of something or somebody else.

It is an interesting question what that something or somebody is – but a question that is academic in both senses of the term. For the two candidates are a) the people or b) their lawful government. Whichever it is, academics could only argue from premises so rarefied as to admit of unresolvable disagreement. Besides the settlement between them, whatever anyone said, would be political and its rational basis 'academic' in the other sense also.

That said, until that apocalyptic day the unresolved question has practical implications. For if the Monarch represents only the lawful government, then if there is *no* lawful government (not even in the absence of any other, the Monarch's own) the Monarch has no powers.

If on the other hand the Monarch represents the people, then in the absence of a lawful government, and until one is formed, the Monarch *is* the lawful government. From a historical perspective, this looks the preferable alternative. For it explains the Monarch's residual role of dissolving Parliament and/or inviting a leader best able to command a Commons' majority to form a government. It also has an attractive glitter in these days of a self-conscious electorate. For it reminds governments that their tenure, no less than the Monarch's, depends directly on those whom they think to serve.

Finally it calls in question Parliament's power (let alone the power of the Commons acting without the authority of the Monarch and/or the House of Lords) to dissolve the Monarchy. For the Monarchy both stands behind and is part of the legal government. The Monarchy therefore cannot be without its consent legally abolished and its role indeed is to ensure that an illegal or ineffective government be replaced by a legal one.

Accordingly until a political crisis overbears historical logic, I prefer the first explanation of the Monarch's powers, that the Monarch holds its power from the people rather than from the government.

For a writer on the House of Lords this conclusion has a direct bearing on the Lords' position. For if the two Houses together (regardless of the wishes of the government of the day) cannot without the abdication of the Monarchy abolish it, then by a closely related line of argument the Commons cannot lawfully abolish the House of Lords without their consent either. For it is the Queen in Parliament as a whole that represents the people; and at bottom sovereignty is of the people. It could be strongly argued that the 1911 Parliament Act was in no way aimed at such giving the Commons such a right, any more than it could be properly used by a government in the Commons to force through a Bill proroguing a Parliament beyond five years.

How far the Lords could escape the Parliament Acts to oppose unwelcome or incomplete reform falling short of abolition is another question. Perhaps that issue turns on whether a proposed reform interfered substantially with the House of Lords' present constitutional role (whatever that was determined by the judges to be) without improving it.

But these are high and dubious questions which one hopes would never be put to the test. For if they were, consensus would have broken down, our democracy would have failed and a political rather than a constitutional settlement would in practice be imposed, with unforeseeable social and economic consequences. It is sufficient here to recognise that both the Monarchy and the House of Lords incorporate both powers and problems which impose potential limitations on constitutional reformers.

Both also have a symbolic role, as the head of State and its principal retinue. The symbolism behind the Monarch both in popular estimation and in constitutional theory heavily outweighs the Lords'. But they are alike in kind since they depend on their roots in Parliament as the people's representative.

It is with their symbolic roles that we are here concerned. But it is not to be forgotten that the House of Lords has important functions even within a working government, while the Monarch's function in Parliament is only triggered by the failure of a government. So neither institution without its consent could be seriously interfered with by a government in the Commons, without causing a constitutional crisis with unforeseeable ramifications. The triple functions of the Lord Chancellor are a parallel case. He combines a senior executive function (in effect already a justice minister) with the chairmanship of the House of Lords and a seat on the chief court of the land, the House of Lords' Appellate Committee. Each function is independent of the other, though under our constitution the Lord Chancellor holds all three. It is he, above all, with the Monarch, who holds the constitution together.

Together the Monarch and the House of Lords hold together disparate sections of the reef. These sections have now grown apart. But their functions – the military, the diplomatic, the civil service, the judiciary, the church, not to mention Ministers and the Commons themselves, heroes great, small and charitable, with gongs and initials after their names – all those that once clung to the Monarchy when it ruled as its advisers and supporters, have now in the Monarchy and the Lords their only common points of contact, except in action. None of these sections is or should be beyond reform. But their fabric is as weird and wonderful and colourful and subtly interrelated – and as vulnerable to change – as any community of corals. This reef with all its rich variety of function and ceremonial to grace it, is the British state.

State ceremonial is not everyone's cup of tea; and it embodies for different individuals different ideas. For some a cup of tea with the Queen is the ultimate memory; some prefer to watch a royal wedding. Some rely on the Cenotaph to keep family memories alive. Some dream of a gong, and by golly they work for it! Like it or not. So why be mean? The honours system comes cheap to the state; but for many individuals it is an inspiration to public service.

Sentiment is the only unifier and inspiration of nationhood. As nations become ever more disparate in themselves and more dependent, economically and administratively, upon each other, a focus for what they have in common is politically indispensable. What is more it is a comfort, a source of pleasure and often a spur to communal, charitable and social action.

It follows that it is only those that would be rid of the lot, those with a single idea which they would if they could impose on our varied and liberal society, who feel comfortable, let alone passionate, about changing very much at all. But even reefs need pruning and have animals in them to do it. It is not beyond our collective wit either to improve what we have in order to enliven it.

But hesitancy to undertake standard maintenance and refurbishment of a venerable system, for fear of hurting what no one can fully understand, has left a daunting list for review.

Refurbishment of the Monarchy is already under way, not unaccompanied by sadness, whether at Windsor Castle or in the decommissioning yard. One may well wonder if the Treasury (and other accountants) are the experts wanted. But anything is better for a reef than to allow it to become a dead fossil.

Next after the Monarchy, the House of Lords stands in line for cleaning and revitalising. A reformer can have no better role model than a cleaner-wrasse.

Reform, though, is generally concerned with the substance behind the symbol, rather than the symbol itself. For symbols have a historical life of their own.

But symbols are not 'image'.

It is sufficiently obvious that modernisation of the image of the Monarchy or the House of Lords has nothing to do with the substance of reform; so that politicians who have seemed obsessed with Queen's image, say, (or with their own image reflected in it) may be presumed to be little interested in the effectiveness of democracy, or at least to see no great need to improve its workings.

What is not so obvious is that 'image' – which means how a person or an institution is perceived in the passing fashion of the day – has very little to do with the potency of the symbol. It is very nice to have tea with the Queen; but approachability is not to be confused with what is being approached. The Queen is human, indeed very human. So by the way are judges despite their wigs or Lords with or without their ermine. Sometimes human, all too human. But none of this has anything to do with the potency of ceremonial when they are engaged in it. That is the very opposite of what is fashionable in my eyes or nice about the Queen or a judge I come up before. Their role in its very essence is to transcend my afternoon or my predicament. Think of a cuppa from the Queen's teapot as like a slice of wedding-cake. Being associated in a wedding, with a slice of cake, does not make me a part of *their* marriage which we celebrate. *Theirs* is the mystery which by our presence we celebrate, not ours.

If by a cuppa with the Queen we became in any way what she is, there would be no point whatever in having a queen at all. It follows that the pot she pours from is of no significance whatever except in so far as it makes us feel at home with her.

So we come to it. When the British talk about the image of the Monarch, they are talking just of what they feel comfortable with. Fine so long as they recognise this and do not suppose the Monarch is just there to make us comfortable. She is there as our head of state – of course, also as head of *our* state. That function has nothing to do with whether she serves still the best Darjeeling or now tea-dust in a teabag.

Analysis of this kind is easiest with the Monarchy, because while there is a government in place the Monarch has no presence except as a symbol of the continuity of the state. This continuity cocks a snook at fashions and image-makers, who are concerned merely with their momentary political acceptability.

Nevertheless Monarchy and other state institutions must grow or wither.

Nobody is suggesting that the very particular pomp of Victorian imperial occasions – which would have been ruthlessly stage-managed anyhow – is appropriate today. Nor even that money is no object in putting it on. What is being said is, state institutions in themselves rather than how we today look at them embody Britishness. We are learning to manage our countryside, for the sake of those who made it and of those who come after us, with respect. So too we should treat our state institutions.

Such a statement invites challenge. If the Monarch represents our state, is indeed the primary symbol of it, why can't we demand any Monarch we like? We can, of course – but should we? Perhaps in framing our demands we should consider less what makes us comfortable with the Monarch, more how the Monarch represents the state we are in and as we would like it to be.

The state is an essential of the British heritage, and it should be treated no differently in principle from other beautiful old things, towns, buildings and their contents, the countryside... Things which represent what is left from the lives and efforts of our predecessors – not just for us, but for those who come after.

There is always a balance to be struck here between fashion and symbol. Many bitterly regret much that was pulled down and thrown away and uglily replaced after the Second War. The fervour of their moment pre-empted the choices of their future. Often available alternatives were not seriously costed. Undoubtedly much that was destroyed could have been modified, not only usefully but more cheaply too. There is a tendency again after this second Labour landslide of the century for fashion to dictate change too much at the expense of the symbol.

Fortunately the fervour this time around is of a different and a kinder kind. The people want to be part of their heritage, to understand it and to be included in it – and 'to cut out dead wood'.

What is dead wood, and what needs to be left as it is or modified? The Monarchy above all, along with other institutions such as the Lords, was earlier billed as an 'obstacle to reform' just because of the difficulty of answering this question in a way that can hope to gain general agreement. We can now see that the symbol of the state has significance beyond the forms in which it clothes itself, but that these forms, or some of them, are themselves part of Britishness.

Perhaps a guide should therefore be to cut out those of our traditions which serve *no* useful purpose – those that cannot be modified to do anything useful at all and which if lost would not seriously thought in need of replacement. To that guide a rider should be added that the symbol of the state is supposed to represent as many sides of our national life as possible; so that what we decide to modify should be changed in the direction of including what earlier has been left out.

Though this approach may be just another way of stating the problem, it may still be useful. Ruling groups, however well-intentioned, weight political representation in their favour. This is *the* argument in favour of democracy as the only fair political system, since it allows for periodic counterbalances. It is also the charter of reformers, who demand continual and vigilant reassessment. The symbol of the state has been weighted too much in favour of some parts of our heritage at the expense of others. Since this is a book about House of Lords reform as a means of improving the people's representation in government, I shall take my examples from the Lords.

The House of Lords has an active function as a legislative and debating House. But from its antique role, never quite defunct, as the courtiers and advisers round the Monarch, it retains a symbolic significance in the state second only to the Monarch.

Three categories of its *ex officio* members, in particular – the bishops, the law lords and the Lord Chancellor himself who presides over the House – derive both their membership and their roles directly from that ancient form of English government, practical roles which have altered remarkably little through the centuries and which even if their House were abolished would survive unscathed under different names.

Even disestablishment of the Anglican Church, a topic outside this book, would not necessarily either affect the bishops' seats in a reformed House or undermine their symbolic role. Indeed it will be later suggested that, whether disestablished or not, Anglican bishops should be joined in the Lords by other spiritual leaders – a proposal, by the way, that many bishops over the years have themselves endorsed. It is wholly appropriate that a Second Chamber that embodies so much of British idealogical heritage should include spiritual leaders representative of all persuasions within our multicultural population, and that the exclusiveness that followed on after earlier victories should now be erased. For the state aspires to represent all its citizens. Those additional leaders would enrich debate, regardless of whether they were in the company of established prelates.

The law lords (who include *ex officio*, among others, the Lord Chancellor and his predecessors) constitute the highest court in the land – a function which would resemble even more strikingly the US Supreme Court if Britain were ever to acquire a written constitution or to entrench some constitutional settlement intended explicitly to be outside the long reach of the Commons. Even without such innovations, they would play a solo and virtuoso part, invidious and unwelcome, if ever a government sought to abolish the Monarchy or the House of Lords without those institutions' consent. But the law lords, like other Parliamentarians, are generalists. They play also a vigorous role in the general business of the House of Lords.

The Lord Chancellor on the woolsack is *ex officio* a very senior Minister of the Crown and in effect a minister of justice. Some would sew this label explicitly into his gown (or someday hers); but whether or not this is done – and the decision would probably turn on some political need to repackage a reorganisation and extension of the department – the Lord Chancellor, by that or any other name, would continue the venerable function of the government's conscience.

In short the law lords, including the Lord Chancellor, have over the years adapted their symbolic roles so aptly to their practical functions in government that whatever symbolic role they might later be assigned in the state their jobs would be practically unchanged. If this cannot be said of the bishops, this is a symptom of deep doubts over who if anyone – and how – is to be a spiritual leader in a multicultural state. Fortunately there are no corresponding doubts about the need for the rule of law.

In other respects the Lords do not seem to have adapted symbol and function as successfully. For British government is – and has been for a long time – sick. So therefore is the state sick in symbol and function. I have suggested that neither is cured by mere refurbishment of image – whether by 'Cool Britannia!' or by Leaping at the Lords). I now would add that a consensus should be sought on how to reform the workings of government before too much time is spent on worrying about its symbol, its ceremonial and protocol, its forms and formalities and all the rest.

There are good reasons for this. The symbol has always followed the fact; and accordingly it has lagged behind it. So it should – for the symbol represents the stability of the state as it changes with society in time. An assault on the symbol unaccompanied by adaptation of the functions of government to present needs is either muddleheadedness or evasion; and when undertaken by a government obsessed by the power of image, it can be presumed to be evasion.

Furthermore when traditions are slashed without a clear sense of direction, things and thoughts will be smashed which our tourism trade now and our successors later may bitterly regret.

Finally the slashing and the smashing will be carried out by a government whose abuse of power is a large portion of the constitutional problem. The government in self-defence is diverting public disapproval from its undemocratic conduct on to the trappings of power. Here I take no party-political stance. For the shaking of Parliament I attribute to Mrs Thatcher. The Blair government is riding the tsunami consequent on the landslide – by contrast has shown so far as a lightweight outfit playing to galleries on the shore. But it is always the people must endure the flood.

None of this is to be taken as requiring nothing to be changed at once if its survival is a nuisance. The House of Lords' oath, for example, is said to be so long and cumbersome that it delays unduly Lords taking up their seats. If this is true, then it should be shortened. If it is true… But perhaps whether it is true is a matter for experienced Lords to judge, rather than for tabloid newspapers and certain new and future Lords who do not much like taking any oath anyhow. A little patience and humility is not out of place even among the governed. Especially when the some of the governors – the Monarch, for example, and some of the hereditary Lords – are displaying a little of these rare virtues themselves. Above all when the people have at last tumbled to the truth, long and professionally obscured by governments, that they, the people, are in the last resort the governors in any event.

The Monarchy is downsizing, the royal yacht scrapped, Buckingham Palace to be vacated as a picture gallery. Many hereditaries have condemned the principle of hereditary power. No-one can at present say what will be the final station of this display of sackcloth and ashes. It is the turn of the government both to educate and consult the people on how government itself should be reformed.

Meanwhile a common view about the heritage aspects of our constitution should also be sought. For not only is it a stabilising factor in a rapidly changing and fragmenting world, comical, pompous and picturesque as all at once it can be. It is also worth good pounds sterling in a whole range of ways (tourism not least). Since shortage of ready cash in an increasingly ageing and self-indulgent population is already constricting governmental freedom of action in all its activities, the hard-headed cannot afford to neglect the hidden revenue that heritage Britain represents.

Some might say cutting the cost of governing is the primary concern of modern government. It is certainly a huge factor in that downsizing of the trappings of state of which the Monarchy is currently the government's apparently beloved and favourite victim. The sheer cost of paying for well-informed Parliamentarians and an effective Opposition is a prime excuse for government's monopoly of the expenditures essential to wielding power or influencing the powerful.

It is still, however, widely understood that downsizing the Monarchy below the glamour line would have serious diplomatic and trade implications. The Commonwealth is still a powerful force for stability and international understanding. Furthermore as states become increasingly interdependent in trade, economics and international administration (of which the European Union is only the most insistent and unavoidable example) the British will rely more and more on their quaint traditions as a part of their dwindling Britishness.

Moreover the British heritage is a motivation for public service which the British cannot afford wantonly to throw overboard. It is also the foundation of a sizable chunk of our tourist industry: public screams would follow on very swiftly from any drying-off of that milch cow. And it is still an inspiration to the young and at least a source of amusement for their seniors, as well as an endless source of profit for the popular press and of ego-trips for TV presenters.

Finally, nobody doubts that the honours system is still, as we saw, a cost-effective method of not paying for devoted public service, whether in the House of Lords itself or local government, in magistrates' courts, in charitable works of all kinds or support for the arts and sport and entertainment. All these require expenditures that the public is quick to demand and for which no government wants to find the funds from the piggy-banks of a hard-pressed electorate. Perhaps the National Lottery should now be enshrined as a late but welcome arrival in the mystique of the British State.

In truth there is a delicious mystery in being British that encapsulates our varied history and aspirations. Much of it is enshrined in pleasing absurdities and symbolised by our strange constitution. There is much good sense too, encrusted in curious survivals, which only those engaged in its everyday workings can appreciate. That is why the paraphernalia of government makes hard nuts for the teeth of reformers, especially those who look for stable reform through consensus.

Consider, for a classic example, the Queen in Parliament as the sovereign representative of the British People. As a symbolic statement – even as a reference to the formal roles played out before the public by the Monarch and the Houses of Parliament – fine. The formula calls attention to the formal structure of the British state to which our sentiments of nationhood can attach. Just because it is intended specifically not to give any indication how practical government does or should work, it has been for many years a statement 'above politics' to which all the British can nod assent. The formula's secret of success is of course that it treats the Queen in Parliament as a unit, and takes no account of the relative weighting of the three components, Monarch, House of Lords, House of Commons. These weights have shifted out of all recognition since, say, the Tudors. The mystic phrase covers as comfortably Henry VIII's supremacy in 1540 and Mr Blair's today, regardless of who is eating out of whose hand. And it relies on the fiction that Ministers exercise power on behalf of the Sovereign to leave out the PM and cabinet altogether.

The formula has retained its usefulness through time and change because it is not specific, because it is a fudge, because it keeps us comfortable with ourselves regardless of practicalities. It is only one of a number of pleasant anomalies in the lore of Parliament which allows our constitution to move without discomfort. We mentioned a while back the Lords' oath. The complex symbolism at the opening of Parliament is another example. One House calling t'other the Other Place, another.

There are, however, a number of touchy and gloomy worries not far below this surface. It is clear for example that most British constitutional traditions are aimed at maintaining a facade of continuity in the face of political change, while allowing the House of Commons a near-monopoly of power. This goes back to the uneasy settlement after the trauma of the Civil War. Ever since Cromwell it has been true that any Parliament can undo the handiwork of its predecessor; and it has been equally true that we British are anxious to defend the faith that we learnt there our lesson and would never allow anything like a Cromwell in Parliament to recur.

So when it is sometimes said, simply, that the Queen in Parliament is sovereign, fine if that is not meant to exclude the people's ultimate right – or at least not meant to say more than that, while a lawful government is in power, no person or persons may challenge it unlawfully. The awkward question is, what rights does the people retain to ensure that it is democratically represented? If the Queen in Parliament is not doing a proper job, what can or should the people lawfully do about it?

For there has been a sudden and irreversible tectonic shift in the people's perception of the role of government. The public is determined that government should explain itself, and be subject to criticism, from day to day, not just at election-time – not perceiving that, by constantly appealing over the head of weak Parliaments direct to government, we are dangerously increasing, not controlling, governmental power.

Having a concept of sovereignty – the Queen in Parliament – which has remarkably little to do with the everyday business of government, has the great virtue of a symbol of state which by its very formality puts the state outside practical politics. But as a definition out of which the idea of British government should somehow be unpacked it is worse than useless. The Queen in Parliament – Hamlet without the Prince. The Prime Minister presiding over a cabinet of Ministers supported by their departments and controlled with ever increasing stringency by the Treasury – in short the government – is omitted from 'sovereignty' (whether or not representative of the people) altogether. It is hard even for constitutionalists, let alone for the public, trying to assess the health of our democracy, to focus on a fiction.

Moreover, which is worse, Parliament, by implication in a concept intended to have form without substance, is sidelined along with the Monarch away from the levers of power. Between Parliaments, as we have seen, the Monarch bears the responsibility of government, however briefly, on the royal shoulders; and no Ministry can govern for a moment without at least the *de facto* consent of Parliament. Monarch and Parliament both have parts without which there just can be no performance. Admittedly theirs are negative forces, forces of control rather than initiation and management – brakes and safety features, say, rather than the engine and steering column – but they are essential to the machinery of government. By consigning them to cloud-cuckooland we are distracted from an audit of their effectiveness as moving parts of the constitution.

Neither Monarchy nor Parliament have fulfilled expectations in recent decades.

The Queen let down in public estimation by some of her family and Mr Major let down by his own supporters in Parliament strike together strange harmonies. Both Her Majesty and her ex-Prime Minister retain personal affection and respect which did not save them from a loss of public confidence in their spheres of operation. 'Downsizing' of the Monarchy (reminiscent of some experiences of King Lear) is a covert acceptance of this unfortunate fact. But it is open to question, once the fact is out in the open, whether it was right or wholly necessary for so much of the Monarch's public esteem to be centred on the myth of a (Victorian) ideal family.

That said, the Queen's family misfortunes have in no way affected her ability, should the need arise, to exercise with full authority and public support her executive governmental role. There *are* tetchy concerns about how the Monarch should respond to certain potential crises – for example whether to call for a general election or for a new prime minister. But these would apply also to the predicament of any elected head of a British state unless some complex set of rules were agreed in advance to make the decision automatic – in which case the decision would not be tailored to the actuality. The Monarch's executive role seems not in need of reform.

For it is not reasonable to expect that any elected British Head of State, elected to carry out the Monarch's constitutional role in place of the Queen could in fact match in the public mind the above-party disinterestedness that Her Majesty's whole life (or her successors') would have prepared her for.

An elected British Head of State would be very largely a political appointment, voted for largely on party political lines, however the election was dressed up. The candidate could not then be trusted – especially by him- or herself – to jettison at will the mental habits of a lifetime, so as to exercise wholly impartially what can only be a political discretion. Nor have some of the nearest parallels – for example in Australia – given any encouragement to a contrary view.

That is why the current Prime Minister's public patronage of the Monarch, though no doubt well-meant and coming at a time when the Monarchy had sunk dangerously low in public esteem, is firmly to be deprecated. Put it bluntly: the Queen has been made to look too much like Mr Blair's poodle; and if those were the only terms on which the Monarchy could in fact survive in Britain – and certainly there were not – its constitutional effectiveness might in a real crisis be seriously called in question. For there could well come a day, say after the next general election, when the Queen, not Mr Blair, is boss.

So while the formal position of the Queen in (as part of) Parliament has led to confusion which has been among the factors obstructing constitutional reform over many years, the Monarch's executive constitutional role has not: on the contrary it is very much alive. It is Parliament's constitutional role that needs urgent attention.

Parliament has become ineffectual as the people's scrutineer of government. The actual monopoly power of government has evaded the public gaze. For the effective government has escaped its stables in a cloud of Parliamentary myth. Parliament's role in that myth is useful, like the Monarchy's, as a symbol of state; but in so far as the myth has let Parliamentarians off their duties, it has been a practical disaster.

How Parliament could and should come nearer to exercising the role which myth assigns to it is the subject of this book.

This is not a role, however, which all Parliamentarians would welcome – especially the ambitious ones. For government takes its key support from its MPs. So indeed does the Opposition, even if the Opposition's muted voice as a government in exile makes both unity and what it says of very much less importance to the public than what government says and does. MPs do not relish the thorny road of clear independent expression of the public interest – often in the faces of their leaders -which leads generally to the bottom rather than to the top.

Party unity is such a prerequisite of electability that a search for a voice for Parliamentarians which will not undermine either their careers or their parties is the most urgent of current tasks – and in the British context the most difficult.

Parliament is the prime obstacle to the reform of Parliament.

Look at Parliament's own views of itself (views, because there are opposing interests and perspectives between the two Houses), Government's and the Opposition's self-interested views of it (which coincide with party interests), and the views of a disenchanted public (for whom politicians as a class are among the least-respected of professionals). All those, in short, who should be pressing for deep reform of Parliament in the interest of British democracy have their own reasons for leaving the balance of political power where it is.

But the reformer's cause is not lost. For the mind-sets opposing reform among the powers that be and the public they are to serve are diametrically opposed to each other. Those that have power and jobs want them undisturbed, while the people do not know either how to assess or how to improve the performance of their supposedly devoted servants.

Meanwhile the levers of reform stick to the hands of those who have no urgent motives for reform. No doubt Parliament (the House of Commons anyway), if it had the will, could mend its ways without legislation. The government is already billed to initiate 'reforms' (and the Opposition to oppose them) which will strengthen government's hold on government. MPs are content with a role in Parliament which turns them into multicoloured flocks of sheep, for fear of being wolves preying on their own kinds. Behind them all stand Kafkan party machines whom not even their leaders fully control or call to account; and in front of them a public mesmerised by their media outriders.

Governments can never be trusted to act as watchdogs of the constitution. Either they are strong, so that reform may weaken their hold; or they are weak, so reform is outwith either their aspiration or their power. Oppositions for this purpose may be classed as exiled governments with no power whatever, unless they join with government in some loose coalition (when they are useless as either). MPs, cowed by their parties or their ambitions, generally lack motivation, in any case. But at present their frustrations or downcast self-esteem is expressed in antipathy either to a strengthened House of Lords or to the institutions of the European Union, which because of MPs inherent weakness they see as their potential competitors.

It is nonetheless incontrovertible that the people are being short-changed by both government and Parliament. The British, however, are rightly wary of change until they see clear benefits and will slough no skin until the new is felt growing within. Therefore any programme of reform must be seen growing out of the constitution we have. Earlier positive and new growth in both Houses has been identified. What now is needed is the focus of government's and Parliamentarians' energy on these growth points. This is not politically possible until the public demand it. A clear programme put before them may well arouse the sleeping lion.

The House of Lords, of all the main institutions of government, is perceived as underperforming and has in fact been making the best of the meagre resources at its disposal. Two reasons in one for reform here. The public would like it to be composed and empowered to do more; and the Lords have already shown themselves to be outgrowing their scope.

Commentaters often point out the political obstacles to reforming the Lords before the Commons. But this objection dissipates in the face of proposals in which the reformed House of Lords is seen as the forerunner of Parliament reformed as a whole. The Commons, in the scheme proposed, would profit from the teething troubles of the Lords and could indeed feel encouraged to put new facilities to better, though slightly different, effect.

Commons jealousy of the Lords is the single most intractable obstacle in the way of a revitalised Lords deriving as we have seen from MPs chronic self-doubt. Put crudely, the Commons would object to any rearrangement of the Lords which increased their influence without a countervailing increase in that of the Commons. It has apparently occurred to nobody that this stand-off is misconceived. For the two Houses should be complementary rather than in competition. Nothing is a more telling symptom of Parliament's ineffectualness that this failure of the two Houses to cooperate.

Because a modern British government is so overwhelmingly powerful between elections, there are no equivalent misgivings about Parliamentary reform on the Blair government's part. They are simply under no pressure to make concessions to an ineffective Parliament if change might make their control even a little less awesome.

Hence the unholy alliance between the government and the Commons (which even Mr Hague, with a temporary power failure in his own engines, is making little effort to ram) to make piecemeal changes to the House of Lords – which none deny will improve its democratic facade and none pretend will improve our democratic works.

The Lords, being short of territory, have modestly established themselves in the untenanted ground of non-contentious legislation and amendment and in the altogether vacant lot of European legislation. To date, both government and MPs are content with the *status quo*. As a legislating arm, the House Lords does, without taking any credit whatever, much careful and tedious laundry for the government, saving overworked MPs that trouble. In its European Communities Committee, it at least has a go at analysing, debating and reporting on EU legislation which Tory MPs of the last long administration found distasteful and voluminous.

Neither the Commons nor the government, however, can have much of a shout (except on the dreary ground of cost – which allows modern government to put any constructive proposals at the bottom of any pile of priorities) against a scheme for the Lords which builds on proven strength, which improves popular representation, which would increase the Lords' usefulness to both of them, and which would point the way to corresponding improvements in the effectiveness of the Commons themselves – provided of course the public were convinced of the value of the scheme for the purpose of improving their own role in the control of government.

The current underlying all current reform proposals from whatever source is the people's growing determination to be consulted on and influence policies carried through in their name. Government's reaction (over several Parliaments) has been to appear to grant the first through increased media approachability and to deny the second by the centralisation of decision-making and the manipulation of news. The measure of government's success has been the spacious oxbow round Parliament. Democracy's bastion against the arrogance of government is left silted so far to one side of events that the people have not only discounted Parliament as a primary source of influence but even the expectation that Parliament could ever now be restored as a sluice controlling government policy.Faith in Parliamentary reform is eroded almost beyond repair.

A self-confident electorate, a manipulative government and a crestfallen and discredited establishment – these in the past have generally occurred in the aftermath of violent revolutions; but revolution as a prerequisite for popular government is happily also discredited as bringing in anti-democratic rulers, in love with themselves rather than their professed ideals, and economic mismanagement. Class war is also dropped in favour of picking off the privileged in their sport, for example, or one by one, preferably through tabloid supping on their misdemeanours, or, where this is impossible, ignoring their efforts altogether – along with the poor, the sick and the elderly. Ours is neither a caring society nor a vindictive one, and avoids (besides the virtues) the vice of both – occupational interference in quiet people's lives. Instead it is a self-indulgent society of media addicts and trivial pursuits. It is a society which looks to amusements of the moment to distract itself from looking outside or overseas, and to chat-shows to distract itself from the mirror. It is the comfortable-with-itself society.

How should such a society be represented? For now if ever the people is able to get the government it wants and will get the government it deserves.

These two are as far apart as ever they were. The people wants efficient government; and it wants to be engaged in it. Without an effective Parliament as its strong arm the people is no match for a strong government. Shaking the prime minister's hand or buttonholing a minister on a chat-show is no substitute for informed scrutiny. Nor does watching two hours news a day on TV discernably improve the world. These pleasant pastimes are not participation in government. Freedom demands active vigilance and control requires hard work. If the people still thinks it can delegate those to MPs or to Parliament as a whole, it must ensure it gets the right folk in Parliament and then make sure they have the tools of their trade and clear objectives. The people is in fact as far from the corridors of power as when it hailed Henry VIII appearing from a balcony. It is most apposite that our Lord Chancellor likens himself to Wolsey or his protege, Mr Blair, to young Henry.

The Lord Chancellor, in casting himself as New Labour's conscience, draws attention to his unique position as the triangular cusp of the government, Parliament and the judiciary. His unique position on the Olympian heights simultaneously of the executive, the legislature and the administration of the law harks back to the days when a monarch could be a regular royal king; for he was the monarch's chief adviser in all departments of state. He, above any individual in the realm, is personally responsible for just government, just representation and justice; and with a strong, reforming Prime Minister behind him (if not in his pocket), he is in a position almost unique in this century to deliver.

Lord Irvine has rediscovered the House of Lords. In drawing attention to himself on the Woolsack he spotlights, as their leader, the historic role of the Crown's prerogative advisers. No one contests the Commons' primary historical function in relation to the raising and spending of public money. The Lord Chancellor is – and the House of Lords should assist him – Lord High Everything Else. If one were looking for a formula to express the position of a British Second Chamber rebuilt on the firmest foundations of our history and designed to rectify the failings of past governments, one could not find a better job spec than watchdog of the constitution, than guarantor of fairness in government, representation and the law. This indeed is the function that the House of Lords has, in its better moments over the past century and a half, sought to carry out.

Just how the House of Lords might in practice carry out that function more fully in the next century and get the authority, manpower and resources to do it is the subject of Part III of this book. Here it is sufficient to observe that the creeping failure of the House of Lords to bear its share of the constitutional load has been a primary cause of our weakened democracy. To mark this as failure is not to apportion blame. The Lords would have been superhuman to look beyond the erosion of their influence and interests during the extension of the franchise in the last century to their wider democratic responsibilities. There were some wiser heads among them (Lord Lansdowne and later Lord Bryce, for example) who tried to do so. But on the whole it was inevitable that the instinct of the Old Romans (whom they so much admired) to die in the last ditch rather than adapt their lives to a new dispensation should have prevailed. But having taken a mortal blow in 1911, by their diligence in this century (and especially since World War Two) they have kept alive a tradition of service which could now come into final bearing.

In Part I we traced the outline of events that led up to the 1911 Parliament Act. We noted the Lords' opposition to the extending franchise, the twists and turns of the Salisbury doctrine and its adaptation by the Fifth Marquess after the post-war Labour landslide to a view of the Lords' functions that has survived, just, to the present day. But few would doubt the Lords have been making the best of a bad job.

So it is that when there is serious constitutional thought to be done the Lords are, as the Upper House, nowhere to be seen. The Lord Chancellor speaks as a councillor but is thinking exclusively as a minister, even though, like Lord Jenkins with his constitutional reform committee (who is not even a member of the government) and all members of the Lords, unelected to Parliament.

It is plainly undemocratic – and an affront to Parliament if Parliament were alive to such matters – that the Lord Chancellor with his committees on devolution, human rights and freedom of information should not feel it right to exercise his duties within a Parliamentary framework; and his lip-service to the historic source of his authority serves only to underline the point. The same goes for Lord Jenkins's committee, which is a quango located just where the House of Lords should be.

For if ever there was a subject on which freedom of information about governmental plans should be funnelled through Parliament to the public, it is, surely, constitutional reform. Quangos, with their loose affiliation to ministries via statute (and often looser ministerial control), are themselves mute (and often secretive) witnesses to the weakness of the Parliamentary process. Lord Irvine and Lord Jenkins, who both happen to be members of the House of Lords and charged by the government to improve British democratic representation, should show the way to a non-partisan approach to reform by insisting that their deliberations from an early stage should be brought within the Parliamentary fold. The House of Lords is the traditional forum for such work and has never lost its residual responsibility as constitutional guardian.

The very fact however that no-one in the government (or quasi-attached to it) has thought to use the House as a forum shows the low esteem for Parliament in Whitehall – and the negligible chance that the influence of Parliament over government is among the government's priorities.

In short the weakness of Parliament has been and remains the chief obstacle to its reform as the organ to restrain the excesses of government. As things now are, unless harried by a public aware that it is being short-changed – normally as a result of too generous words in an election manifesto – or unless compelled by an effective and focussed Opposition in the House of Commons, no government of any colour will go out of its way to ensure public scrutiny through Parliament of its doings. It is futile to hope that it will. A Second Chamber with the powers and authority to undertake this work is a prerequisite for its being attempted; and with Parliament as it is this will not happen until the public is awakened to insist upon it.

The Lord Chancellor has a conflict of interest to which he has himself drawn attention. For as leader of the Lords he should ensure above-party scrutiny of what as a senior member of the government he is doing. It may indeed be that his pronouncements were timed to provoke debate on how he is to mastermind reform.

Debate is the key, but of a door to undiscovered country. The fact is that reform in Britain has never been planned in anything approaching a political vacuum. That is only possible when there is a cataclysmic discontinuity, analogous perhaps to a mass-extinction, after a revolution. Such were the birth-pangs of the US and Soviet constitutions. After the English Civil War, and even after the Glorious Revolution of 1688, there was retrenchment. Similarly after the long struggle over the franchise which culminated in the defeat of the Lords in the1911 Parliament Act, there has been over eighty years in which the House of Lords has rubbed along pretending so far as it could that nothing much had happened.

That is the British way. The constitution is occasionally turned upside down and we boast of its continuity none the less.

The British have not been, till recently, accustomed to change for its own sake. What was the Welsh referendum, leading to a Welsh Assembly, really about? Carried by a tiny majority to an Assembly with negligible powers – what kind of nationalist sentiment inspired it? By contrast no one can mistake the drive to Scottish separatism – to redress, as many have seen it, the trick by which the Act of Union was consummated. But all this is a nationalism of sentiment merely. It in no new way assures Scots of their essential interests, whether economic or idealogical. The Scots did not need an Assembly to vote themselves oil-revenues (which are not up for grabs) or an international alignment (out with the EU, for example) or a new religious or ethical orientation.

It is interesting to compare Welsh and Scottish nationalism with Irish nationalism. No doubt here what this is about, over Northern Ireland. It is about grabbing territory, the Six Counties – at least it was until the recent all party talks. With guns if necessary. That is what nationalism used to be about. Grim and not nice at all – but not without a sharp point.

No-one begrudges the Welsh and the Scots their Assemblies. But it is important to recognise the limitations of the motives which inspired them, in order to understand the kind of constitutional debates which are nowadays fashionable, and to distinguish them from what such debates should be for – good government and the protection of essential interests for us and our children's children. The Welsh and the Scottish Assemblies were on offer and nice to have – like goods invitingly displayed in a supermarket (except that they are not understood to cost); but precious few would pretend that they are essential to their electorates or could say why if they did. The Assemblies are a luxury of sentiment – not to be decried for that, but not to be mistaken for bread and butter either. Nor is there any clear plan for their development into a scheme of better government for Wales or Scotland. Nor apparently has there been, either in government or by the Welsh and Scottish electorates, any analysis of the implications for the Union that is the UK. The Blair government launched into devolution with small thought for the Union, no forethought for the integration of the British Parliaments – and worst of all, for this is basic to good government, no concentrated national debate. And England seems to have been forgotten almost altogether. New Labour favours government by diversions.

Whether or not the Assemblies end in statehood for the Welsh and the Scottish – and whether or not within the EU over the next few decades that will count for much even in Wales and Scotland – their function, at present, is much the same as the Monarchy – or Parliament, nowadays, including the House of Lords – for the British as a whole. Or do I mean for the English?

For whereas the Welsh and the Scots have something new and untried, and at least capable of development, the English have lost faith in their institutions even as a symbol of identity, let alone as a basis of democratic government. Otherwise they would not be downsizing the Monarchy, neglecting Parliament, emptying the churches… Indeed if the English were any longer sure what they are made of, most probably the Welsh and the Scots would not now be hiving off. For what are they leaving, missing?

But until the Welsh or the Scots have governments of their own, the British are all in the same boat. The Welsh and the Scots with novelties and the English with their heads in the sand cannot escape the consequences of mistaking the formalities for the realities. British government reform is not a sentimental journey and really does affect all our citizens' essential interests.

Until we as a people ask for it we shall not call New Labour's cosy bluff. Close after the weakness of Parliament comes chatty – but authoritarian – government as an obstacle to needed reform. But until the people ask for it they have only themselves to blame for what they do not get. The British are not good at making a fuss unless they know how to get what they want. That above all is why they loathe party splits, worship strong governments and despise weak Parliaments.

Nevertheless the British paralysis is all-pervasive, probably in the absence of an obvious enemy. For the enemy is within: it is our indecision over Europe. At a time when nationalism is everywhere overtaken by instant communications and financial imperatives, unless it is a symptom of repressive and inward-looking regimes or a creature of sentiment, it is hard to fix unified priorities. Europe is the juggernaut on our doorstep.

Do we want in or out of Europe? And in or out of what Europe? It is, I believe, an all-penetrating uncertainty about this dread subject that accounts for the triviality of current British political debate. There is no dodging this one. It is a comet fully visible in the sky and computed to be coming straight for us. What Britain cannot afford to do is to say: anything we do, they (the coward's 'they') will undo. We need stronger institutions, not weaker ones, if we are not to be over-whelmed.

Good government is better than a defence; it is salvation. For the EU is no enemy. It represents in its threatening aspect no more than the cutting edge of international competition, such as Britain has no longer an empire, nor any other economic advantage, to shield us from. In or out, we need a working government machine.

It has been said that Parliament is itself the primary obstacle to its own reform. We can now distinguish two strong strands leading to this conclusion, whose interweaving has contributed much to the complexity of the problem – the formal versus the substantive place of Parliament (the Queen in Parliament versus the Queen-in-Parliament) in our constitution. The combination has made it impossible to confront Parliament head-on even if there had been consensus even as to the need, let alone as to the appropriate means. A two-pronged but simultaneous attack is essential, if guerrilla ploys and diversionary tactics are not to make the tangle more baffling than it has ever been. It seems to have been sub-liminal recognition of the complex and systematic nature of Parliament's inade-quacies which has tempted the public to watch unconcerned the Labour gov-ernment prepare to dismantle the formalities of the Queen-in-Parliament on the one hand without strengthening its practical role (of controlling the government) on the other. For the entrenched interests the public must confront in order to modernise both the formal and the substantive functions of Parliament are daunting if not overwhelming.

First – to take the substantive weakness first – there is a new government with a huge majority untroubled by a unified Opposition. It is moreover a govern-ment beset by control-freaks and media-manipulators, whose first concern is to fiddle with the formalities in such a way as to appeal to an electorate dissatisfied with Parliament while ensuring its hold on power is tightened.

Second, there is the House of Commons who have in the past bitterly fought for substantive supremacy and now do not exercise it in the public interest they claimed it for. Nothing suits the Commons better, as a creature of the executive and power-hungry party machines, than to see a House of Lords that is also turned wholly into a creature of prime ministerial patronage. This is not even an issue for Commons' Oppositions to get excited about, confident that their turn will come soon or late.

On the other hand Parliament (still in the wider sense) as the symbol of state-hood has compounded its practical weaknesses with a fuddy-duddiness that has ceased to amuse. The gorgeous ceremonials of coronations, weddings and funer-als (which were themselves primarily relics of 19th-century imperial spin-doc-tors) have turned sour through the unhappy marriage and death of Diana Princess of Wales. Nothing is more unsettling to an already uneasy public than a fairy-tale with an unhappy ending. The hereditary peers, long uncertain of their role in an unreformed House, are but peripheral public victims of a bigger tragedy. Their interest, long-recognised, to ensure that their departure heralds a stronger Parliament is likely to be washed away in a flood of other tears. Tears for a broken dream.

Meanwhile a runaway government and an underpowered House of Commons hope to divert attention from their own failings by downsizing the Monarchy and tinkering with the House of Lords.

One might think, with the cards stacked as they are, the chances of responsible reform infinitesimal. Fortunately – not so. For underlying equally both of Parliament's weaknesses, formal and practical, is Europe, that dread dragon. I believe it to be generally if dimly perceived that there is one but a great beast: the same beast that tore apart the Tories and earlier frustrated those who hoped that the British Commonwealth would replace the British Empire as both our glory and our trading partner – that beast now lies in wait for any British Parliament that fiddles with the news or lives in the past. It is that perception – and general uncertainty how to deal with it – that allows government to play at reform in the sunshine and live with its stable unmucked out.

The technical problems concerned both with Parliament's links with the EU institutions and also with devising a Parliament to operate in a new environment we come to later. But Europe is no mere technical problem. Europe, itself just the continent nearest us in a shrinking world, cannot be ignored by government, Parliament or public. For it is a challenge both to our statehood and to our essential interests that media manipulation cannot magic away.

"The Treaty of Rome is the supreme law of this country, taking precedence over Acts of Parliament," declared Lord Hoffman as a High Court Judge in 1990. So we do not have a 'supreme court'; we have only a 'supreme law' – and one not of our making! The House of Lords (as a court) has nibbled round the edges of Hoffman J's ringing platter (by limiting the Treaty's supremacy to cases where intent to override Parliament is clear and by 'direct effect'). But even these tit-bits are denied by implication of the European Court which now holds (Case C-106/89: Maerleasing [1990] ECRI-4135) that the British courts must always interpret national law in the light of the wording and purpose of Community Law, whatever the date of the national law. Supremacy is likely to be interpreted by the European Court as automatic. [See, for an excellent summary of the constitutional position of EU law in UK, *Lasok 6th Ed'n* 1994].The monster is out in the open.

It is a bathmat that constitutional change, whatever constitutionalists may propose, is invariably disposed by political necessity. This is even more true than in those developed countries such as ours without a written constitutional law. For political necessity is the only sure way here to make reform stick. If Parliament can always undo the work of its predecessors (even, by the way, the 1972 European Communities Act, to take us out if Parliament in its wisdom so decrees) then short of political necessity no reform is safe or stable. No Parliamentary reform which fails to confront the very substantive fact of Europe is worth a row of beans.

It happens that the reforms suggested in this book presuppose the UK's continued membership of the EU. Also that the reforms would in fact easily fit the UK's needs if we came out. But either way substantive reform is politically unavoidable.

Westminster is being flooded by Lord Denning's 'incoming tide' of European law. But the ocean out there is economic and financial encroachment which governments are powerless to stave off. The House of Commons for the most part have been content to play Canute in deckchairs on the South Coast telling the waves to go away.

Besides their distaste of any change that affects their position – which has discouraged demands for the tools for the job – MPs have also been genuinely unable to assume the extra workload that responsible monitoring of impending EU legislation would necessitate, even by liaising fully with their MEP brethren. Indeed the cold-shouldering by parties of their MEPs has gravely affected their effectiveness in bringing British concerns before the European Parliament.

Up till now the weakness of the EP has been an excuse for its neglect by busy MPs. For the EP, so far, cannot (with limited exceptions) initiate legislation in partnership with with the Commission; and only the Council of Ministers can agree it. But the main results of fortress Westminster have been a *carte blanche* for Euro-zealots to plan a federal Europe and a cloth of gold for our Ministers outwith the writ of the British public. Moreover the fortress has been far from impregnable; and if it has not been taken that is because it is, across the Channel, thought hardly worth the trouble.

A secondary result has been a vacuum into which the Lords have moved and out of which they cannot be ejected without throwing away what little influence Parliament retains in Europe. The House of Lords' impressive record in European Affairs will be reviewed. The composition of the Second Chamber has much assisted review of EU legislation from a non-partisan viewpoint.

That record is one pillar of reforms proposed here; for it has wider implications for the functions proposed of a remodelled House. One small recommendation will be the *ex officio* Lords membership for MEPs; but that is no more than a crumb to feed a multitude. The public is being starved of a European future.

Any attempt by the House of Commons to grab what they have been shown unable to eat would soon be seen as sour grapes. Which is not to say that a committee system closer to the US congressional committees might not also be modified for use by the Commons, as is proposed here as the other main pillar of Lords reform.

In short EU institutions must increase and Westminster decrease. Mitigation of this trend cannot be left to governmental messages of goodwill across the Channel, which the Blair Government will soon find ring as hollow over there as Mr Major's. Putting off EMU to the next Parliament with promises of feasibility studies has already been met with ridicule in the EU (though not by the British public who are not impressed by those who insist on running before they walk).

Time perhaps to draw a few strands together…

The Monarchy with the House of Lords as retinue remains a useful symbol of statehood, though too redolent, especially in their 19th-century ceremonial detail, of celebration of our imperial past which the myth was fashioned to fit. By contrast the notion of the Queen-in-Parliament is worse than useless – misleading – as a description of how British Government actually works; for it perpetuates a myth of control by Parliament of government long overtaken by events.

Government supported by its party machine and obedient MPs is much too strong for Parliament. The formula by concealing this has long been an obstacle to reform essential for the public's representation.

Nevertheless the Monarchy, as supported by the House of Lords in its ancient role, never quite defunct, as the royal council, remains the guarantor and guardian of constitutional government. The Monarchy steps in when there is no lawful government to ensure that one is elected.The House of Lords, by contrast retains its role of ensuring regular Parliamentary elections. The House of Lords has more than retained – it has actually much since World War Two increased – its secondary legislative function, outstandingly in relation to vetting EU legislation.

But the Lords' (and the Monarchy's) continuing symbolic and practical constitutional roles should not be taken to protect traditions and practices which now serve no useful purpose whatever. Their remaining on the shelves long past sell-by date is a symptom more of indifference than public attachment. It detracts in fact from the institutions' continued usefulness. The antiquated look of some institutions, however, which is a relic of past practicalities serves to preserve them above day-to-day politics, which no republican system could.

A distinction needs to be kept in mind, though, between symbol and image. The British should beware of a Monarchy, for example, in their own image. We should look at our institutions as on the same side of the mirror as ourselves and separate from us. We should also beware of changes proposed by governments primarily concerned for the perpetuation and increase of their own power. This has led recently, for example, to condescension by the Prime Minister to the Queen – condescension inappropriate to a Monarch who can in particular circumstances be turned into the PM's boss.

Similarly increasing underperformance by the House of Commons since World War Two as scrutineer of government policy should lead reformers to expect over-zealous conduct by the Commons in protection of their superiority over the Lords. The election of MPs to Parliament, while increasing their individual authority (and responsibility) in no way exempts them from looking at Parliamentary reform, including reform of the Commons, as a duty to their electorate and not a protection of their privilege as the superior House.

So reform is inescapable. All that is now in issue is how well it is to be done. Eradicating the hereditary peers without taking this unique opportunity to rebalance the wheels of Parliament would be the act of a government of control-freaks posing as populists. For Europe is on our doorstep and the public is faced not only with a Westminster government long since spinning out of Parliamentary control but with a superior Brussels government of which there has never been any effective Parliamentary control. Popular paralysis has been bred by successive governments unable to propose what to do about it. For in or out of the EU, Britain's world is little of what it was even a couple of decades ago.

The Welsh and Scottish Assemblies, desirable in themselves, are truly a symptom of the dissatisfied, in the face of an irresolvable threat, brushing up their image: image, since an image takes at least a generation to be ingested and form a symbol of identity. The English have not even got as far as that, unable to stay where they are and unwilling to move.

In the past the symbol has always followed the fact of change, like a crab's shell preserved in a museum after the animal has moved on. The shell has the advantage then that it is away (at least in theory: the separation is never complete) from the political knockabout. When even shells crack with time and need repair, shell maintenance does nothing for the health of the animal. But it can generally be done without any painful experience. What is exceptional in Britain now is the delay both in maintenance and in substantive change. The shell has never been properly detached and maintained for its new use; and the animal is having to make do in a new and less favourable environment.

Responsible reform accordingly must be driven by political need but sensitive to our history in a way to preserve, in a turbulent moment of our economic history,what of the symbol is still a usable focus of British nationhood. It is the difficulty of balancing the effects of two altogether separate but simultaneous operations that has discouraged calls for constructive change. For those who have been most aware of the practical imperatives have been those most afraid of losing the imprimatur of history on our institutions.

Political will always follows diagnosis. Already a few wise heads are demanding that the Monarchy and Parliament need to be downsized for a European role. The Dutch Monarchy is sometimes cited as a paradigm. Others are demanding a more positive attitude to EU institutions. The trouble is, downsizing our Britishness is not at all the way to reconcile the public to a European future. We need to downsize our government by developing a counterbalancing Parliament (size is always relative!). Confident in our Britishness and with our political institutions in prime working order, we should be equipped to control our European environment also, of which, in or out of the EU, we are willy-nilly a part – and if we try, a big part.

There are worms at the kernel of our constitution – at a more sharply focussed look at some anomalies in it. Many of these result from the well-meaning attempts of statesmen to cure ad hoc problems which could satisfactorily be solved only by more draconian measures which at the time were not political possibilities. The two primary examples – the Salisbury Doctrine as a way of delimiting the spheres of activity of the two Houses; and the referendum as a method of testing public opinion. These and others might come alive again within a firm framework: at present we have none.

At the same time we have arrived at a moment of deep confusion in our history. For a crisis of identity coincides with a time of uncertainty about the practical efficacy of our institutions. But this is no coincidence. Both these discomforts have been long a-coming. We have been lazy about both: probably if they had not been simultaneously acute, we should have tried to sweep them both under the table once again with *ad hoc* palliatives. Indeed the Blair government is trying to do just that – for example with human rights legislation (by a direct import) and freedom of information. The latter demands in truth a reappraisal of how government works and a systematic approach to making its policies known and debated. What is on offer is a right for individuals in the vocal minority to quizz officials about papers – useful, no doubt, but going no way to systematising open government.

Unfortunately, coming together, these sicknesses are harder to cure than they might have been singly. For a government with a strong majority may be well-placed to refurbish its own image in the reflected glory of a penitent (though dignified) Monarchy and a weak Parliament. It is the worst possible government to curtail its own powers in the interest of deeper democracy. What sanctions does it see for its continuing neglect, that it should make itself (in the short-term) less effective?

This underlying attitude is well illustrated by the evasion of House of Lords reform by the Thatcher government interested only in conveying a populist message through the House of Commons (which was rendered for a while as powerless as the Lords).

History may well as things turn out judge that the last chance for a thoroughgoing reform of Parliament was missed as an aftermath to the St John-Stevas reforms brought in after the Tory success in the 1979 general election. His departmental committees as Leader of the House were among the most constructive democratic reforms of the century (and were adapted by the Lords for their EU work). In the 1980's the House of Lords would have co-operated with some enthusiasm in some programme such as is recommended here. The Lords have long advocated reform that would balance a reorganisation of membership against the democratic authority that an elected Second Chamber with a clear constitutional function would have. But in the end it is the public that gets reform done, since the public is the beneficiary.

The people could yet wake up in time.

2. REPRESENTATION

We have looked at the underlying obstacles to reform, in a general way. It is otherwise difficult to understand how such a need could have been so long neglected. The primary blame must attach to the Commons whose obsession with elected infallibility has supported governments' natural drive to force through their policies with the minimum of hassle.

This combination of interests has conspired to inhibit the strengthening both of both Houses – of the Commons which is under government and party control, and of the Lords which might disturb the Commons' cosy relationships.

Labour's class prejudice against the Lords, so aptly illustrated by their deputy-leader's attacks in January 1998, makes it even harder for the new government to look at Second Chamber reform with the cool eye that the public interest demands. Labour, relying on a huge majority and mistaking the direction of the new public insistence on hands-on political participation, has a manifest desire to rubbish the Lords whatever their actual and proven contribution to the Parliamentary process.

Public trade winds might have dispelled the doldrums but for two persistent factors: a) a complacency that the Queen in Parliament has matters in hand where the Commons is publicly elected and b) a subliminal understanding that serious Parliamentary reform requires a harder look at the European Union than the people feel ready for.

These anti-democratic trends will become clearer when sins of omission and other failings are pointed up.

a) Government and the House of Commons

Parliamentary sovereignty – the Queen in Parliament – has for over a century been taken to mean in effect the supremacy of the House of Commons. For the Monarchy only steps in when there is no other effective government and the House of Lords' powers were curtailed by the Parliament Acts. It is in the context of the Commons' overriding constitutional power that Dicey's famous dictum (which is still regarded as a classic statement of the law) is to be read: "Parliament has under the English Constitution the right to make or unmake any law whatever; and no person or body [has] a right to override the legislation of Parliament" (Macmillan, 10th Ed'n 1959, at page 39).

For the view that this overriding power of the House of Commons is dangerously anti-democratic we need go no further than the distinguished law lord and and law reformer, Lord Scarman, as long ago as 1974: "The Parliament Act 1911 ... remove[d] from our constitution an important check on legislation and introduce[d] and imbalance at its very centre... " (*English Law, the new dimension*).

Since 1974, however, a worse imbalance has cankered the root of the British system: the government has hijacked the Commons. As Donald Shell, the leading commentator on the Upper House's recent performance, has put it: "Part of the purpose of Parliament is to hold government (and all its bits and pieces) properly accountable; and in this the lower House has done badly."

For Philip Norton, this failure is primarily one of will, rather than of system; though most would agree that either must lead in practice to the other. After rehearsing the impediments to MPs carrying through their job – MPs party domination, fear of dissolution, government's superior information and so forth, he concludes: "Government supporters lack the resolve to submit their leaders to sustained investigation; opposition members lack the facilities to do so."

Where Parliamentarians sleep and the public raise no fuss, governments have no motive for putting things right. As put in his lapidary fashion by Bernard Crick: "Abuses which are not likely to affect which way people vote are not likely to affect governments."

At this stage of the argument it is essential to be clear what is meant by control, scrutiny and 'investigation'. It is not proposed that Parliament ever has or ever should wrest from government the levers of power, only that without fear or favour Parliamentarians should be able to argue with government on equal terms. The point was put in classic terms by Bernard Crick: "Control means influence, not direct power; advice, not initiation; criticism, not obstruction; and publicity, not secrecy."

The best that the Commons have come up with in the last half-century to rein in the career of governments have been the committees initiated by R H Crossman in the late sixties, grown from the much earlier precedent of the Public Accounts Committee, built on, as departmental Select Committees, by Norman St John-Stevas and carried on by Terence Higgins, as chairman of the Liaison Committee, (both later ennobled) right to the end of the Tory raj. These will be looked at in detail later, and their positive contribution considered. Here only the fundamental limitation of such a committee structure need be referred to, that is its need in practice to proceed in an adversarial context on a consensual basis. S A Walkland strikes at these committees' heart: "The movement for a strong committee system in Parliament ignored one of the most elementary findings of comparative legislative research, that the strength of a legislative committee system varies inversely with the strength of the party system in the legislature."

Crick again points out the consequence: "Much of the most effective Parliamentary control of the executive takes place in the committees of the Government Party itself, not in the official proceedings of Parliament itself."

Moreover such evasions of Parliament are the germ of New Labour's rule by 'concordat' (see Michael Ancram in *The Times*, 4th March '98) – by vague understandings between powerful individuals outwith any Parliamentary framework.

It is hard to find more damning comments on the ineffectiveness and the closed doors of Commons procedure.

It follows from these weighty criticisms that the Parliamentary reformer has to take on both the government and the House of Commons, the two bodies whose power and responsibility should make them his allies. An emasculated House of Lords with such opponents ranged against it cannot do much more than court martyrdom; nor does its traditional role as guardian of the constitution have attached to it any of the necessary corresponding powers.

In no field has Commons complacency left the government freer rein than in EU affairs. "In our relationship with the European Community, Government has retained its sphere of authority more effectively than has Parliament." As we shall soon see this is partly the result of the structure of the European institutions, which give government, through the Council of Ministers, the lion's say. But the House of Lords has put the Commons to shame in the field, so that the Commons at one stage actually interfered with the Lords' initiatives; and since then the powers of the European Parliament have increased and are increasing. It is with the EP that Westminster needs to build relationships (if only, for a start, by welcoming MEPs as in some way colleagues) and has so far resolutely refused to do so.

Parliament's difficulty with the EP was recognised from the start. The Special Report of the Procedure Committee of July '73 warned: "...entry of Britain into the [EC] presents a profound challenge to many of the established procedures of Parliament... which could leave Parliament substantially [weakened] *vis-à-vis* the executive." Geoffrey Rippon's suggested joint committee of both Houses failed because only the Lords had the time and inclination. Nevertheless the Foster Committee of February 1973 whose brief was to 'consider procedures for scrutiny of proposals for EC secondary legislation' had recommended as an objective 'to restore to Parliament responsibilities for, and opportunities to exercise its constitutional rights in respect of lawmaking'. The Committee expressed itself adamantly opposed to the executive's establishing or modifying laws in negotiations with other governments.

The House of Commons did not listen – even though, for Labour, Edward Short (now Lord Glenamara) accepted the Foster Report. Consequently the House of Commons Select Committee on European Secondary Legislation has only a restricted brief 'to inform the House of proposals of legal or political importance... to debate a proposal... and to point out the matter of principle or policy... and the changes in UK law involved.' The Select Committee to be was no more than a sifting committee; for the Commons to ignore or listen to, as they chose.

As we shall see, all was left to the Lords. Within their limited capabilities the House of Lords took up the challenge. But before we consider their adopted function, there is a question to be addressed – how on earth Westminster's muddle with the EU institutions was allowed to grow, to the detriment of Parliament's and the public's involvement in affairs which intimately concerned them.

The EU institutions and British government institutions have been from the start a bad fit. (See, on this whole subject, *Westminster and Europe*, ed. Phil

Giddings for the Study of Parliament Group, Macmillan '96.)

Most policy initiatives originate (officially at least) in the Commission and are adopted by the Council of Ministers, after consultation with the European Parliament. In fact, as a result of the Maastricht Treaty, the EPs role is now, as we shall see later, much enhanced: that could now be used to increase Westminster's involvement, had the Commons insisted; but as yet it has not occurred to them to do so. Nevertheless it is in the Council and the Commission that initiatives and trade-offs are agreed, and decisions made; and it has all along been difficult for Parliament to get a hearing, even if it wanted, early enough to make useful contributions to policy.

It is to this mismatch of institutions, which has increased government's role at the expense of Parliament in a strategic area of British affairs, that is at the root of much cross-party discontent with the EU's structure and, consequently, all its works. On top of this comes the supremacy of EU law over UK law, the direct result of the Rome Treaty. Finally it is never to be forgotten that foreign affairs have ever been Parliament's weak link in relation to government, since 'abroad' has been the preserve of the government, as heir to the royal prerogative – a weakness which government has perpetuated by the mystique of diplomacy and state secrecy. No wonder many Parliamentarians hide in their bunkers when Europe is mentioned.

The revered Bagehot spoke of deceit as a necessary precondition of 'running a free and democratic country'. No one suggests that international negotiations should be handled on open fax. But as Lord Keith has put it in a leading case: "It is unacceptable in our democratic society that there should be a restraint on the publication of information relating to government, when the only vice of that information is that it enables the public to discuss, review and criticise government action."

But the pretensions of government, most blatant perhaps in foreign affairs, are sly but all-pervasive, as any Sir Humphrey will confirm (and illustrate). Government's claim always to know better than their public is way out-of-date – more out of date in fact than the House of Lords. For it has never been a *necessary* consequence of not being elected that a Parliamentarian will be out of touch with the electorate. The Lords, for example, in necessary humility have often been more responsive than governments. But it is a necessary consequence of hugger-mugger concealment (if not frustrated by leaks) that governments do not communicate with their electorates; for that is the intent of the concealment. Except of course when governments engineer their own leaks.

The failure of the Commons to grasp European affairs, and government's monopoly of Euro-power, is but the most disastrous and most insidious example of the unholy alliance between government and Commons that reform must tackle.

b) Mandates and Manifestoes

There is a firm Tory view that the Salisbury Doctrine, discussed at length in Part I, is part of our constitution. But an agreed formulation of it is hard to arrive at. In its simplest form it is claimed by the House of Lords as its remit for dealing with issues, mainly in legislation, that come up to it from the Commons: issues settled by a general election and adopted by a government majority in the Commons should not be reopened in principle by the Lords. A version of the doctrine applies the converse. Issues *not* settled by an election *must* be taken up by the Lords. The words 'settled' and 'taken up' are intentionally vague: it is only too easy to spoil the force of the argument by stating it in hard words.

The justification for the Doctrine, in the last century as in this, was the very real one that a government with a clear Commons majority can do very well as it likes. It can in particular dismantle beyond the capability of any subsequent Parliament to rebuild.

> Not all the King's horses and all the King's men
> Could put Humpty-Dumpty together again.

The practical refutation of Dicey's theory that any Parliament can undo the work of its predecessor is the plain fact that one Parliament can make such a muck, particularly of the constitution, that no subsequent Parliament can clear it out. Herein lies the temptation of governments to change first and think afterwards, that change done badly is at least as likely to stick as change done well; and irreversible change at least wins a place in history.

But the Salisbury Doctrine was avowedly a Conservative's response to Liberal agitation for change. What became a charter for the Lords was never binding beyond the reach of subsequent repudiation on the Commons. No refutation can be clearer, as we saw in Part I, than Lord Addison's response to the doctrine at the time of the 1949 Parliament Bill.

From the start the Doctrine had to face what Bernard Crick much later called the 'stark unsuitability of the House of Lords to set itself up as a superior judge of what is public opinion.' But during the electoral struggles of the 19th century when the doctrine was formed the two Houses of Parliament were at least in theory 'coequal partners'.

Since the 1911 Parliament Act that status, for good or evil, is irreversibly changed. Moreover to persevere in holding to equality of that kind in the face of public sentiment pointing steadfastly in the opposite direction is to miss the objective justification for the House of Lords as it has continued since. For insensibly, under pressures slowly applied in the British way, the Upper Chamber has been preparing itself for an altogether different constitutional role, although the Lords must be partly to blame if the public's view of the new growth has been obstructed by dead wood.

The New Labour landslide marks a sea-change and a false start. There is both a new self-consciousness among the people and a mistaken expectation that Mr Blair will satisfy it. It is ironic that the most high-handed government for decades should be regarded (for the moment and because it is poll-rated highly) as responsive to popular feelings. To their old consciousness of their rights the people have added a confidence that they are adults to exercise those rights for themselves; but they have not the faintest idea how in practice to do this or what tools they need for it. The House of Lords is an obvious target because it represents something out of date. How it offers the public a door to participation it is the task of reformers to demonstrate.

Government has never been above the law, that is, beyond the reach of the people. In the very same year that James I was asserting that he was, Coke CJ (in Bonham's case, 1610) was denying it. The result of this little clash of principles was King Charles's head chopped off forty years or so later.

But in Britain government derives from the powers of the monarchy and has been separated off only in stages, often so gradual as to be insensible, in step with political change.

British constitutional history has been a game of Grandmother's Footsteps. When, occasionally, she has looked round, there has been a political crisis. Otherwise the people without drama has slowly approached the goal of power.

Meanwhile power has been divided among various of her offspring – ministers, the judiciary, the Commons, even the Lords and the Bishops – who have remained clustered round her as her government.

Separation of powers has in the UK accordingly been the slow and unripened fruit of pragmatic evolution. In Britain it is in truth a reflection of the gradual separation of functions – as we can see by reference to the Lord Chancellor's position. It is untidy, but our own. That is why our constitution is unwritten. Baldwin, who manipulated it as skilfully as any this century, thought it could not be written, or not at least by him. So it starts from the opposite end of the known world to the USA's written dogmatics. This is not to decry the American solution, unless to question if it is democratic to leave politics' ultimate principles in the hands of lawyers. But British constitutional change has been in no way haphazard, either. It has its own internal logic too.

But our very flexibility imports the danger of intolerable distortions which our tradition of tolerance allows too long to self-extend unchecked. Moreover we have not developed clear mechanisms for correcting them. This gap in our armoury leaves too much scope for governments, in the short run, to manipulate to their advantage. Party domination of the House of Commons has left governments free reign to bully MPs and to ridicule any attempts however modest or peripheral by the Upper House to call government to account.

The Queen in Parliament shall once more be sovereign; and government shall once more through Parliament be made answerable to the people. Any reform programme is a mockery that does not keep this guiding star in the centre of its horizon.

But in the meantime the losers out of this cosy arrangement between government and its party in the House of Commons are the people. The people know it too. The trappings of power and hereditary ermine and all the rest (especially sleaze and sexual peccadilloes) may be more titillating political fodder. But when on a good day people sit back to think, they are aware that run-away governments are a more present threat than the tabloid on the doorstep and the newscaster in the living room.

A MORI poll in the spring of 1995 found three to one in favour of the view that Parliament has insufficient executive control. That is a democratic imperative for reform of Parliament as a whole that no disagreements about the manner of reform can obscure.

It probably was true when the third Marquis of Salisbury said it in 1869-72 that 'the nation takes no interest in politics' – even while 'the nation is our master [in the House of Lords], though the House of Commons is not'. But this theory of the absentee master most certainly no longer applies. That at least is one paradox that time and resistance to reform has removed.

The 'stark unsuitability' follows of the Upper House setting itself up as a 'superior judge of ... public opinion' – though not exactly for the reason Bernard Crick gave. For it is Parliament as a whole that from its unresponsiveness has become the inadequate judge. By contrast, therefore, the later dictum of Lord Salisbury, in 1883, gains exponentially in force, as the people make their final scramble to touch the skirts of government, that 'the only arbitration possible between classes is... the cool and deliberate judgement of the generality of the nation.' It is now the very eagerness of the people to participate in government that makes it difficult for the constitution to cater for that 'deliberate judgment'.

In Part I, the history of the mandate theory, expressed in the Salisbury Convention, has been recounted from the middle of the last century to the middle of this. Whether it is an established provision of the British constitution is dubious but still often asserted. The legality of the 1949 Parliament Act partly hangs upon it, since the Act was passed without the Lords' consent in the teeth of the Convention. But as we have seen during the Second Reading debate on the Act, Lord Addison, to some surprise, bluntly repudiated it – and then omitted to apply his repudiation. Nevertheless as late as July 1996 after the Lords' debate on reform, Lord Carter (a Labour whip from '90-2) wrote to the Tory Chief Whip inquiring if the Convention still held in Tory eyes and was told it did. Thereby it would appear Lord Carter affirmed the Convention too.

So we may, if we wish, assume the Convention holds. But even if it does not, it has guided Tory peers on a course of moderation towards the Commons that has contributed much in Parliament itself to the Lords' credibility and respect. But the Convention has serious defects as a practical guide for the Lords in their relations with the Commons because of the ease with which government circumvents it.

The Salisbury Convention grew out a stand-off between the two Houses in the election reforms that followed the 1832 Reform Act, as the Commons gained in representational respectability at the expense of the Lords. For as the Commons became progressively more representative of the people, as a result of the Herculean efforts of the Liberal reformers, the basis of House of Lords membership remained unchanged. Up till 1911, therefore, Parliament remained systematically unstable; thereafter Parliament remained stable but, as Lord Scarman has pointed out, permanently out of balance. A constitutional relationship evolved in such circumstances is unlikely to be comfortable. It is to the lasting credit of the Lords and their pragmatic flexibility that they have made it work after a fashion to this day.

Meanwhile however there have been fundamental debits to public representation by and in Parliament. For the weakness of the Lords has been shadowed by a quite separate weakness of MPs. The power of the cabinet, the prime minister and the party – not exclusively, but as a trend, in that order – has grown out of all proportion to the powers of Parliament to control them.

What was hailed by Lord Hailsham as an 'elective dictatorship' in 1976 (where he meant a government uncontrolled by the elected Parliament) has become billed in 1997, in an equally catchy and inaccurate phrase, as a 'presidential style' of government.The Prime Minister admits to disliking his Parliamentary appearances and can govern through announcements in the media without being called effectively to account in Parliament by reason of his party majority.

But this *de facto* arrangement in no true way resembles the US Presidency to which it is likened. For in the US the executive, vested in the President, is, as the basic feature of the system, judicially separated from the legislature in Congress. Such was the express intention of the Founding Fathers in order to avoid the very ills and injustices from which the UK is suffering, that is to say, those flowing from direct control of Parliament by the government. It is disputable how far in practice such a separation of powers, even in the US, is either complete or desirable. What is certain, however, is that the debate, on all major issues of legislation, finance and general policy, between the US presidency and Congress is much deeper and searching than anything Parliament can match.

It is true that 'separation' of powers is far from the only reason for the successes of the US system. Other features Britain might well imitate. One such is the secretarial and research facilities available to Congressmen. The Reith Lectures of Sir Douglas Wass, *Government and the Governed*, in 1983, are well worth revisiting on this whole subject. Here is a comment on the imbalance between the facilities available between government and Opposition: "I believe there is a good case in principle for improving the efficiency of the Opposition by providing it with the staff to do its job properly." The same applies to all MPs now – and to the Lords also.

Another feature of US success more germane to our situation are the Congressional Committees which gained autonomy in crucial fields of policy as early as 1822. As Presidents have grown more powerful, the Committees have done more than anything else to ensure that, again in the words of Douglas Wass, 'the majority does not silence the minority'.

But a third, but harmful, feature which has been absorbed here along with (and part of) the 'presidential style' is the 'spin' first converted into a science by Kennedy to win his thin majority over Nixon in 1962. In this sophistical (and sophisticated) use of advertisement techniques the projection of appearances – of political and personal image – is all. Every move, every word, in a campaign is planned to avoid any spontaneity which might by its clumsiness (or directness) lose some constituency of support or another. Kennedy's expenditure on his election entourage was lavish. His machine was recently described by Brian Walden as 'awesome'. Its effect on the fair debate of political issues in the US and elsewhere has been awful. (See eg J A Maltese, *Spin Control*, Univ of Carolina Press '94). Nixon himself was not slow to understand and later analyse, in his Memoirs, the implications of Kennedy's method:

Modern presidents must try to master the art of manipulating the media not only to win in politics but in order to further the programs and causes they believe in; at the same time they must avoid at all costs the charge of trying to manipulate the media. In the modern presidency concern for image must rank with concern for substance.

No clearer explanation of 'presidential style government' can be found.

However Kennedy's most successful disciple (before Clinton) was another idealogical opponent, Ronald Reagan, 'the great communicator', who '...shrewdly transformed his landslide victory over Carter into a *"mandate"* (my italics but Maltese's inverted commas) – for his political agenda. He then proceeded to present to Congress a tightly constructed legislative package with clear-cut priorities.' (p.179).

'Do we want to control the message? Of course we do!' (George Stephanopoulos). So spinning soon takes over government altogether. As Fred Barnes (in *Spinning Grief*) said of Clinton in August '93: "... he spins when the truth would serve him better. But once spin control becomes common, it soon becomes a habit, then a way of life."

That such is the blueprint of the manner both of New Labour's coming to office and of its early days in it scarcely needs pointing out. The UK has inherited the 'presidential style of government' from the US with none of the safeguards – neither the separation of the executive from Congress nor Congress's Committees.

The import of spin without system from the US has been an epidemic with no countervailing strengthening of the body. Few would believe the import unintentional who remember Labour's comments about its review of American methods at election-time. But the notion of a British President cannot work without the *institutionalised* removal of government from Parliament, which is in political theory anyway a dubious exercise. In the British system it would finally undermine Parliament; and Parliament is already tottering. It would also require a fundamental review of the judiciary (with a Supreme Court and a written constitution?) at a time when the juduciary is the main constitutional function operating beyond reproach. Worst of all, it would bamboozle a public already struggling with ill-thought-out reform initiatives already on the rollercoaster. An Executive President for the UK is to be rejected with all his works – save one, his minder, his Polonius, a working Parliament.

For Parliament does need, in both Houses, some means of calling government to account. The separation, right from the start, of the American President from Congress made strong powers of Congress as scrutineer quite unavoidable. James Madison, in particular, was haunted by man's taste for bullying his neighbour and by his fear of tyranny by the majority over the minority. These he saw as the endemic threats in society against the individual – against the very ideal of liberty which gave his constitution birth. The UK with its elected dictatorship has been manoeuvred into just that position and has much to learn from in principle from Congressional scrutiny and control of its President.

Meanwhile there is a vacuum which by manifesto and mandate New Labour is ruthlessly exploiting *à la* Reagan. The above diversion turns out after all to have been no digression. For it both explains how Parliament came to be over-run by government and points to means which may forestall walkovers in future.

The Salisbury Convention started life in a raging storm between the two Houses. It was an attempt (and an extremely shrewd and lasting attempt) to find a *modus vivendi* which allowed the Lords to put a brake on constitutional change while taking account of electoral reality. For, as the Duke of Wellington put it, better a bad law than a revolution. But the Tory bias in the Upper House put its legitimacy at the hazard from the start. Moreover the effect of the Convention was systematically uncertain. For only too often it gives paradoxical results. In a nutshell the Convention requires the Lords not to frustrate the will of the people as expressed in a general election and to oppose everything else. The word 'oppose' here is intentionally tendentious. The Lords has *always* its general duty to scrutinise and control government: this is a form of opposition. But in practice the in-built Tory bias in the Upper House has made its 'opposition' look to its opponents like constructive criticism of Tory governments and obstruction to all others.

In short the Convention was and is widely seen as unfair, not because of its terms but because of the unfair composition of the House that has adopted it. The fact a whole succession of Tory Leaders in the Lords (for example Lord Carrington) have applied it with scrupulous moderation has not stopped politi-cal opponents from attacking both it and the Lords as a whole with less scrupu-lousness. Besides, most of its words might be in inverted commas. What is meant by either 'the will of the people' or 'expressed in a general election'?

None but party bigots or politicians under pressure would deny that a gen-eral election is fought on so many issues of policy and personality that the elec-torate's views on any one of them is virtually unknowable. The electorate is only required to – *can* only – express a general preference, on balance, for a team and a general programme.

Consider for example: a) an election manifesto should be only 'broad policy' instead of 'being written like an advertisement... [and] after the election treated as a pronouncement from Sinai... reverenced as Holy Writ'; and b) 'an unelected Chamber has no right to take its own view on an issue which has been before the electors'. Between these two dicta – of a) Lord Hailsham in 1976 and b) of Mr Callaghan on the Dock Work Regulation Bill (Hans 18 Nov '76, col 1560) – cool reflection must favour Lord Hailsham. But then, he was out of office at the time and Mr Callaghan was Prime Minister.

In fact the Salisbury Doctrine has been turned by Labour opponents on its head. Labour equivocates on what is decided in any general election to preempt all political argument – to claim the 'will of the people' exclusively for them-selves on every possible subject. Labour apply the simple expedient of throwing something of everything into their election manifestos, including parts of the kitchen sink, without serious thought and explanation. They then attempt to shut the Upper House out of comment and debate on any subject whatever – 'beef on the bone' or what you will – except when the House accepts government amendments wholesale.

This is buffoonery, ridiculous. It brings not just Parliament but, in the medium term, even a surfing government into contempt. It is the *presidential* elective dictatorship to which Parliament's ineffectiveness has brought us – and at the time in British history when it is least appropriate. For the Blair government, spinning like Aladdin out of his bottle, does its utmost to shut Parliament out of debate at the very moment when the public has the strongest will to take part in its government.

The mandate of government is, and always has been, to act on the general principles under which it was elected in the light of a continuing dialogue with a Parliament vividly conscious of public opinion in all its diversity. That puts government, Parliament and the public continually on their mettle, on the *qui-vive*. For that a workable constitution is essential – after that, let the liveliest win!

Government is at an *impasse* with Parliament. The two Houses are not working satisfactorily together or with government. And because of party interests neither House nor government has as its primary goal the righting of these relationships. So the grail of reform is an enigma wrapped in a mystery: Parliament is not only the obstacle to its own reform but the agent of it. Government which has for fifty years (at least) profited from Parliament's weakness is ill-equipped both morally and in motivation to put it right.

Both parties since 1979 have exclusively seen Parliamentary reform as a calculus of government's convenience against electoral advantage. This is why the Thatcher government did nothing after its first year to ensure that either House increased its control of government; and why Labour's sole irreversible aim is to remove the hereditaries (which are both unpopular and feared by them as a potential hindrance to their less carefully-thought-out legislative plans).

Both Labour and the Lib Dems would be unconcerned if Lords reform never got beyond this stage. That way Labour would find Parliament an even easier ride. That way the Lib Dems, whose ideal of a wholly elected Second Chamber may be unattainable (and might be no much of a brake on party control of Parliament), will be compensated for its disappointment by a referendum on PR for the House of Commons. That referendum the Lib Lab coalition is expected to win; and whatever its democratic respectability (as clearly tending to one person one vote) that result can only increase the Lib Dems seats in the Commons, whatever it does to the quality of British government.

To work as it should Parliament needs to be a self-righting organism and should not require outside interference at all. But it clearly is not and does. But at present the only pressure it is under is from government, not from the people who are being short-changed. The Thatcher government did nothing for eighteen years. The Blair government rushes headlong into referendums galore with no thought either for complexities or for any overall plan, carefully canvassed with the electorate, without which any substantial change is necessarily irresponsible.

At last we have arrived at the root. The constitution cannot be left as it is; and it cannot be responsibly changed without a consensus based upon a clear reckoning of its shortcomings and an agreed plan to overcome such of them as we can.

There is not even educated agreement about methodology. If there were, Labour could never without popular revulsion have embarked on piecemeal change. Consider:

Step 1, 'if it works, don't fix it.

Step 2, 'if it doesn't work, find out why.'

Step 3, 'when you know what's wrong, decide how to fix it.'

Step 4, 'fix it as economically as you can.'

Elementary. Isn't it? No plan of reform can be arrived at without diagnosis of what is wrong or carried out before it is arrived at. Government has avoided this exercise because the result of such a study can only be criticism of government's abuse of Parliament and Parliament's connivance at that abuse.

Parliament is not working. We have arrived at a diagnosis in principle but not in detail. We are somewhere nearing the end of Step 2.

Parliament is not carrying out its democratic function of controlling government. And both have found it convenient, to the detriment of public representation, to leave the *status quo* or to propose changes which will not cure the sickness. In particular Labour have long ago passed the judgment that the House of Lords is not operating 'as effectively as it should'. But they have carefully laid the blame for this at the door of the hereditaries, whose undisturbed position at worst cannot be more than a symptom of both Parliament's and government's lazy-mindedness over many years. This sickness we can now define as a progressive strangulation of Parliament by government.

Other symptoms beside the anomalous hereditaries – the craze for referendums instead of public debate led by Parliament, confusion about what governments gain from a general election, public mistrust of politicians and all their works, the public's bypassing of Parliament through the media – all these will pop up as we analyse further the sickness. But it is essential to distinguish symptoms from the workings of the disease – Parliament's lassitude and anomalies from the internal nasties which are their cause. For the aim must be to propose a self-righting structure that will not permit of such lazy-mindedness in the future. The function of the structure itself is to bring public pressure, in all its diversity, on government through Parliamentary scrutiny and debate.

Governments have progressively avoided such pressure, in the Commons, through party control of MPs and, in the Lords, by playing upon their lack of elective legitimacy. Governments have gone a fair way to using all Parliament as a rubber stamp for policies for which they claim a mandate. These policies are whatever they have referred to, however vaguely, in their election manifesto. But if by any unlucky chance government has not covered all possible eventualities, particularly near the end of a Parliament, we have seen how Lord Addison rammed through the 1949 Parliament Act. Government simply claims a mandate for anything for which it can get a Commons majority.

This amounts to UDI by the Commons – a unilateral declaration of independence from Parliament as a whole. The 1949 Parliament Act itself was of doubtful legality, being a desperate means in no way put before the electorate, of attempting to force through legislation towards the end of a Parliament which was not even used for the specific purpose for which it was forged. Undoubtedly it was carried through with no regard for responsible public debate. Fortunately when the structure of Parliament as a whole is under scrutiny, a return to 1911 (if that were to be part of an overall solution) would present no difficulty – as for example the Home report proposed in 1978. But that will not be the solution recommended here (or rather, at most, only a small part of it).

The 1911 delaying powers were intended as no more than a stop-gap before a 'popular' chamber was introduced. It will helpful to ask what a popular second chamber might now be expected to do. But that is an inquiry for Step 3 – and Part III of this book.

Meanwhile a quick look at the delaying powers in the context of their 1911 introduction. The Lords had been operating for many years under an early version of the Salisbury Doctrine. Under this, in effect, the Lords, in exercise of their right of legislative veto, could not attack in principle issues settled at a recent general election but they could and should amend to ensure effective and fair legislation. On any other issues the Lords had a free hand to amend, veto or wreck as the Tory spirit moved. Sometimes on these other issues Lords claimed it was their duty to oppose. That could be taken as a duty to veto any legislation not sanctioned by a general election. This is absurd unless taken as rhetoric. No House can do better (or properly less) than to look at issues and legislation each on their individual merits. We shall take this as what was meant.

There was a fundamental flaw in this solution. It did not depend on the inbuilt Tory majority in the Lords, since that, as has later been shown, can be handled by tact and self-restraint. It centred – and still centres – on the inevitable prevarication about what is and what is not settled by elections. General elections are so much the product of a diverse multitude of issues and a diversity of opinions that it is unsafe to deduce more than generalities from their results. In practice governments have wanted to claim a free hand for anything they want to do and Oppositions have tended to doubt whether elections settle anything at all. Elections are a general snapshot. Time moves on; situations, requirements and public opinions change. "Events, dear boy – events!" None was more responsive than Macmillan to changing winds. But neither governments nor Oppositions can ignore them. So, as Lord Addison pointed out, this argument cuts equally both ways.

The arbiter between these opposite interpretations can only be Parliament – a Parliament with vigour and teeth. In conjunction with a Parliament acting 'as effectively as it should' other possible palliatives are to be considered. Referendums and fixed four-year Parliaments have already been mentioned. But the barometer for government of the people and its interests can only ever have been Parliament. Now barometers have themselves been replaced by very much more sophisticated meteorological systems of forecast and analysis. The understanding of weather patterns has been vastly improved by the systematisation of hugely increased stores of available information. Forecasting has improved, however, not only from the availability of such information but from forecasters' keenness to use it. But the parallel increase in political information government has, and Parliament has not, taken both the facilities and the care to use.

There are many reasons for this and most of them, predictably, are to be laid at governments' door.

First, of course, governments who are primarily judged by unanimity and spending policy are not about to put high on their agenda the expensive dissemination of information which might persuade the public, MPs or their own members to question to good effect what government does. With such ammunition not just Opposition MPs but brave hearts on their own side of the House might enliven Parliament business by requiring governments to give a full account of their policies.

Secondly, Whitehall's monopoly of policy preparation would inevitably be challenged – probably by civil servants drafted in to brief MPs on the underlying issues behind Whitehall's own recommendations. Think what Sir Humphrey would think of that! More information available to MPs and through them to the public would also greatly enhance the public's demand for open government and would incidentally go far to reduce government 'spin' and even media control of information dispersal. The public would start again talking to Parliament direct; and Parliamentarians would be expected to have answers ready.

Thirdly, a Parliament supplied with and competent to handle such information would be more expensive to run. Government can block almost any constructive reform that takes account of new systems of debate and analysis on grounds of cost. In fact Whitehall empires would be dismantled (especially quangos) as a result and some personnel transferred to Parliament itself. But this is a consummation hardly to be wished by the government machine already hounded daily by the Treasury on its excessive use of paper clips.

So – what price an efficient democracy? It is no exaggeration to say that a Parliament ready and able to speak to government on equal terms is a prerequisite. Nor do I believe that faced squarely with that proposition would the public disagree or believe they now have it. The complexity of public affairs and finance is huge and growing. The volume (volumes!) of annual legislation has long been outside Parliament's capacity to monitor. This is no criticism of Parliamentarians whose Herculean struggles in this field have only not been matched in the broader control of government. A cursory look in any public library at the number of annual volumes and their hideous thickness will confirm the exponential increase in legislation, that constitutes cruelty not just to civil servants but to Parliamentarians also. It is small wonder that government has no true concern for Parliamentary reform other than to ensure a compliant Second Chamber to complete what the Commons have not the time, capacity or facilities to do.

Where Parliamentarians – and especially the Commons – have been at fault is their anxiety not to publicise their inadequacies for fear of annoying parties or public. In no field is this truer than Euro-affairs to which we now turn.

c) Parliament and Europe – and Referendums

Labour's EU referendum of 5th June 1975 was of still incalculable importance both for the UK and for Parliament. To the Question, "Do you think that the United Kingdom should stay in the European Community (Common Market)?", 17 million voted For and 8 million against. (For a detailed discussion see: *The !975 Referendum*, Butler and Kitzinger, 2nd edn, Macmillan 1996).

As we have seen in Part I, referendums had been on the political *tapis* since the 1890s. The principle has been supported by a long succession of prime ministers. But 1975 was the first occasion on which a nationwide referendum was used to test national opinion on a major political issue.

Opinion on the propriety of the whole proceeding has been sharply divided from the time to this day. Two apparently quite separate but equally weighty objections have continually been raised.

The first was strictly political: all three main parties campaigned vigorously in favour despite vigorous agitation against by sizeable minorities in both major parties. Consequently those not in favour have frequently thrown doubt on the whole referendum process, undoubtedly feeling (if not alleging outright) that the whole proceeding, in any case an innovation, was rigged to produce a Yes result – while leaving insoluble problems for government, people and Parliamentarians.

The second objection concentrates from a very different point of view – the constitutionalists. It is most eloquently put in S E Finer's Introduction to his edited collection of essays: *Adversary Politics and Electoral Reform*, Anthony Wigram, 1975, pp18-9. It is intriguing that his introduction seems to have been written on the cusp of the referendum itself – his preface is dated All Souls College Oxford 8th July 1975 – so it is impossible to be sure internally whether it was written after the referendum result or before. The main thrust of his collection was electoral reform by way of PR but his comments on referendums stand independently of his more doubtful conclusions from his diagnosis. Professor Finer's writing is so concise and compelling that it is impossible to avoid quoting quite a chunk. For he connects the referendum issue to devolution which subsequent events – the affirmative 1997 Welsh and Scottish referendums – have joined even more intimately than they stood in 1975.

"...in its effort to retain its fief in Scotland,... the Labour Party committed itself to a much larger measure of devolution than even its Scottish Labour Party desired, and in the end forced this wider scheme upon it – simply in order to guarantee the few additional seats it needed (so it thought) to win the Election. The result of this surrender has been to promote the establishment of regional assemblies in Scotland, Wales and Northern Ireland, whose appetite... will grow by what it feeds on. Thus, the unitary nature of the United Kingdom is in jeopardy, and this, in turn threatens the sovereignty of Parliament."

"But Parliamentary sovereignty is also is also threatened from another quarter by the use of the [EC] Referendum. Although officially 'advisory', the Prime Minister had to equivocate as to whether or not its conclusions would not be 'morally' binding upon the MPs... why should not [this] be done ... for any major issue that divides a Parliamentary party into two irreconcilable camps...? ... The Referendum is the Pontius Pilate of British politics. It permits and was intended to permit a party to take two wholly incompatible views and meantime... stand back ...on the grounds that it was not a party issue at all, but one for "the People". And finally, and associated with this very device, the collective responsibility of the Cabinet... has had to be set aside with an 'agreement to differ' … on this one matter because in the words of its Prime Minister 'we are united on everything else'."

This critique of the Labour government in 1975 strikes me as devastating in 1998 when so many of Professor Finer's points return to haunt us now.

a) Party domination, not to say government's and the Cabinet's evasion, of Parliament,

b) assisted by the specious appeal via referendum over the heads of Parliamentarians to "the People";

c) the threat to the United Kingdom and to Parliament from ill-thought-out devolution,

d) even, by implication, from EU domination of Parliament –

All these issues stand out, though interwoven, in a few lapidary lines.

Party divisions over the EU remain bitter and unresolved. A big factor in Mr Major's election defeat lay in his attempts at concealment less successful than Mr Blair's. But the gravamen of Professor Finer's charges bears upon Parliament's weakness, compounded by government's irresponsible appeals by referendum to the People.

Referendums, as Butler and Kitzinger point out, are imperfect devices for making basic decisions. The legitimacy of the verdict may be compromised by the timing of the contest or the phrasing of the question, by the level of the turn-out or the margin of the victory – even by who is allowed to vote. Indeed all or some of these vices were present in both the Welsh and Scottish referendum decisions.

But, handled fairly and with genuine regard to what the People actually wants, referendums need not be evasions of Parliament: provided they are used as the culmination of responsible, full and informed debate both in Parliament and (preferably simultaneously) in the country. So far, however, no such a procedure has been tried in the UK. Governments and their parties have been too concerned not to lose face by attracting contrary verdicts, and too anxious to ensure that there should be no Parliament that might not be pliant to their wishes. In the result and so far, the use of referendums, on devolution and EU membership, has done nothing for public representation and has worsened the predicament of Parliament.

Government's conduct *vis-à-vis* the EU is only the most short-sighted example of their persistent policy of preferring compliance in Parliament to efficient democracy. Before considering EU treatment in more detail therefore, both as an example of a deep malaise and in its own right, we need to put referendums also into the context of the abiding problem of Parliament's relations with government on one hand and with the public on the other.

Essentially, governments have sought to use the referendum as either a supplement to, or a replacement of, their mandate to govern through Parliament. The mandate itself is inseparable in history and theory from the struggle between the two Houses in the half-century or so from 1867. From then on, the brief 'golden age of Parliamentary government' was replaced by a new era shaped by domination of the parties with monumental figures such as Gladstone and Disraeli at their heads. (For an excellent summary see V Bogdanor's

Introduction to his *The People and the Party System*, CUP '81.) From the start the Commons had the moral high ground: they were elected and the Lords were not. The Upper House all the same had to maintain its claim to represent in its way the people, without being the House of Commons' echo.

The Salisbury Doctrine, later the Salisbury Convention, is best, and most fairly, seen as a temporary expedient, so successful that it has lasted for more than a century, to maintain a balance between the waning Lords and the waxing Commons. The Convention has allowed the Tory-dominated Lords to do a continuing and useful job. But its very success has been an obstacle to deeper change. For the Doctrine was never designed to foster co-operation between two Houses of a unified and working Parliament. In its original form the Upper House recognised not the Commons but the people as 'master'. Accordingly the Lords determined to 'yield [their] own opinion only when the judgment of the nation has been challenged at the polls and decidedly expressed'. But being an expression primarily of party interest in the Tory-dominated House, the Doctrine inspired its equal and opposite adversarial counter.

> Under the rule of democracy, the control of government, in the view of the Radicals such as Joseph Chamberlain, ought to pass from the Commons to the electorate. Parties should appeal to the voters on the basis of particular programmes which would bind their actions in government. MPs should be under an obligation to support all the items in their party programme; for the electorate could be assumed to have endorsed them all. In this way the voter would gain more influence over government policy, but the role of Parliament would be further diminished. (VB op cit p6)

In the right corner, in blue... In the left corner, in red... Both sides were taking advantage of the too flexible nature (in fact the unclearness) of the British Constitution. But in the long run if it came to a contest of extremes between Lords and Commons, the Commons were bound to win; and the Tories have long known it. It is regrettable that Tory governments have repeatedly failed to initiate change in a climate to suit themselves, so as to keep in trim the best features of Parliamentary government. Burke's famous dictum applies, above all in an unwritten constitution where organic development is unfettered: reform is still a prerequisite of preservation. The result of Tory laches may be a serious loss now to our British heritage, to our constitutional and cultural diversity – and above all to the diverse representation that our varied and pluralist culture demands. The Home report in 1978 was specific on the point: "We do not believe that leaving things just as they are should be considered a viable option for the next Conservative government." Such advice from such a source might have been expected to carry weight. But in the Thatcher years the nettle was left to spread all over the field.

Neither the Old Tory nor the Old Radical solution fits the requirements of a modern democracy whose complexities can only be served by a Parliament well-briefed and in touch with the people.

The referendum was an early attempt by Tories to break the impasse that the Radicals' view of government had engendered. For if it was unfair of the Lords to resist anything not clearly settled by an election it was equally unfair, for example, for Liberals to found both their policy and their majority on a sectional Irish interest. The referendum proposal, like the Salisbury Doctrine before it, was the best resource available to the Tories in a losing constitutional position. But it was not adopted nationally, as we have seen, until 1975; and its habitual use now runs all the old hazards with little of the countervailing advantage.

For the advantage of a referendum is to focus public opinion on a particular issue, especially a constitutional one outwith central government policy. But this can only be done when public debate, both in Parliament and outside it, has fairly isolated issues in the context of an overall scheme of action (or, in the cases of devolution and the EU, of the constitution as a whole). Otherwise a referendum is just a cop-out, for the government, for the government party and for Parliament *en bloc*. Parliament and the Cabinet in particular are relieved of their responsibilities and thereby taken out of the constitutional process. And hurry or botched debate allows government to fudge the way a referendum is carried through and so the result of the referendum itself. So it was with the referendums in 1975 and 1997 – on European integration and Scottish and Welsh devolution, surely the two historic constitutional issues so far decided this century.

So referendums are no substitute for responsible Parliamentary government.

This comment might expect the retort that nobody thought they could be. But the referendum has been frequently proposed as at least a partial solution for a difficulty that Parliament has never since Cromwell (who could almost be described as the House of Commons' founding father) fully overcome. Said he: "I am as much for government by consent as any man; but if you ask me how it is to be done, I confess I do not know."

For if one listens to the red corner a general election decides everything; if to the blue corner, it decides practically nothing at all. For the heirs to the Radicals one need only stuff one's manifesto with a few vague words on every subject, or if one does leave something out (like Lord Addison's India Act and thence to his Parliament Act also) then say that circumstances have changed, so as to justify any government action or legislation whatever that a Commons majority may secure. One the other hand, for those unyielding Tories one need only refer to the shotgun effect of a general election to justify almost any Opposition. Meanwhile the right of the public to representation by Parliamentary government is ignored by all those happily engaged in the Parliamentary fray.

The referendum does offer in principle a public decision by rifle shot. Where an issue can properly be divorced from standard government policy – and in constitutional reform, government is almost the last initiator one should trust – the referendum can be part of a scheme to be adopted, provided it is hedged about with safeguards which in practice government are loath to adopt.

If one lists these safeguards it is not difficult to see why. Governments have adopted national referendums as quick fixes for intractable problems, although by contrast the Euro referendum of 1975 was an evasion of intractable party problems that split the Cabinet on crucial policies in most fields of government. And the 1997 devolution referendums were rushed through, in a bid for cheap popularity, with no responsible scheme or analysis of aims, implications and consequences to back them up. All three have yet further weakened Parliament's control of governments and of public debate; and because they were botched they have weakened the United Kingdom as a whole. If that is a fair sample of the ways governments are to use referendums, they should be banned until the UK has a Parliament ready to prepare them.

After thinking through these fundamental but unsolved problems with Parliament's representation of the people before government, one is at least spared continuing amazement that they remain open issues. But there lies uncovered also hope. For larger than all of them looms the grandest of them all – Europe. Not even the Westminster ostrich can look the other way for ever. For Europe is itself the outrider of a shrinking world. Either by circumstance or design the British Constitution shall be changed, if not in a twink, certainly within a generation.

Not until Westminster's failure to come to grips with the European Union has been analysed will we have completed Step 2 of our inquiry. For in no rich field of policy has Parliament more miserably failed. But for the sustained efforts of the House of Lords since 1974 it is almost no exaggeration to say that Parliament would have no role whatever in representing Britain in Europe.

For nearly twenty years out of the quarter century of missed opportunity, the House of Commons under Tory leadership has done virtually nothing to adapt to the 'incoming tide' of European policy and legislation. Tory MPs out of government have mostly contented themselves with yapping from the sidelines, with their government occasionally impeding what the House of Lords was trying to do.

There have been extenuating circumstances. MPs have generally in their curriculum vitae en route to the Commons no particular experience in European affairs or need for it. European habits of thought and law are foreign not just by being different. Across the Channel they have been taught to think and argue from the general to the particular, while we Anglo-Saxons, despite the Norman invasion, have ever persisted in arguing from the particular to the general. No matter that no argument is complete without completing the full circle: Europeans do think differently, at least in the order of the steps they take. One of the few genuine arguments for a written constitution is the thought that the British would be forced to think in generalities as a matter of course and so understand better their European neighbours. But I for one prefer the British approach to practicalities, if only as a counter to the inflexibility of the generalists (whether those putting Britannia in the cooler or headlong into the EMU).

Besides, government's inheritance of the royal prerogative in foreign affairs has never cascaded down to Parliament. That is no doubt one reason why Lord Bryce in 1918 proposed a role in foreign affairs for the reformed House of Lords. Whitehall – ministers and the Foreign and Commonwealth Office together – has guarded with obsessive zeal from the outside world, and particularly Parliament, anything that could possibly be labelled foreign, diplomatic or confidential. So successfully has government done it that it has scarcely dawned on a British soul that, by reason of the Rome and subsequent Treaties and our adoption of them in Parliament, we are part of the European Union in so intimate a fashion that European affairs are our own domestic affairs.

Finally the EU institutions seemed at first specifically designed to keep Parliament out. The Commission, charged initially with a virtual monopoly of policy initiatives for the implementation of the Treaties, is by its very constitution almost outwith any political control, let alone the control of member state Parliaments. Until Maastricht the European Parliament was itself sidelined – farcically – from the cosy caucus of Commission and Council of Ministers who between them took all decisions of importance. Anyway MEPs were cold-shouldered as aliens by Westminster.

"The House of Lords Select Committee on the European Communities [set up in 1974] was not expected to become... not only the predominant Select Committee in the Upper House but also the major forum for Parliamentary scrutiny of Community policy within Britain. Nor was it anticipated that its careful, thorough and non-partisan approach to scrutiny would contribute so much to the enhanced reputation of the House of Lords." Donald Shell is generally recognised as a firmly non-partisan authority on the House of Lords. His considered judgement is not to be controverted.

It remains a mystery, even after their Lordships' studied low profile over years, even after the Commons' distaste for Euro-affairs is taken into account, the extent to which the Upper House's consistent contribution has gone unrecognised. Nevertheless the public is at risk of losing Britain's main channel to Europe outside government communications.

The Select Committee on the European Communities was set up in the teeth of opposition from the Tory Leader of the House, Lord Jellicoe, who preferred the notion of a Standing Committee, believing that 'the investigatory and inquisitorial procedures of a Select Committee would be too long and would be difficult to staff'. But Jellicoe lost – that time.

The Select Committee was set up with subcommittees and wide terms of reference 'to consider Community proposals... to obtain all necessary information and report on those [proposals] which raise important questions of policy or principle and on other questions to which the Committee consider[ed] the special attention of the House should be drawn'. The main Committee acts as a liaison committee and receives and approves subcommittee reports. Around 800 documents are received annually by the Chairman from government plus ministerial memos of legal, financial and policy implications and the timetable for government response to the Council of Ministers.

By April 1991 the volume of work astounded even Whitehall; and the Jellicoe Committee complained of a need for more speed and selectivity in the Committee's proceedings and this plea was endorsed by the 1st Report from the Select Committee on Procedure in 1992-3, despite a tied vote in the Lords (HL, 11 Jun '93).

But the reasons for complaint are instructive: 'there may sometimes be a danger that a report will become too much a critique of domestic policy in isolation from its European context' – per Lord Waddington, Leader of the House, to the Jellicoe Committee. In other words the Lords were trying to connect British trends with European, even possibly making, as Parliamentarians, policy suggestions of their own. One is inescapably reminded once more of John Biffen's mild comment: "In our relationship with the European Community, government has retained its sphere of authority more effectively than has Parliament." Small wonder with government that sort of a friend of the Lords.

It is not just in the House of Lords that government has turned the screws on European involvement. For the European Parliament, through the Single European Act of 1986 and the Treaty of European Union of 1993 ('Maastricht'), has been gaining steady ground in policymaking powers within the EU. But meanwhile the British Government has been seeking to maintain its monopoly of imput into EU affairs through the Council of Ministers. That has meant the exclusion of EU affairs not only from the Lords but from the Commons also.

The increased powers of the EP has combined with the supremacy of European Law over the Law of member states, including of course the UK, to decrease the influence of the Westminster Parliament not only in European affairs but within the UK. The EU is within the UK, no less than the UK is within the EU. It follows that it is imperative for the UK's people to have Parliamentary representation in Euro- affairs no less than in 'domestic' affairs. It is however the case that the British Government has shut Parliament out of scrutiny and control even more effectively in Euro-affairs than it has in domestic. And that the House of Commons has acquiesced equally in the one shut-out as in the other.

Let us remind ourselves of the underlying sickness of our constitution – that Parliament has neglected its duty to represent the electorate by its abject failure to control and scrutinise government policy – this time in the words of Lord Scarman, retired law lord and by general consent the most distinguished law reformer of his generation:

"The *de facto* separation of the three powers [executive, legislature and judiciary] has not proved strong enough to restrain the inexorable progress of the executive to the dominating place in the constitution." ("*Power House*", *Guardian*, 6th June '88). The government's muzzling of Commons and Lords in Euro-affairs is just the most comprehensive and insidious example of the executive's overbearing of Parliament.

As we have seen, Select Committees were set up in both Houses to review EC legislation, although the Commons' brief was more restrictive than the Lords'. As the Lords got stuck in, the MPs walked out. By 1988/9 concern had grown such that there was a Procedure Committee Inquiry into the Scrutiny of European Legislation in the Commons. For example debates on the European Legislation Committee's Special Reports were sparsely attended after 10pm and became little more than 'a forum for Eurosceptics'. (See generally *Westminster and Europe*, ed Giddings and Drury, op cit). The PCI concluded the European Legislation Committee's sifting function was indispensable and complained debates often came too late (ie after the Euro Council had reached a 'common position'). Similarly in the PCI's view the 6-monthly retrospectives by White Papers on past "Developments in the Community" were useless and should be replaced by one-day debates before the half-yearly Euro Summits. Even these in no way suffice.

Parliament should have been concerned with something more than a perfunctory monitoring of an international organisation whose day-to-day operations affect most people's daily lives in many ways. But two debates a year in the Commons, their rubber-stamping a few documents and leaving the rest to the government was hardly a satisfactory formula for Parliamentary scrutiny of EU policy and legislation. It was into this vacuum that the Lords delicately stepped.

The House of Commons has only itself to blame. Sir Terence Higgins as he then was, Chairman of the Liaison Committee, proposed that there should be European Business Sub-Committees of the Departmental Select Committees that came within his remit. This proposal was turned down. The Commons did not want this extra burden on their Select Committees and thought they would be 'diverted' from their main work.

Similarly the PCI stopped short of allowing the House to refer Euro questions to the Select Committees.

Finally, involvement by Members of the European Parliament in Westminster scrutiny was 'summarily rejected', even after the co-operation procedure of the European Parliament with Council and Commission gave the EP a much enhanced role in EU legislation.

All the PCI could do was to cry weakly for better communications between Westminster and the EP, adding a plea for ministers not to enter the Council without MPs collective views. John Wakeham, as Leader of the House, rejected even these modest views, except that is, the twice-yearly debates and Special Standing Committees on EU documents – but even these were reduced from five to three, on the ground that the Committees shifted debate from the floor of the House. On 28th June 1990 there was a full debate approving the three Euro Standing Committees (since reduced to two). But the Procedure Committee which reported to the House in 1991 concluded:

"The new Committees were intended to remain firmly as a deliberative part of the House's legislative role, distinct and separate from the investigative activities of the Select Committees. Hence our firm recommendation against equipping Euro Standing Committees with powers to send for persons, papers and records."

So the Committees were set up and smacked down; and the House of Commons, overstretched and defiant – and under the thumb of government – abnegated their responsibilities like naughty schoolboys.

Meanwhile both PCI and ELC repeat that the effectiveness of any input that Parliament may nevertheless deign to make depends on governments not agreeing to legislation before Parliamentary scrutiny (such as it is allowed to be) is complete, including, if necessary, full debate in the House. But even this admirable sentiment is repeatedly frustrated by the regular interstate trade-offs in the Council of Ministers. The public deserves better. A scandal remains, and nothing done.

d) The Lords – Constitution Guardians?

It is an old idea, not originally partisan Tory nor capable of precise translation into our epoch, that the Lords, as the monarch's (sometimes) trusted advisers, should stand guarantors of the constitution.

It is striking that Walpole, who kept the Tories out of office for a generation, spoke against and killed the 1719 Peerage Bill (that sought to ban new creations) on the ground that the Lords must continue as the monarch's protectors. For then as now the monarch represented the constitution, though already then only sovereign in Parliament. For Walpole, the peers were 'guardians as well as ornaments of the monarchy...[to be] augment[ed] as a proper balance against the democratic part of our constitution, without being formidable to the monarchy itself, the support of which is the reason of their institution'.

But it was Victorian reaction to the French Revolution and its Napoleonic repercussions, to which over port Tories liked to link the Great Reform, that shaped the House of Lords as it still stood at the beginning of our century. The Duke of Wellington saw the Lords' assent to distasteful legislation as a necessary concession to prevent revolution. Looking back across to his German roots, but also forward, Prince Albert saw the Lords as an assembly of notables advising government.

Much of 'traditional' interpretation of the Lords' ancient role is in fact neogothic, but for that reason closer to being intelligible for ourselves. There is a clear line of descent in such ideas to Bernard Crick's formula (however different in intended application) in *The Reform of Parliament* (2nd ed'n revised 1970):"It is for the Commons to use the Upper House as a policy-making body uses committees of consultants, advisers and scrutineers."

A strong benthic current cuts right across party lines. It is the view there is a crucial imbalance in the checks and balances built into the 1689 constitutional settlement that somehow a reconstituted Second Chamber should be resetting. The final Obstacle to a new settlement – after confusion about how the constitution works which we have seen exploited by ambitious government and lazy Commons – is disagreement not on the sickness but on how it should be cured.

Waters mingled can never be returned to their constituent molecules. I do not think it possible to dissociate altogether the underlying disquiet, which is general, about constitutional imbalance from the very particular party interests of the Lords. That is no less of a puzzle now than was the last desperate deal that Balfour offered Asquith as an alternative to the emasculation of the Lords in 1911: by referendums, to separate Irish Home Rule from the one programme in return for separating tariff reform from the other. Politics is the Parliamentary ocean, the isolation of particular streams by referendum an artificial device. But the worry is general and genuine and can only be laid to rest by some consensual reform that restores Parliament.

For the sake of the future we must assume that reform will remove the obscuring injustice of the Tory in-built majority in the Lords, so as to leave a little clearer the non-partisan component of Tory thought. That component is encapsulated in Lord Hailsham's phrase 'the elected dictatorship'. This has been here expounded as the consequence of Parliament's reneging on its primary task of controlling government. The fear of it underlay from the start the Tories' view of the Upper House and the Salisbury Doctrine. (Again) this is no partisan point. For the Tory government once in office (and Lord Hailsham in particular) seems to have forgotten the force of its own moral. Once in the driving seat it motored on happily regardless – and ultimately contributed to its own catastrophe.

There have been rumblings of discontent about the ascendancy of government over Parliament for many years. It is probably unilluminating to affect to decide when it began. If M. Duverger is correct it is a necessary and so far unsolved concomitant of the UK party system and dates back, therefore, to the titanic duel of Gladstone and Disraeli. Nevertheless a long perspective allows a revisit to the Salisbury Doctrine in a new context. The gravamen of the Lords' charge against the Commons was a tendency to trigger-happiness. Once in office the elected government would do what they liked, regardless of public opinion and needs. This became a progressive danger the later a government got into its term of office. It was only a corollary of this that led to a claim, which Lord Salisbury sought to apply to almost any argument, that elections decide no specific point on any specific issue.

It is a sad feature of the rough and tumble of politics that Oppositions carry their arguments to absurdity and then forget them altogether in office. It is sophisticated buffoonery to deny that a government comes to office with a core programme or that as an administration progresses its election victory becomes less determinative of its mandate, especially when unforeseen events require unforeseen measures. There is of course ample room for vigorous debate as to what constitutes the core programme or as to the moment at which a government may be expected to get out of synchrony with its electorate. These are matters of judgement in particular cases, ultimately for the electorate itself.

Constitutionalists can only prescribe for generalities. There may for example be a case, as improved communications ever increase the speed and impact of events, for fixed four-year Parliaments; for more cooperation between the two Houses and, when that fails, frequent isolation of constitutional issues (in particular) after thorough Parliamentary and public debate, by referendum; increased delaying powers in a Second Chamber, especially towards the end of an administration – whether or not restricted to non-Money Bills. All these have been debated and will be again debated here. But it does seem that the root weakness to be cured is Parliamentary scrutiny of a government's programme in a way that allows for continual public pressure throughout a term, without frustrating effective government – and that only some kind of Second Chamber can ensure this.

With this conclusion we end Step 2. But there is a coda – in fact a mystery. If a Second Chamber has been so clearly necessary and for this purpose, how is it that for so long reform has been delayed? One can understand that governments and the House of Commons, delighted with a slack rein, might resist giving a Second Chamber the *powers* to carry out the job: but how ignore the need for the job itself? The response is, of course, that, within the limits of their powers and in a pragmatic and unsystematic way, the Lords are in a quiet way already attempting the job. Their powers they in fact seldom use; but their influence is out of all proportion either to their powers or their use of them. They are already aware of their function.

The Parliament Acts left the House of Lords an unfettered veto on the prorogation of a Parliament beyond five years. Important as this reserve power is – for despite public opinion a failing government will go on as long as it can (think of Mr Major) – it has never been used. But few doubt that the Lords would use it if necessary – and without party fear or favour. Moreover if this power did not reside in the Lords, it would have to be placed in the hands of either some kind of supreme court (by whatever name it was called) or some *ad hoc* equivalent of the House of Lords as we know it. Meanwhile nobody for this purpose would want to change the House of Lords as it is.

The Parliament Acts, which replaced the Lords' veto on Commons legislation with the delaying power, also left the Lords' veto on subsidiary legislation untouched. This power is also seldom used; but its retention is often attacked by Labour who still smart under the rejection by the Lords of the Southern Rhodesia (United Nations Sanctions) Order 1968. It is a weird irony that Labour anger over this high-handed action by the Lords more than anything else (other than pressure on Parliamentary time) frustrated the last serious attempt at consensual reform of the House of Lords. (For this period of relations between Lords and Commons, see *The House of Lords and the Labour Government, 1964-70* by Janet Morgan (1975)). The continued retention of the veto is however strongly advised because of government's predilection for passing 'skeleton' Acts. This procedure leaves the meat of legislation to subsidiary legislation which thereby effectively bypasses Parliamentary control (somewhat as quangos, the creatures of government departments, also tend to do) – see eg Lord Glaisdale's Debate on *"The Salisbury Doctrine"* of 19th May 1993, HL *Hansard* vol 545, col 1780).

Then there is the issue of the 'elective dictatorship' which, though coined by Lord Hailsham, has drawn critical attention across the political spectrum. This complaint is directed against overmighty governments solidly supported in the Commons. Majorities can and frequently do tyrannise over minority interests. This perception above all moved the founders of the US Constitution (especially James Madison) to insist on the 'separation of powers' to ensure minority rights.

A constitution on US lines does not seem a serious contender. Even abolitionists seldom favour an executive outside Parliament, a second House that can block a Commons' budget and a Supreme Court to interpret a written constitution. Few would doubt that we can learn something from the Congressional committee system, which does inhibit too hasty government. But the British electorate who have got so far little further than thinking seats based on heredity alone are out of date are unlikely to support imported solutions when there are alternatives to hand which can be home grown. The EU as a system of imposed foreign government is already more than enough to swallow.

The 'elective dictatorship' is none other than the direct consequence of Parliamentary Sovereignty, which has developed through the years via sovereignty of the House of Commons, then cabinet government, to, finally, prime ministerial government supported by a posse of party-minded MPs. Which of these three contenders, virtually alone or in combination, is the supreme element probably depends on the style of the party leader who is the Prime Minister of the day. Certainly however neither House of Parliament has for generations truly balanced the power of government.

Nevertheless individuals and committees in both Houses have exercised much influence over the years. It is difficult for the public to assess how much, or how much indeed the present system allows for simple and effective development. For one need only remember the House of Lords' self-started achievements in European legislation to see that Parliament already has many tools to hand, if it would (and could) use them. Parliament can and does organise itself and can, as we are told, make and unmake any law. But there is another resource, quite as significant, in the House of Lords – the calibre of many of its members. If their influence in debate and legislation is unquantifiable, and depends much on individuals' authority whether as lawlords or ex-cabinet ministers or as experts from the top of nearly every imaginable profession, it is powerful, varied as our pluralist society requires, and capable of development.

How all these ideas can be combined will be considered later (in Part III). What stands out here is the public's difficulty in assessing how far change to the House of Lords' composition and powers is really necessary at all, provided the hereditaries' unelected voting rights are made the ritual (and titular) sacrifices to democracy. Why is it beyond MPs, in whose hands practical power resides, since they have done their best to make the Lords powerless, to exercise more effectively their Parliamentary duties? The truthful answer to this is: it never suits the governing party to let their MPs do so, and the public so far has not seen the need. This is the result of clever media manipulation by recent strong prime ministers, Mrs Thatcher and Mr Blair, obviously, included. The final and killing obstacle to reform has been the public's indifference to the need of it.

Indifference, however, is itself instructive. It shows just how successful government has been in diverting public debate out of Parliament and into the media (where it is much easier to 'spin'). The public has not in fact seen Parliament in working order, certainly not since World War II. Indifference to what Parliament might be able to do is only natural. It can only be overcome by the presentation before the public of a workable scheme for Parliamentary control of government that gives the public both a better-informed and a more active say in policy and its implementation.

Tabloid reporting and the public's immediate access to 'Tony' and friends are of the most superficial kind (however flattering), rigorously simplistic when not intentionally vacuous. It has its place in the continuous electioneering that brilliant new communications have fixed in the firmament. But, for bringing public pressure to bear on governments, it should be eclipsed by the glare of politicians, professional and briefed, who can both lead and learn from public debate.

Even if we were not threatened by government-led reforms which will only strengthen, through party control, government's hold over Parliament, the public interest would make deep reform imperative. Ever-increasing international interdependence (of which the centripetal tendencies of the EU is but a symptom), together with the exponential growth in available information on almost any topic, is relentlessly adding to the responsibilities of governments as surely as it is subtracting from their power to influence events. The result is to push the public ever further from useful influence. There is no remedy for this other than the ordering of information through Parliamentary debate at an ever earlier stage in the international decision-making process. Again, Parliament's already perceived tendency to arrive too late on the EU-legislating scene is but a symptom of a wider and a deeper malaise. The world is beginning to pass Westminster by; and that is dangerous both to our essential interests and to our democracy.

A working Parliament is in no way an impossible machine to engineer and then to put in place. The motivation is already in place. For the public is fiercely interested in participating in government, perhaps as never before. The determination to be rid of Parliamentarians with no qualification beyond birth is an indication of this. But the public has been taught to look for quick and easy fixes. Of this the Scottish and Welsh referendums, that were put in no workable overall constitutional context, were proof. To boot out the hereditaries without a better replacement could be only the next example of legislation first and thought afterwards.

To light a common will to a renewed democracy, we need only to bear sharply in mind the means to this end that we have been missing; and for that we have several hundred years of Parliamentary experience to draw on. Sketching out one possible way of filling this pressing need is the subject of Part III, which now follows.

Part III

Solutions

HEADNOTES

FOR PART III

Chapter 1. Commons and Lords
MPs golden silence and feet of clay – too much indigestion – government's isolation: losing the people – Lords' contributions to debate: War Crimes, hurrah! Poll Tax, alas! – Thatcher undermining the Lords – legitimacy: hereditaries and life peers in same boat – judges in Parliament: some morals – Lords off-balance – blow Lords' achievements: why not abolition? – Commons' longings – a fair cop? too many Tories – too much nitty-gritty, and Lords doing it – Lords and Commons to cooperate on EU committees – 'factitious ire against backwoodsmen' – Lords regulars, a healthy mix of views – legitimacy? – Lansdowne – and Bryce ('18) elected/appointed peers: JSC of 2 Houses – Labour's two-tier House ('68) – and so to Home ('78) *Hoc voluerunt*: they asked for it! – New Lab minimalists, in context – after the landslide… time for change – to a popular Second Chamber – so eliminate abolitionist option – fresh start *ab ovo* could not command informed assent – no Republic, please – Public close to Parliament? No: 3 eclipses of Parl't a) 'Parliamentary Sovereignty' – but the judges call ministers to account – judges and human rights – Parliament restricted to resistance of getting Bills through – b) PMs' manipulations – Thatcher rules alone; Blair Charming manipulates – Diana, Princess of Wales – c) populism – info revolution – newspaper magnates above election – government secrecy and insensitivity: Hong Kong and Montserrat – popular access to government? – and access to Monarch.

Chapter 2. A Parliament Among the People
The aim – a popular Lords – not even Parliament on its own can form a consensus on its own future – referendum limitations – constitutional change not for government's comfort – need for popular consultation – government's plan: how NOT to do it – quango of quan-

goes – shelving what counts – New Labour's old uncertainties – another way of 'incremental reform' – building on experience – contrast: 'so far, so good' – Lords' job spec – and reorganisation analysis -

8 questions, a) to h) – a method – legitimacy: Lords given a bad name to hang 'em – a) Lords productive: so fewer MPs – work split, 2 Houses, 2 Jobs and how it works – broadening Lords' Committees – b) logical extensions of what Lords already do – policy formulation and administrative scrutiny – policy-sharing between Parliament and government – 'information is power': so equalise info – root of devolution is need for attention –

3 Lordly extensions: a) foreign b) human rights c) what government forgot – Parliament sidelined from national life – Lords' extended cooperation with Commons: policy development – parallels to Lords' debating – fields beyond legislation – c) and d) Parliament's need for research help, to match (also) media – e) have we the peers we need? – for pluralism, multiply – Lords' varied scope – European Convention on Human Rights – Parliament's abdication from handling media – Lords (sometimes) a-party-political – law lards in debate – f) working methods and authority – election dogma: Lords as guardians against shoddy thinking – Lords and EU – changes in Lords: developmental v structural – reform hereditaries' voting rights – political before economic structures (in importance if not in time) – making EU democratic – Europe: Lords' ECC – EU rules UK, OK – so strengthen Westminster to represent British identity – imposition of EMU to suppress political debate – Lords' potential *vis-à-vis* EU – Lords in financial planning (not only in Europe) – limitations of Commons Select Committees – Lords' committees: vertical and lateral development – g) financial implications – to Parliament a share of civil service support – Treasury to exaggerate expense – concealing a lack of government will – h) the bull's-eye: 'a Parliament that can represent the people to government on equal terms' – contrast US system – 3 theoretical limitations to Lords' self-development – after functions, a first look at a Second Chamber's powers

Chapter 3. Pastures New
Advantages to Commons in cooperating with a functioning Second Chamber – calculus of delaying powers versus referendums and length of Parliaments – written constitution (?= codification): ? AOB for later – ground-clearance, other eliminations – no 'supreme court', so no extra-Parliamentary legislation – summary, recommendations so far – no full circle to 1688 – instead, updating Bryce 1918 – Lords to

rerun old race – how not to alienate Commons – summary of Lords' powers, and 'guardianship' – need for consensus after debate led by Parliament – others' overconcentration on composition -

the Commons stand secure – long and short views – prerogative and foreign affairs – interplay of new committees: preleg and SSC's – 3-way communications, public, government and Parliament via committees – pooling of resources, extra expense well spent –

constitutional reform as Parliament's first test case – till now, media, not Parliament, as mediators – constitutional debate: 2 Houses' committees – unstranding the timid Westminster whale – government monopoly of preleg –

new system explained – preleg split between Houses – après-legislation Admin Affairs and Local Government – other new committees: eg foreign; law (constitution, drafting, parliamentary confidential info, etc) – updating early Salisbury 'referendal' theory – illegality of dismantling Parliament – need of procative procedures/ committees – Lords' coordinating committee – more ministers in Lords? – coordination of Parliaments (EP and nationals) – devolution: unity in diversity – ? a Second Chamber for EU ?! -

Chapter 4 – Towards a Renewed House of Lords
From now on, concentration on Lords' composition – complementing the Commons – election doesn't do the job – justice revolves round money – the people's aspirations – Parliament has failed electorate – constitutional creep – Pelion on Ossa: Blair on top of Thatcher – from propaganda to policy – under overmastering PMs – moth-eaten ermine – to elect or not to elect? if so, hereds and life peers? -

Selection and Election: how to find the Lords we need? – a) 1918, b) 1968, c) 1978 – or an amalgam? – Bryce: elected 3:1 appointed – Lab 230 Voting Peers + NVPs – Home's 400, elected 2: 1 appointed, staggered elections by Euro-STV – farewell to Lord Bryce – appointees in profile – no pale Commons reflections – appointees' role to strengthen committees – 12 new committees listed – 'lordables': profile of VPs to be elected – by-elections – more young and women; but no ageism – first select for Lords' functions; then elect – aim: separation of 2 Houses' functions integrated into single Parliamentary system – crossbenchers at the party – the Second Chamber's longstanding 'guardianship' function – peers' influence stronger than their votes: defence against power-hungry governments – phased election – selection screening.

1. COMMONS AND LORDS

Analysis of the obstacles to reform indicates not only the interests that over the years have impeded it: it is a guide to setting out what to do when the conjunction of political events happens to make change of some kind inevitable.

Throughout the century there has been an uneasy alliance of government and Commons to maintain the *status quo*, against the interest of a public, increasingly vocal about its rights and opinions, in better representative government. Governments stay in power so long as they maintain a facade of unanimity. They only fall when they split. It is fortunate for public choice and influence that being nothing if not human, politicians often do. But a government's fall means not only loss of jobs for government MPs but the imminent prospect of, for them, a less palatable government. MPs may be forgiven for believing that they open their mouths to shoot themselves in the foot.

The result has been a House of Commons too regularly docile and a shrill, intrusive and populist press (and other media), ever more aware of their role as the organ of public opinion but unable, from the very health of their individualisms, to orchestrate informed debate. Probably somewhere sometime every necessary piece of information, every possible intelligent view, is given. But who ever collects and collates them, and then presents them for criticism by others? Outside perhaps the cosy Whitehall club?

Informed public debate requires more than availability of information and free expression of opinion. Nobody learns efficiently about anything by having a mish-mash of facts and information thrown at him. This is the truer the bigger the mish-mash. The 'information revolution' is no recipe for informed debate.

Available information in fact increases the influence only of those with the time to order it – and then to manipulate it. The exclusive political beneficiary of the information revolution has been the government machine.

The losers – and they have been slow to see their own plight – have been on one side the Commons and on the other the public. We have seen the resistances that hold MPs back – too much work, too little secretarial and research help, the sticks of the party and the whips and the distracting carrots of advancement. We have seen also occasional public frustrations, often shrill, expressed in the media – whether for example from fox-hunters, beef-on-the-bone-eaters or from single mothers.

But governments also suffer, through time, from their very success in stifling debate. In power they always forget it; they quote first their manifestos and then themselves. They bask in their majorities and in the flattery of their foreign peers. They surf events to admiring crowds.

And so it is that snip by snip governments cut themselves off from their electors. The mutual lifeline between governments and their MPs has long been recognised. But the umbilical cord from public to government is regularly forgotten – except in election year, by when it is often too late. Forgotten by governments, but not, after the event by commentators, or in election year by Oppositions.

Only through effective and structured debate can governments be brought up short by public opposition. In our democracy debate means, primarily, Parliamentary debate. For good reasons, which have been seen, the House of Commons cannot bear this burden alone. The Commons are too close both to government and to daily events. British democracy cannot work without a better briefed House of Commons to keep government in order, and a Second Chamber to redress the imbalance that day-to-day pressures force upon the Commons.

Two current examples from the Thatcher era are trotted out, and they are good ones – the 1991 War Crimes Act and the poll-tax (coming into force in 1990). It is no coincidence that both items of legislation illustrated both uncertainties about the peers' functions and weaknesses in the current powers and composition of the House of Lords.

There is broad consensus on the reasons for Mrs Thatcher's fall as Prime Minister. Her government was unresponsive to public (and private) opinion. This unresponsiveness was best illustrated by the poll-tax saga.

The government rammed the tax through in the teeth of loud warnings that it was both unjust and unworkable. It was forced through the Lords by the Tory government's calling in the hidden and generally sleeping Tory majority of 'backwoodsmen' – Tory peers who take no regular part in government and are in no way qualified to carry a complex and controversial issue affecting the daily lives of the entire electorate. Within two years of her Act's coming into force Mrs Thatcher was driven from office by her own MPs, concerned for the poor electoral prospects of her government which her beloved tax had foisted on her party.

It was disrespectful to the House of Lords, and calculated to undermine what legitimacy and authority it still had, to use it for legislation in this manner. Nobody would accuse the Prime Minister of naivety. She must have been aware that, whether or not the legislation was a success, the use of inexperienced hereditary peers as cannon-fodder could not redound to the honour of the House and therefore to the honour of Parliament as a whole. No doubt, convinced of the good sense of her government's business, she did not care overmuch.

There was little new in this. For many years the weakness of Parliament has fed the pride of prime ministers; but usually the victims have been backbench MPs. What was unusual in the case of the poll-tax was the degree of abuse of anomaly in the Lords and the clarity with which pride led to a fall, because the legislation itself was so soon shown to be ill-judged.

In the event the Prime Minister (and many in the country, not to mention her party itself) suffered from an imbalance between prime ministerial and Parliamentary powers which resulted in a political catastrophe. So far as the government was concerned, it was able comfortably to ram its legislation through a docile House of Commons, and that should have been enough.

Opposition in the Lords was taken as just an irritant to the government and an insult to the elected authority of the Commons. The Second Chamber was accorded by the PM and her obedient servants no function in such high matters. It may well not have occurred to a busy and rampant PM to consider seriously whether or not the regular attenders in the Lords, whom the hereditary 'backwoodsmen' were corralled in to overrule, had a serious point.

It is the calling of prime ministers to be busy and rampant where they can: that is how they get their work done. It is the fault of the constitution when they are not brought up short before a blunder. Here the weakness of the government MPs and of the attendance rules in the Lords conspired to stifle well-founded public criticism in the noisy and over-insulated corridors of power.

If Tories now feel that such criticisms come from the disaffected among their number they might do well to remember Mr Blair's strictures in 1991. Unless they wish to credit the current PM, then not long Leader of the Opposition, with unusual sagacity and foresight, they must accept that their Prime Minister took the poison pill of unconstitutional power and paid, with them, the price.

Events moved fast after the poll-tax legislation came into force in the spring of 1991. Within a few months Mrs Thatcher was out of office and succeeded by Mr Major. It was he who inherited not only the poll-tax but also the War Crimes Bill which he saw through into law the same year. On him fell Mrs Thatcher's mantle. He wore it in less dashing style; but so long as the force of his MPs were with him, his power was no less. Nor was his use of it very different.

The War Crimes Bill had long been in trouble in the Lords. Apart from the post-war Labour Government's second Parliament Act of 1949 (which shortened the House of Lords delaying powers from two years to one), the War Crimes Act 1991 is the only statute which has gone through the whole procedure of the 1911 and 1949 Parliament Acts, which restricted the House of Lords' delaying powers in the first place. It was introduced in 1989 and went through all its stages in the Commons before being rejected in its entirety by the Lords. It was then re-introduced without substantive amendment in 1990, whereupon it was rejected again by the Lords, this time at second reading and passed straight into law.

However the Lords' opposition to the War Crimes Bill was of a very different calibre to the 'backwoodsmen' support for the poll-tax. Distinguished lawyers, including lawlords (acting as debaters, not as judges), and experienced men of affairs joined with members of acknowledged good sense of all persuasions.

They considered the introduction into the courts of a novel jurisdiction to catch crimes committed abroad more than a half-century before, when certainty of evidence could only be dubious and the cost of prosecution exorbitant, an abuse of the judicial process, which, if ever used, would tend to discredit judicial procedures in general. In fact no successful prosecution has ever been brought under the legislation.

None of this deterred the government's using a sledge-hammer on the House of Lords to crash their legislation through. Nobody could pretend that the War Crimes Bill was central to the Conservative Government's programme (as the poll-tax legislation, however flawed it may have been, undoubtedly was); nor that the opposition in the Lords was of a calibre and expertise within the field disproportionately lower than the Commons. The carrying of the Bill was a crude demonstration of Commons and government power.

It was also a major factor behind the thinly veiled hostility of the judiciary to the Tory government in the last years of its term. For whether sitting in Parliament or in court, judges cannot but care about abuse of the constitution – a good reason why they should continue to sit in both.

Most of the morals one needs to draw for House of Lords reform nestle in these two unhappy episodes. Here are some of them.

a) as presently constituted, the Lords cannot carry a point of principle – whether central to a government programme or not – against a government supported by the clearly expressed view of the Commons, whatever the merits or authority behind a proposal or amendment; and this is no less true under a Tory than under a Labour government. Against a government supported by a Commons' majority, the Lords have no constitutional legitimacy;

b) A Tory government will not hesitate to use against the Lords even that weapon hateful to Tories, the Parliament Acts, to enforce its view when supported by its elected majority in the Commons;

c) Conversely a Tory government will not hesitate to abuse its entrenched hereditary majority in the Lords, even against its regular supporters there, by calling in irregular attendees to force through its measures;

d) The present House of Lords is subject to humiliating frustrations in its Parliamentary role of watchdog of the government (or the people's guardian of the constitution). Governments of any colour can manipulate (when they have secured the cannon-fodder) Lords' attendance and can use the Parliament Acts to bludgeon the Lords' best judgment, even in issues of secondary importance falling within the Lords' special expertise. Or where manipulation is not available, a determined government (of whatever colour) will simply ignore the Lords. These frustrations are well known to have discouraged peers of proven ability from attending;

e) Manipulation on occasion both illustrates the absurdity of the hereditary peers' currently unsystematised function and further weakens the Lords' constitutional function as a wing of Parliament in the control of government;

f) The House of Lords is accorded no function gratefully by a government with a majority in the Commons beyond the convenience to itself of an obedient revising chamber, that is, of carrying the government's own amendments;

g) Any function beyond a revising chamber to be carried through by the Lords will require, if only to command governmental respect, constitutional reform which i) confers electoral legitimacy on members and controls their composition and attendance and ii) ensures adequate powers interlocking with the

Commons. Moreover this requirement is no criticism of what the Lords can or could do under their current dispensation: it is a simple reflection of governmental Machtpolitik.

In the above no special mention is made of the life peers as such. But in practice they are no better armed than hereditary peers, whether regulars or 'backwoodsmen', to do a responsible job. Analysis of voting structures shows that life peers have on occasion constituted a large proportion of the Lords' opposition that the Tory government wished to overbear. Life peers in government's eyes have no more legitimacy than do hereditary peers.

Under a Labour government, however, the voting balance is different, though, in principle, only because they have no sleeping Tory majority to call on. So far the Blair government (in the person usually of the deputy premier Mr Prescot) has needed to do no more than breathe out threatenings and slaughter (especially when there is a vote, however reasoned, against the government) against hereditary peers – for hereditaries are overwhelmingly Tory supporters – and to create a bevy of life peers to redress a Tory majority even among life peers that has grown up under eighteen years of Tory government.

Legitimacy – how ironic – is what the Lords now are most in need of.

The tried distinction of many peers has been much praised in the Science and Technology Committee; just for example one might mention their reports on Greenhouse Effect (1990) and Resistance to Antibiotics (1998). And peers' examination of EU legislation goes far to fill in the gap left by lack of time and interest by the Commons. As a revising chamber in the process of legislation they have won the respect and praise – and more to the point the use – of successive governments. Undoubtedly also as a back-up team they lend a little solidity to the public's view of government, especially when they stand out against the government of the day. A recent example of this was the Lords' opposition to the Home Office's policy on criminal justice and the treatment of prisoners.

But all of this together in truth goes no further than the first part of the way to justifying a continuing role for the House of Lords. It is evident that all the Lords currently do could in principle be done by the Commons. Some in the Commons would already say it should be; and there will straightway be more of them if proposals are seriously entertained for widening the scope and increasing the effectiveness of the Second Chamber.

Against them can be urged (unanswerably in relation to the EU): that if they could have, they should have; that if they haven't only because of lack of time and resources, well, if not they then there was nobody else in the position to vote themselves what they needed; that if they haven't because of some lack of opportunity, calibre or interest among their members, then it was up to them to brief themselves and then to ensure themselves the Parliamentary time to get issues debated and legislated: many of their own number think there are too many Commons members as it is, and more of them think there are too many on the government payroll.

A new career would now be open to under-used and under-rated backbench MPs: they should undertake the current duties of the Lords and be properly remunerated there for. As a sidewind of their new duties MPs would be then less dependent on the wolfish smiles of the whips and the crumbs of government office for a useful and well-remunerated career.

But these comments evade the political reality: that the Lords are there. They are useful and come cheap; and in fact they do much of the nitty-gritty grind that MPs would otherwise have to do, and don't like. Besides they have already more than enough of their own.

It is nonetheless timely to remind the House of Commons of the additional burdens that would fall on them if the House of Lords were abolished. For undoubtedly the Commons could be reformed so as to shoulder these burdens, and almost as undoubtedly the Commons would not relish them.

Even so, whoever does the Lords' present job, all Parliamentarians would profit from more secretarial assistance – in fact from a secretariat.

Furthermore few doubt that the Commons too would work better, whether the Lords were there or not, with such a secretariat; or that if the Lords got it, so, in double-quick time, would the Commons.

Remarking on the Commons' view of the Lords' current activities does have further point. The fact that the Commons would not enjoy the Lords' work does reflect on their current morale, especially of the Tories' morale until recently in government and now in Opposition. Low morale of the Commons contributes to inadequate performance. The Commons does, as we saw, have its own EU Committee, though it has a narrower brief than the Lords' brother committee.

If under the Tory government now consigned to history and now in Opposition the anti-marketeers (or what is left of them) had troubled themselves with the hard work of making the EU work – in the absence, as even some of them would admit, of any reasonable alternative – instead of using their noise to bring down their own government, they could have contributed to the Lords' patient review of EU legislation and certainly have won more of a hearing in Europe for their criticisms than they achieved by letting in the Opposition party to do it with their own different slant instead.

It is hard to resist the conclusion that much of the heat with which anti-marketeers attacked their own government was generated by frustration at being denied too long as back-bench MPs enough to do. It is a time-honoured ploy of prime ministers to keep their able but disenchanted colleagues quiet if not happy by giving them ministerial responsibilities. One out of the last government would probably now be Leader of the Opposition if the shouts of his supporters had not cost him not just office but his seat also. It would be a useful outlet for the energies of anti-marketeers to be required to test their views against their opponents in detailed debate.

So far as concerns the EU at any rate it is here suggested that the Commons and Lords committees should cooperate under the wider Lords' rules. This is in fact an adaptation of Geoffrey Rippon's recommendation, rejected long ago, by Tory government. The combination of committees should 'shadow' a minister of cabinet rank (possibly in the Lords) with a senior colleague in the Commons. The committees' reports should be accorded regular debating time. And as many Tory anti-marketeers as possible should be detailed to serve, paid for regular attendance, and given the secretarial and research assistance to make attendance productive.

The House of Commons as at present constituted cannot do without the Lords; their interest and the interest of governments of all colours is solely to retain a complaisant House of Lords that will rubber-stamp their afterthoughts on legislation introduced in the Commons and carry the burden of non-controversial government legislation introduced in the Lords.

The only difference in view between the Commons' representation of the two parties concerns the hereditary peerage. Their inbuilt Tory majority the last long Tory reign showed itself prepared to abuse – but would prefer it to remain in place. Labour naturally want it removed.

So far as it goes therefore, within the rough and tumble of day-to-day politics, such partisan attacks by Labour on Tories in the Lords are not unreasonable, especially since the Thatcher government often treated them in practice little better. The government, when it cannot seriously complain of what the House of Lords does, need only attack the Lords who do it. For the Upper House is so unrepresentative in its composition that its actions need not be taken seriously by a hostile government. That makes a nonsense, as most of all parties agree, of the Lords's role. Parliament is brought into disrepute when reasonable decisions can be rubbished without regard for their merits.

A glance at the Lords' composition will swiftly explain this. It is helpfully set out in 'Second Chamber' by Lord Carnarvon and others (1995). At that time there were 755 hereditaries eligible (82 had not applied for a Writ of Summons) plus 15 hereditary peers of first creation (including for example the Prince of Wales). Life peers numbered 376 of whom 65 were women. To those should be added 26 senior Bishops and 24 Law Lords.

A distinguished analysis of the Lords' composition, performance and voting habits was done for the 1988/9 Session, *The House of Lords at Work*, by Shell and Beamish. (OUP 1993). Their study has been the basis of much subsequent thinking on House of Lords reform; and this section leans heavily upon it.

The Lords of the time were, as now, overwhelmingly Tory but no government push-overs, despite Mrs Thatcher's attempts to make them so. The authors record that Lord Denham, Chief Whip, was told by the Prime Minister that she expected no defeats in 1988/9 and would reverse them if there were. Thus of government defeats in the Lords in '87/8, 9 survived, 4 were compromised and 2 overturned but in '88/9 only 4 survived, 3 were compromised and 5 overturned – though in practice there were often concessions in advance of defeat.

It is impressive the degree to which the Lords have been (and are) willing and able to resist party pressures. "There is no ego, no constituency, power-push to persuade the Lords to vote in any way they do not want to. They are very independent." (An anonymous peer.) "The House of Lords has a mind of its own and no single party can rely unreservedly on its support." (An anonymous bishop.) But it is important to put such expressions of independence in both Parliamentary and party perspective.

For the Lords' treatment of legislation coming up from the Commons in the last period of Labour government (1974-9) was largely responsible for Labour's NEC Report of 1978, *The Machinery of Government and the House of Lords*, which advised abolition of the House of Lords.

Labour at that time accepted that unicameralism would enhance the powers of an executive supported by a whipped Commons majority. But they claimed that scrutiny would be satisfied by more open government and by greater pre-legislative thinking. In view of governments' persistent manipulation of Commons' majorities before and since, such optimism is firmly here repudiated as a combination of dogma and wishful thinking. But the frustration from which it sprung was sharp and genuine.

For between 1974 and 1979 Labour, with a wafer-thin Commons majority for part of that time, were defeated over 300 times in Lords' votes; and the propor-tion of government amendments carried in the Lords fell from 95% under the Tories earlier to 75% now under Labour. The Lords are not to be criticised for vot-ing under Labour in accordance with their consciences; but theirs are prepon-derantly Tory consciences and this is plainly unfair – and bad for democratic control of government.

On the other hand under neither government have the Lords often frustrated government legislation in principle either by voting down Bills at second read-ing or by wrecking amendments (though what constitutes those often depends on political perspective...) The outstanding exception is the (Tory) War Crimes Bill which was voted down twice by the Lords and then had the dubious dis-tinction of being the only Bill since the 1949 Parliament Act (itself of dubious con-stitutional validity) to be run roughshod into law over the heads of the House of Lords.

So one is left with a feeling when Labour accuse the Lords of wanting to infect the public with beef-on-the-bone and so forth that the Commons often mix in with their criticisms of the Lords a generous seasoning of fractious and factitious ire. Especially when it is remembered that the Lords spend twice as much time on government legislation (which is traditionally taken on the floor of the House) as they do in debate – and that for a pittance.

Not all, by any means, of hereditary or even life peers regularly attend (this has itself been a source of not always fair criticism).

Non-attendance (by peers of all categories) has confused the issue, whom and what peers represent, in two different ways. Firstly the large number of heredi-taries, who could attend but almost always do not, are – with the ever-present exception of the poll-tax – little more than theoretical exaggeration of the Tory imbalance in the House. These occasionals are the least worthy voting members, by common consent. For their appearance, whatever their sterling individual capabilities, cannot be based upon up-to-date familiarisation with the House and upsets its already variable micro-climate. These 'backwoodsmen' by overbearing the regulars in the famous 'poll-tax' vote did much, unwittingly, to precipitate the expected reforms.

However their potential clouds the workmanlike ways of normal sittings. For on a normal day 60% or so of attendees will be regulars (those who attend a third of sitting days or more); and Shell and Beamish have shown that over twenty years – since in fact the aborted Labour reforms of 1968 – the regulars have con-stituted about one half of those Tories who attend almost at all and two-thirds or more of their Labour and Liberal counterparts.

Moreover the 'crossbenchers' who accept no party whip but regularly attend have over the same period numbered around 50-60 and with Labour and Liberal together substantially outnumbered the Tories. This has made for a healthy mix of views in debate, especially when fortified by law lords and bishops on particular topics – even if crossbenchers have in practice tended to divide in the lobbies mainly on the Tory side.

It was respect for the variety and distinction of Lords' contributions – their constitutional diversity, that increasingly typifies our pluralist and libertarian society – that moved the Labour government not to insist, in the 1968/9 negotiations, on a Lords working majority over crossbenchers in addition to those who accept a party whip. What made sense in 1968 as a principle has grown in authority (and should be built on) now that the 'elective dictatorship' is firmly in place in the Commons and the electorate by contrast has grown in self-consciousness and variety of demands on government. More British homes are becoming castles every day.

Variety of views, however, in either House does not commend itself to party-minded governments. It is above all what bicameralism offers – a check on ambitious governments with strong Commons majorities who ride rough-shod where they can over minorities they dislike, even though harmless to their neighbours.

It is strange at first sight in view of British cultural diversity which is reflected, though in a distorted mirror, in the Lords, that reform proposals for almost a century have concentrated so unremittingly on the composition of the Lords, to the neglect of a Second Chamber's functions and the powers required to carry them out. The reasons are twofold: a) (obviously) governments' wish to keep all power in the Commons where they control business; and

b) (less obviously) an unspoken assumption that electoral reform in the Lords must track the political history of the Commons in the last century and so rear the renewed Second Chamber as some party-political rival to the Commons. We return later, when proposals are considered, to this unfounded assumption, belied as it is by the proven aspirations of the Second Chamber as it at present is. Meanwhile government politicians are, as usual, mesmerised by their need, where they can, to control Parliamentary business – against the public's democratic interest.

Faced, as the Tory government was, by opposition in the Lords, a Labour government is certain to be no more tolerant of resistance to their measures than were their predecessors. But having no 'backwoodsmen' to call on (or blame), Labour, under pressure in the absence of a cosy deal with the Opposition, are likely to aim their attack at the very idea of having a Second Chamber at all. There is a strong undercurrent from all parties in the Commons that runs counter to an effective House of Lords. Neither governments nor Commons like sharing power. A government with a well-whipped Commons majority suits both and the ruling party structure also. Interference in this cosy alliance will never be welcome. The stronger the government's majority and the higher a prime minister rides, the truer this must be.

So far Labour have concentrated fire on the hereditary peers (easy meat indeed!) and shelved serious reform to a Labour administration at some unknown future date. Piecemeal reform, where Parliamentary control of government has in fact broken down, is likely to be more palatable to government than to its people, at least when they wake up to it. But removal, or severe restriction, of the hereditary peers will at least show up the deeper problem represented by the life peers. For as government and/or party appointees they have no more legitimacy than hereditary peers when standing out against the Commons. This much was shown in fact by the Tory government's handling of the War Crimes Bill.

To round off our sketch since legitimacy is so generally thought of almost exclusively in terms of composition, it will help to bear in mind the three main sets of official proposals on composition from the last century or so – a) the Bryce report of 1918 (set against Lord Lansdowne's last Tory offer before the 1911 Parliament Act), b) the 1968 Labour White Paper, and c) the 1978 Home Report. This summary will also serve to put the wider discussions that follow, on functions and powers, in context.

a) After the second Tory election failure of 1911, Lord Lansdowne, the Tory leader in the Lords, made his last ditch proposal to Asquith: the Lords' powers should remain intact in return for changes in composition of their House.

Especially at this late stage, any such deal was the last thing Asquith wanted and wholly non-negotiable: it could only augment the authority of the Upper House when the supremacy of the Commons had not yet been finally settled. But taken on their own and in retrospect Lansdowne's proposals look reasonable enough. There was to be an Upper House of around 350 peers: one third elected by MPs; one third of government appointees in proportion to the Commons' state of the parties; and the last third hereditary peers who had held important office. A revised version of this became government proposals of 1922 which likewise got nowhere.

What is most interesting about this scenario is its obvious relation to the House's composition as it has in practice grown with life peerages since. It is a pleasant if unprofitable speculation how history might have gone if Lansdowne had not waited to lose the general election before putting forward his proposal.

However the proposals remain in the historian's drawer. But they were much in the minds of Lord Bryce's Committee which sat only a few years later to reconsider the future of the Upper House in the new context after the 1911 Parliament Act.

Nevertheless Bryce took a startlingly different route – one that looks as prophetic on composition as his proposals were on function. The scenario of Lords' reform is shot through with insistent flashes of *déja vu*. If Lansdowne showed where the Lords might have got us today, Bryce showed where we might yet consider going.

His Committee's proposal was for a House of 246, three-quarters elected indirectly by the House of Commons on a regional basis and the remaining quarter by a Joint Standing Committee of both Houses.

b) But their times were unpropitious for both prophets. Then between the world wars came a period of Tory domination when (predictably) House of

Lords reform fell down the ladder of priorities. Thus we come via the 1949 Parliament Act and the 1958 Life Peerages Act to the 1967/8 session which was billed, on 31st October 1967, to include 'legislation to reduce the present powers of the House of Lords and to eliminate its present hereditary basis'.

This phraseology is interesting since it makes plain Labour's priority then to reduce the Lords' delaying powers (from a year to 6 months) over its determination to eliminate the House's 'hereditary basis'. In the former issue of powers the Labour Government proved inflexible (and added a provision to abolish altogether the Lords' powers of rejecting subordinate legislation) but not in the latter. In the Interparty Conference that followed several schemes of composition were discussed (including one comprising exclusively appointees); but on composition the 1968 White Paper contained moderate proposals. The White Paper was full of high-sounding Labour intentions for the Lords' functions – to which we return later – not obviously to be satisfied by cutting its powers; but concern here is only with proposals on composition.

The nub of these was a radical division of the Upper Chamber into Voting Peers and Non-voting Peers. The 230 Voting Peers were all to be life peer appointees (but might include a good proportion of re-ennobled hereditaries of established distinction). The remaining hereditaries would sit out their lifetime as NVPs but would not be replaced. Some life peers who were not made VP's would continue as NVPs. The distinction between the two categories depended on the crucial issue of the vote: NVPs were not disfranchised from Questions, Motions and Committees. There capability to influence remained intact but not to impede government legislation. In retrospect, the exclusive appointment of VPs looks like a significant (and unwelcome) addition to government patronage; but that effect of the proposals was not seen then as undesirable as it is now.

The idea of a two-tier House remains on the table for development but has not so far recommended itself to peers (despite their already weakened voting powers). Lord Hailsham was often very emphatic on the point. The point is bluntly put by Donald Shell: "Would peers who could not vote still bother to take part in the proceedings of the House? This problem is a recurring one for any scheme of reform which involves two-tier membership." But influence is, for some public spirits, better than not being around at all and attitudes change as alternatives are closed out.

c) Nevertheless (as we have seen in Part I) the two-tier route was not chosen by the Conservative Review Committee who reported under the Chairmanship of Lord Home in 1978, despite the influential precedent of the 1968 Interparty Conference. Consequently the Committee's proposals have the advantage of simplicity and clear lines. Strong reasons must be adduced by anyone wishing to go beyond or outwith them.

The Committee after considering various options decided upon an Upper House of mixed membership. The House would be limited to around 430 salaried members sitting for six or nine-year renewable terms. Two thirds would be elected by Single Transferable Vote. The remaining third would be prime ministerial appointments made in consultation with a Committee of Privy Counsellors. This

Committee would include distinguished party members who themselves recommend as well as advise on members. During the transition from the present to the future balance of the House, the appointees would comprise life peers together with fifty hereditaries who would sit for life without succession. To these would be added a smaller number of bishops and law lords than heretofore – 16 and 12 respectively. All would be styled Lords of Parliament. But the peerage would continue as a courtesy outside Parliament. Those peers not LP's could vote in elections and stand for the Commons.

It will be seen by reference both to Part I, Chapter 2 and below that all the issues on composition of the Upper Chamber are covered or arise by some kind of implication out of these three paradigms. But their combination of variety with good sense indicates how difficult it is to select, develop and put together from them a scheme on composition that satisfies as well as may be within the constraints of practical politics whatever we think the renewed House of Lords' functions and powers should be.

The incoming Labour government had every reason for their determination to make some change in the hereditaries' voting status, for fear of what they must see as unfair Tory interference in the Lords with Commons' legislation. But the Labour reaction is not just to attack the hereditary peers, but to counteract the Tory majority with the creation of Labour life peers – a ploy that can be extended ad *infinitum* – so as to shelve responsible reform to the next Parliament.

It is no consolation for the discerning public that the Tories have only themselves to blame. First the Tory government abused the Lords; and then the Tories in the Commons destroyed themselves over Europe instead of making the best of what may well be a bad job when they had nowhere else to go. So much is history; and what the Tories did wrong, that at least the incoming Labour Government shows every intention of putting right. It was wrong to pack the Lords virtually off the street to force through controversial legislation. It was silly and irresponsible to oppose government policy from within its ranks without having a rational alternative. And it would be silly now for Tories to oppose New Labour schemes for reform without having their own scheme ready.

Said Caesar surveying the field of die-hard dead after his victory at Philippi: "Well, they asked for it!" However such reflections are an indulgence if directed to the past; they are only instructive if directed to explaining first why the House of Commons is not capable by itself of fulfilling its task of monitoring government and second how the incoming Labour Government falls into sore temptation to abuse the constitution in its turn.

For the Labour Government, like its Tory predecessor, regards its MPs as there to serve the government; and to pack the Lords with its life peers is really no more than to overflow government manipulation out of the Commons into the Lords. The incoming Labour Government has suffered in Opposition from Tory abuse of the Lords. Not even Tory die-hards in the Lords, if indeed more than a handful remain, would defend intervention by 'backwoodsmen' into controversy. Now out of resentment and to curry immediate favour with its supporters it is bent on eliminating this anachronism before considering what to put in its place.

The convenience to Labour is obvious and certainly calculated: during the current Parliament the government will be subject to even less Parliamentary restraint than its Tory predecessor. With a huge majority and riding high on a tide of populism, Labour expects to disport itself on an open field without serious challenge. Such fiddling while democracy burns is currently called 'minimalism'. It is no substitute for policy.

The fact is however that minimalism – and only especially since the Civil War in the mid-seventeenth century – is the history of the British Constitution. The settlements under Charles II, William and Mary, George III, Edward VII/George V, then under Macmillan and recently Thatcher all confirm this. The only possible exception is the last Labour Government to come in with a huge majority, after the Second War; and the vision of their radicalism has faded with time until it is repudiated even by their direct political descendants. To put it politely, we are almost infinitely flexible; less politely, we prefer to alter course without perceiving it. This by the way is conservatism with a small 'c', not Toryism. Tories prefer not to change anything at all if impromptu resources will serve.

Unfortunately governments in the short term profit from this in abusing the caution of electorates by acting without restraint. That is how Thatcher fell. Her name is Ozymandias: "Look at my works, ye mighty – and despair!"

It happens that this year, 1997, when this book is being written, the constitutional lines are unusually clearly drawn. A long Tory administration has fallen that manipulated Parliament (as all governments do where they can) in a way that ultimately contributed to its own destruction. A new government has come in with the usual mixed motives of reforming zeal, indignation and revenge, but with the overriding interest (which triumphs with governments but less often with MPs) of doing as little as possible with Parliament, so as to maximise its Parliamentary control.

Immediate change is accordingly inevitable, but, unless diverted, no less inevitably of the wrong kind.

Clarity is unusual in British politics, especially in constitutional matters; for we are minimalists where we can be, and the calculus of continual infinitesimal change is generally hard at any moment to sum.

Occasionally, however, an unusual event – this time the heavy fall of an extraordinarily long administration – concentrates minds. At such a time the prospects, even in the United Kingdom, of responsible constitutional reform are unusually bright. Prolonged disenchantment with Tory rule in the west and north, while England remained predominantly Tory, has already within a few months contributed heavily to Labour's referendum victories, though the effect on Labour's future representation in Westminster when England awakes to its shorn skin remains to be seen. Since the one kind of policy that governments never forget (and least of all this one) is the manipulation of votes, it would seem that they probably rely on the side-effects of their PR deal (with the Lib Dems of March '97) to give them a countervailing electoral advantage.

The time has come for far-sighted reform of Parliament itself. Even with a strong new reformist administration we have seen the difficulty of achieving this. For only Parliament as a whole can reform itself and this includes at least both Houses together, if not also their relation to the monarchy. But the lead must come from a Labour administration with a huge majority. The temptation to manipulate rather than to reform, in the spirit of its Tory predecessor, is for Labour as sharp as may be.

The Salisbury Doctrine (analysed at length in Part I) bumped satisfactorily along for over half a century. It was a fine resource pending the implementation of the intent behind the 1911 Parliament Act. Now the British must be grateful, and, some with regret, move on – lest worse befall.

For the alternative on offer is a short-term fix which leaves an overwhelming government careering forward with no braking system in place. That may suit the Blair Government early in the day; but excessive power, like any other excessive pleasure, is both an aphrodisiac and an accelerator of age. Besides the public deserves better than a self-indulgent government; and a strong government has no need of such cheap satisfactions.

Let us again consider those prophetic words in the Preamble of the 1911 Parliament Act. The Act was to "substitute for the House of Lords as it at present exists a Second Chamber constituted on a popular instead of hereditary basis". We do not need to acquit Lloyd-George of all people, or Asquith, of manipulation – a favourite indoor sport of all prime ministers – to adopt that intention as a watchword for the best part of a century on.

But achieving a popular Second Chamber is not even in principle possible without a thorough review of Parliament's functions as a whole. It is at this point in reasoning that the question has to be faced finally whether the United Kingdom needs a Second Chamber at all – or at least whether it is ready to consider the question.

To take the second variant first, abolishing the House of Lords would soon concentrate minds on the first – a review of the Commons that would be left; and the stronger the government, the sooner this would be true. For governments would consistently, and the stronger the sooner, overreach popular support; and the populist tide, already running at the full, largely in fact because of the weakness of Parliament and the pull of the populist press, would soon enforce a change.

Probably, however, the change would not tend towards a Second Chamber at all (or not anyway in the first instance) but towards proportional representation in General Elections (instead of, possibly, just in Second Chamber, Northern Ireland and Euro-elections – to give three live examples). This at least would have the virtue of approximating party representation in the Commons to sentiment in the country on Election Day. But this is not at all necessarily a prescription for good government.

It seems certain that without a strong Commons majority there could never have been carried through the Thatcher economic reforms, stemming from the early days of the Tory administration. Despite the fashionable denigration of that administration because of the insensitivity of its latter days, those reforms – which grew in fact out of happy experiment – are now accepted by the new government, which would indeed not otherwise have been elected.

Moreover those reforms have been and are being adopted with appropriate modifications all over the world, and in some very unexpected places. (Mongolia is perhaps the strangest.) By the same token radical constitutional reforms of the kind being recommended in this book could not be examined and carried through except by a government, such as the present one, enjoying a large majority.

For a secure government has no need to play the numbers game, and the daily deals that go with it, to ensure its majority. Such a government would probably never arise under proportional representation. There are times when a strong government is needed. Indeed these moments occur much more frequently than popular mistrust of governments will generally allow the country to credit.

One such moment has come now when radical constitutional reform is absolutely necessary.

Analysis of missed opportunities by the United Kingdom will tend to substantiate the proposition that they occur under governments with weak majorities or towards the end of their term. The failure of the Macmillan government to take the UK into Europe when it could have helped to form the mould will be seen by historians as the most crucial governmental mistake of the century.

But strong government also requires a strong Parliament to scrutinise, to debate, to keep it in line with both popular support and with good sense.

In any case, in fact, Westminster is already under threat from Brussels and Strasbourg. It was appreciation of this threat with no clue how to counter it that was at the root of the Tory anti-marketeers revolt that achieved no more than the ruin of their own government and the eclipse of their party. Nevertheless any government operating in a weakened Parliament will represent British interests less well in the European Union; and this will be all the truer of governments with the small or uncertain majorities that proportional representation will tend to perpetuate.

This book supports strong government underpinned by a strong Parliament. Abolition of the House of Lords would probably foreclose that option for ever. A single House of Commons proportionally representative of public opinion is a poor alternative. Moreover it would soon come to be regretted by politicians no less than by the public. Abolition of the House of Lords without replacement by another Second Chamber is accordingly to be considered only if no Second Chamber could do the essential job of complementing the Commons in the control of government. I for one am convinced that this is not so.

The only hint of a reason for House of Lords abolition now is the opportunity for a fresh start. Otherwise the siren voices advocating yet another fudge, in a government at last seised of the complexities, will be almost irresistible. The House of Commons, once a potential rival is finally eliminated, will be the first to complain that it cannot continue to operate as is by itself. Abolition of the Lords would at least ensure reform of the Commons. Only a little less certainly it would result also in the formation of a Second Chamber soon afterwards.

However a Second Chamber starting from scratch would be of a different kind from that advocated in this book. The root with the British past would have been cut. Since the plant would have no evolutionary past, it could only be genetically engineered by reference to other constitutional systems of which the British would have had no experience. Unfortunately however no Second Chamber without a history could be set up without a major new constitutional settlement in a written law very probably also affecting and most probably abolishing the monarchy, as an historically essential part of the wholly remodelled Parliament. It is exceedingly difficult to see how such a settlement could be genuinely assented to by the British People.

Assent to change requires not just public debate, but some clue about the effect of the change. It is possible to have an inkling of change grown from current experience, such as is advocated here. It is impossible to foresee the results of an altogether new dispensation, based it has to be added on what could only be doctrinaire principles. Unless the change to the House of Lords as it is be inspired by the public's need to have issues properly debated and government's actions scrutinised and controlled – and neither Commons or the Labour Government are showing signs of any such immediate concern, then the motive for replacing the hereditary peers with a further crowd of life peers can only be a thirst for popularity supported by government convenience – the perfect recipe for the 'elected dictatorship' warned of by Lord Hailsham in 1978, sanctified into perpetuity.

Elsewhere I criticise the craze for referendums as a substitute for responsible government after informed public and Parliamentary debate. But a referendum on a change on which informed public debate is in principle impossible because no relevant information can be available is nothing short of absurdity.

In fact even a General Election called on such a proposal would not only be profoundly unfair on the electorate but of doubtful constitutional validity. As has been elsewhere said, only Parliament can reform Parliament. Any Bill from the Commons, whether or not enshrined in a party manifesto before a General Election, which purported as part of an altogether new constitution to abolish the House of Lords and/or the Monarchy without the consent of both would not be capable of being passed into law; nor would there be any constitutional reason for either the House of Lords or the Monarch to grant any such consent. That is one issue, almost the sole issue, upon which the Monarch and/or the hereditary peers, whether from the backwoods or not, would be constitutionally justified in standing out against the Commons and the government.

There is even a respectable argument for applying this line of thought to the current proposal to remove the hereditary peers without any plan agreed by Parliament as a whole for their replacement within a workable democratic scheme.

Abolition of the Lords and/or the Monarchy would be a populist revolution leading direct to a British Republic.

The last attempt was made to convert Britain into a republic was Cromwell's in the aftermath of his victory in the Civil War. It was not a success. Nor however altogether was the Restoration of the Stuarts which led to the Bloodless Revolution and the Bill of Rights under William and Mary in 1689. From this ultimately flowed our constitutional monarchy, with its residual powers – one of which is undoubtedly to prevent the Commons hijacking Parliament. The

Monarch retains the right to consent or no to the appointment of life peers, as was seen in the discussion of the political manoeuvring leading up to the 1911 Parliament Act. *A fortiori* the Monarch retains the right to consent or no to the abolition of the House of Lords.

The weakness of Parliament and the overwhelming Commons strength of the Labour Government has recreated the backdrop to a possible revolution. But nobody thinks – or almost nobody and certainly neither government nor the Commons thinks – that the people feels the need of one.

The people simply wants to be closer to government – closer to the monarchy, to Parliament, closest of all to Mr Blair, as prime minister. This wish is primarily the result of Parliament's failure, particularly the Commons' failure, to bring the people into Westminster by intelligent debate and scrutiny of legislation. It is hardly an exaggeration to state that if the people wants a revolution at all it is not the Lords and/or the monarchy that it feels irrelevant, but Parliament in itself and as a whole.

The role of Parliament is so ancient that it is taken for granted, so venerable that its slow eclipse has not been noticed. There are three reasons for this, three different satellites round Parliament, which itself moves round the people.

a) The first is 'Parliamentary Sovereignty'. It is such a truism that Parliament, as the Queen in Parliament, is 'sovereign' that it has hardly been noticed that it has progressively ceased to do its job of representing the people. Quite apart from senior judges' interventions in debate and legislation, the judiciary has been a more effective Opposition in recent years that there has been. They have developed a system of judicial review of all aspects of governmental activity long latent in the common law from earlier isolated precedent in the interest of disadvantaged individuals. Ministers have with progressive frequency been brought up short for abuse of statutory powers, where previously ministers would have been – and still could be – called to account in the Commons.

The explanation of this has not been far to seek. Statute law is now so over-whelmingly complex that judges themselves frequently confess difficulty in understanding it. To complain of ministers' actions in detail in the Commons would generally be a bewildering waste of Parliamentary time that is already over-limited. It would also be ineffective since ministerial briefs prepared by dis-tinguished government lawyers, even when demonstrably wrong, would be more convincing than any riposte available to MPs.

The tendency of judges in court, in place of Parliament, to call ministers to account is accentuated by the progressive swamping by statute law of the Common Law itself. Judges have compensated for their progressive scrutiny of ministers' adherence to statute law by disclaiming the right to develop further the Common Law itself, except in cases where statute gives no guidance.

Those (including judges) who say that judges no longer make law are sharply refuted also by the enormous and continuing development of the law of negli-gence since before the Second World War. This has been a huge contribution to the protection of the individual from other individuals and governments also. But it took place in a statutory void. Where individuals' rights are plainly infringed by unjust statute, the judiciary plays reverend lip-service to the sovereignty of Parliament by finding against the luckless individual and recommending Parliament at once changes the statute, like a schoolmaster telling the head boy to redo his prep.

This parody of justice has now been enshrined in statute as the appropriate treatment of the European Convention on Human Rights when inconsistent with earlier statute. This nonsense is the direct result of Parliament's dictating a statute before its direct results (this time conflict of the ECHR with earlier statutes) have been patiently analysed. Parliament has institutionalised a procedure for legislating in the dark.

But the clarification by the judges of their function *vis-à-vis* both statute and common law is a major hidden change. It is a good example of the British way of adapting the constitution to changing circumstances.

But such adaptation can equally have results not immediately perceptible. The balance between the judiciary and Parliament has changed.

The judiciary monitors government under statute but no longer relishes developing the law itself. Lawyers are unfortunately too accustomed to stepping into mess and clearing up, so far only as is possible and too late. They are not perhaps as readily aware as other practical men and women of the need to forestall mess. If ministers' implementation of statute cannot be monitored by Parliament as currently constructed, it stands to reason that Parliament as currently constructed is not fully capable of legislating either.

A Parliament that does not analyse the effects of legislation and is not thereafter effectively capable of calling ministers to account is a watchdog losing its teeth.

But the direct censure of ministers is a matter for the Commons to amend its procedures to ensure – which would not prevent them consulting a Lords' Law Committee (if there was one, as I think there should be) on the constitutional and legal implications of such procedures.

For the creeping control of government by the judiciary that led to open recriminations, especially in home affairs under the outgoing Tory government, has contributed mightily to the protection of individuals from overmighty government. But it has done nothing to underpin the functions and reputation of Parliament. In fact by criticising ministers often in the context of their very own legislation on the one hand, and by abdicating their ancient role of developing the law as they go along on the other, the judiciary has done much to develop public awareness of governments' agelong tendency to overreach, while further undermining Parliament's traditional role of controlling it by informed scrutiny. Towards the end of the last administration the government and the judiciary had adopted a stand-off; and Parliament as a responsible curb of government was almost nowhere to be seen.

For this unsatisfactory 'balance of powers' the long Tory government was largely to blame, both by trespassing on to what the judiciary had seen as their preserve by statutes which on high principle the judiciary claimed never to dispute and by refusing to take seriously the judges' informed criticisms in Parliament – that is in the House of Lords.

The classic case of this is of course the War Crimes Bill of which much has earlier been made. There was also, however, persistent judicial opposition, repeatedly voiced in the Lords by senior judges, on criminal justice and sentencing policy.

Parliamentary Sovereignty has become a synonym not for Parliament's role but for a government's right to force through its legislative programme, untrammelled and untroubled by Parliament itself or by any effective opposition.

This is not to forget the resistance that applies to anything at all to be put on the statute book. Whether a Bill is to be introduced in the Commons or the Lords, both at the preparatory stage in the departments and in the Office of Parliamentary Counsel and during the passage of the Bill in all its stages (through both Houses, unless it is a money Bill), much detailed work is put in within government, mainly, it must be added by civil servants rather than ministers. But even civil servants' energies are finite, especially in these cost-cutting days; and ministers themselves, to retain the respect of Parliament, are expected to understand and retain ever greater weights of information and argument.

Often, too, especially when controversial, policy behind a Bill will have been explained in a White Paper, which may have been the subject of formal Parliamentary debate.

Always before a Bill is taken to the government's legislation committee to be slotted formally into the government's Parliamentary programme, the Bill's effects on policy, on other legislation, on MPs and others' known sensitivities will all have been analysed; for the government cannot escape the testing of Second Reading debate. During the passage of the Bill government afterthoughts, occasionally inspired or at least influenced by Opposition comments, will be drafted into amendments by the draftsman of the Bill.

All this hassle, especially behind the Parliamentary scene, constitutes a genuine brake on the arrival of ill-considered legislation on the statute book. No doubt drafting mistakes and anomalies with other legislation occasionally occur, as the legal professions and particularly judges delight to point out. As the jigsaw becomes increasingly huge and intricate, fretting new pieces to fit becomes ever more difficult. But in general, with few exceptions, what the government meant gets there, and not without a deal of hard thought and hard work.

Nonetheless this labour is primarily a love affair of government within itself and nothing like the shared travail with Parliament that it should and could be. That is to forget who is Parliament's master – the people. In the end against the Tories they rose in their wrath. And so the people should and so they always will – and so prime ministers forget. Theirs is the country, not his or hers.

The eclipse of Parliament leaves the Prime Minister's light to shine more brightly in the people's eyes. This is fine when he sails with the popular tide, but leads to disaster when it turns on him. For then he has no firm support in his sails, no advice to turn to so as to counteract the flood. For tides change like a pendulum, though just sometimes they alter the shoreline for good. But winds are variable as currents, only experts may foresee them; and it is winds that afford a safe course on particular bearings in difficult waters. Prime ministers need Parliament when the going gets rough.

b) So after the first moon that interposes between people and Parliament, the myth of Parliamentary sovereignty, which in truth is the people's, we come straight to the second which is in conjunction with it. This venerable moonface is the manipulation of Parliament by prime ministers.

It is interesting to contrast the styles of Thatcher and Blair, while noting the identical result, the invisibility of Parliament. For Thatcher was a bully and Blair is a manipulator; but their intent is the same, to keep Parliament quiet by appealing over its head to the people – while keeping the people comfortably uninformed and out of the decision-making process.

For Thatcher it started with her treatment of her ministers. Any opposing views to her own, however closely reasoned, from ministers, however loyal, were brusquely, with them, brushed aside.

The line of Mrs Thatcher's able ministers in disgrace (and of other able MPs whose outspokenness earned her displeasure before they even began as ministers) became a procession to an executive coterie of such confusing greyness that her government seemed to have no personality at all except the strident colours of her own clothes. It became impossible to think of Thatcher as a team captain at all.

Nobody was visible but herself. When Geoffrey Howe did at length stand up to ramble over his miseries, the mere shock of surprise at the squeak of a mouse was sufficient to unseat her. If she had allowed criticism or even occasionally welcomed advice, let alone engaged in dialogue with her Parliamentary supporters, the mealy-mouthed attack of her ex-Foreign Secretary and Deputy Prime Minister might have been hardly heard. For it was primarily an attack on her personality rather than her policies; and on Europe the Tory force was with her, not with him, as the sequel soon showed.

Thatcher MPs were whipped first with her order paper like naughty children. Many allowed their personal admiration of her to get the better of their judgment for a long time. Meanwhile her ministers' performance was judged solely on their capacity for getting complex legislation through. Many were very good at it, even when it became increasingly unpopular – which nobody seemed to notice, since adverse comment from her own cohorts was not welcomed. MPs role was to cheer at question-time (at which her hectoring was both effective and inimical to rational thought).

It was plain at the time that nobody was more surprised than herself at her fall, which she construed as a massive conspiracy of betrayal. It is the illusion of leaders that they think their lieutenants owe all their glory to them; for this is only true when leaders promote the wrong supporters. It is Parliament's place to keep prime ministers in communication with their electorate. Most MPs whatever their failings as statesmen (for that, opportunity would be a fine thing) retain an acute sense of which way, or more often, ways, the wind is blowing. Prime ministers at least should see through their own mystique; and if they listen to their friends they have no excuse for not doing so. But in the elation of the chase with streaming out behind them the ever-lengthening crocodile of camp-followers, a sense of perspective becomes harder to retain.

Where Thatcher hectored Parliament, Blair bids to ignore it altogether. For the moment he is favoured by a decimated and shell-shocked Opposition. But he has only to be seen on a brief holiday in a French gite for his ministers to be thought inept and his honeymoon over with the people in the person of the press.

The press: under Labour it is they that have replaced the Opposition; and more malleable even than MPs of any party ever were. Thatcher used to rejoice in being seen alone, as it were, among the crowds. Isolation was in the end her downfall. Blair manipulates his potential opposition. He flatters them, as Labour prime ministers of old flattered the trades unions. His chief adviser is 'a spin doctor' – a minister without portfolio whose office is to manage relations with the press. Blair rejoices to be seen with other protagonists, whether they be other European leaders or the royal family. If he falls in public esteem, so will they with him. He has the wit to recognise that mutual reflection generates the brightest light. The people is being prepared for the unspoken thought this is his Europe, even his royal family.

Such rule is more absolute than ever Thatcher could have aspired to.

Thatcher, in her zealous impatience to act and to run things, behaved as if she and her government were the only thinking mortals in the realm. Especially she thought Parliament was there to do her bidding. Since this was not so, she annoyed people, first in the main Parliamentarians, then in the country. Blair is cleverer than she – or perhaps only more anxious to hold on to power rather than to use it. He asks the media what platitude the people most wants today and serves it up generously with a school-boyish smile; and because he is a chameleon, it is a smile in which all the world can see itself.

The most startling example of this is the tragedy of Diana, Princess of Wales, a gift which his friendly press were determined should run and run.

The press lets it be known that the Prime Minister is her Majesty's trusted adviser, as if there was something new in this. That has long been the Prime Minister's job; but most (except Harold Wilson, who also genuinely admired the Queen) have kept this role to themselves as a tribute to the monarch's dignity.

To highlight the contrast between the Queen's privacy first on holiday and then in mourning in Balmoral with Blair's brilliant visibility transported from his holiday in France with providential timing to Westminster, the impression is contrived that the Prime Minister should be given the credit for the princess's funeral arrangements also. (In fact the arrangements were done, and very beautifully, by the Dean of Westminster.) The Queen is thus cast as the unfeeling mother-in-law and the PMas some Sir Lancelot riding to the rescue (after her death).

Prince Charles then consults the Prime Minister (no doubt among others) as, after a profound private and public shock he is in duty bound to do, about future relations between the monarchy and the people. So it is that we find that suddenly the Prime Minister is managing not just the press but the monarchy also.

All this happens during Parliamentary recess. It is perhaps most significant of all that on the one side the Queen is viciously criticised in the media for not subjecting her family – and particularly the young princes – to the public glare in the few heavy days before the funeral; but nobody in sight suggests that Parliament might be briefly recalled in tribute to the princess, and the royal family as a whole, to reflect the overwhelming public response to the tragedy. For who cares about Parliament? What is Parliament for, anyway?

c) So we find that third satellite eclipsing Parliament, populism. In fact it is much bigger than the other two – the myth of Parliamentary sovereignty and its manipulation by prime ministers. It both influences them and in its seasons eclipses them in their turn.

Populism is a difficult phenomenon for the constitutionalist to pin into its proper place in the scheme of governments. The people in a sense is the play and its backer, its writer and its audience also.

But in a developed democracy the people has no formal role but to appoint the actors at election time. Direct and day-to-day participation by the populace in government or Parliament ends in a bitter confusion of voices – demagoguery in place of elected dictatorship (whether or not presided over by a monarchy) as Ancient Athens and Revolutionary France in their times have shown.

The people must be heard, nonetheless (and how!) What is not so clear is what account government should take of it. This is not at all to say that the people must be governed against their will for their own good, although governments have at election times tended to treat electorates like children or dominions being trained up for self-government. Such was the politicians' flattery appropriate to the times, when people thought MPs wiser than themselves and had anyhow, too, much too much to do earning their living and caring for their families to want to be bothered with running the country.

Now popular sentiment is different. The immediate availability of information through newspapers, the BBC, now the internet and – above and behind them all – television has affected a profound and irreversible change in public consciousness. The first sign of it was the delight in local radio and BBC chat shows where the audience wanted to give their own answers. Next came a widespread interest in local government, such as only a generation ago would have been lampooned as Uncle Tom Forrest of the Archers round the parish pump. Now we have regionalism – Scotland and Wales first, but England's regions will soon be shouting; and Northern Ireland would long have been so, had not the majority seen their very political existence as dependent on their umbilical cord to the mainland. Finally all Britain signed individually and in person the books in memory of Princess Diana.

The people wants to share in government – or does it? That is the puzzle. Undoubtedly the people wants to be heard, but is it more than in the sense that we exclaim at the TV in the drawing-room?

The people wants to be taken more into the government's confidence; it wants its feelings taken into account during Parliaments and not just at election times. So it always has. But common sense is as insistent as ever that the people does not want to be the government.

The change is this, that the vast sudden increase in the availability of information and in the ways that individual voices can now be heard has not been matched by openness and responsiveness in government. There is nothing new in what the people wants: there are just new ways, that governments ignore to their peril, of their getting it.

We have found Parliament (and even sometimes the monarchy) stuffy and unresponsive, and governments unnecessarily defensive and secretive.

Meanwhile we have been conscious that huge issues of which more is understood (even by us) than ever before – such as poverty, wars, environmental pollution, illiteracy and ill-health – are going almost by default, certainly with little or no communication between government and people.

Simultaneously the media, spotting a huge gap and with an eagle eye on circulation figures, have been ever more vociferous in playing to the gallery.

It is striking that this phenomenon has been even more evident on TV and radio than in the newspapers. Newspapers have slanted progressively towards populist presentation, certainly; but the danger from them seems more of an oligopoly of political attitudes peddled by magnates, often not even British, without accountability, but with their own political predilections and business agendas. The brightness of the media often makes Parliament not more visible than the moon in the day.

More significant is the increasing stridency of TV and radio presentation and interviewing. The Radio 4 Today Programme, for example, which used to be my particular favourite source of news, became for a while so aggressive, rude and hectoring of any poor Christian or other victim thrown to the interviewer that I for one could not bear the massacre; and this though, as often others, I was as impatient as the interviewers with the evasions with which politicians or ambassadors provoke them. The sport of such interviewing is not to elicit more information, but to draw blood by forcing admissions from leading questions (often unfair) – admissions that intelligent listeners have learned long since to infer for themselves; and the point of it is to have the so-and-sos answer us in our own living-room.

Accessibility of information and a microphone is what the British now insist on; and there is no earthly reason why they should not have it. Government should come to us and we should be able to get at government. Not before time the new government is to introduce its own Freedom of Information Bill in the 1988/9 session.

Whitehall hates this idea, of course – especially in those great ministries of state, the Home Office and the Foreign Office. Ministers and civil servants have time and again misused the protection of overriding public interest and security just as a cloak to save themselves embarrassment and public accountability.

This has been an ancient tendency: all that is new is that government can no longer get away with it. One of the primary causes of friction between the judiciary and the executive in the past twenty years has been the judges' refusal to tolerate the abuse of secrecy when it prejudices the just interests of individuals.

The tendency of government to try unsuccessfully to keep its distance from the governed has been seen to apply no less in our few remaining dependancies than in the United Kingdom itself. A large part of Chris Patten's media success as last Governor of Hong Kong, and of his acrimonious brush with the Foreign Office, lay in his striking a new balance between the management of Hongkong opinion and inter-government negotiations with China which threatened the Foreign Office's long-established methods of diplomacy.

In that case however a new balance would have tested to destruction the wisdom of Solomon, since China was even more wedded to the traditions of hugger-mugger understandings (and misunderstandings) than the old 'China Hands' at the Foreign Office themselves. It may well be that Hong Kong would indeed as they (undiplomatically) emphasised, at least in the short run, have achieved better terms on hand-over had Patten played to China's rules. The point however was that the Hong Kong public would not have seen any reason to trust Patten's policy had he done so.

Unfortunately however for the Foreign Office, they spoiled their case against Patten by accusing him, if not falsely at least unprovably, as having leaked secret information in putting his side of the case to the British public. Consequently how to deal profitably with China became inextricably muddled with the Governor's rectitude instead of with his media policy. A proper balance between the public's right to know and the subtleties of diplomacy has still to be struck in the Foreign Office as the Montserrat episode shows.

The island was a disaster area after a serious volcanic eruption, and threatened by more and worse. The Labour Government made reasonable – some might claim generous – offers of assistance. The island's politicians loudly demanded more. The British Government refused.

The minister, Clare Short, roundly claimed the British Government had offered enough, thereby lending unintentional support to the island's opposition politicians – and adding fuel to the general conflagration. The minister's handling of the affair was, in effect, swiftly disowned by her superior, the Foreign Secretary, who ordered a wider-ranging policy review.

But what incensed Monserrat was not just, perhaps not even mainly, the British refusal to increase the original offer of assistance. It was instead the minister's refusal to come to see for herself. It was felt that whatever her judgment, based on no matter what policy or facts, her simple refusal to appear so as to be faced by the Monserrattians in their misery, constituted in itself an unreasonable and inhuman response to the disaster. More than anything else a minister's duty was to be seen, to interact with those affected by her decisions, whether right or wrong.

Popular access to government was the issue.

The parallel is striking with the criticism which fell upon the unfortunate monarch for not immediately coming south from Balmoral to lead, before the funeral for Princess Diana, the public display of mourning in London. The people was indifferent to the feelings of the royal family. They were troubled and wanted to see that their monarch was troubled also.

By contrast Queen Victoria, after the death of her husband, Prince Albert, hid her royal visage from the British public for many years until she was winkled out of her shell. This caused even at that time bad feeling and much lessened the monarch's popularity. The difference between the public's reactions in the two cases is the great longsuffering of the people then and the extraordinary impatience of the people now.

It is however equally instructive to notice how little else has changed in long over a century. Being visible and publicly responsive is a considerable portion of government's stock-in-trade.

Since the Falklands Debate before the Task Force was sent, Parliament, despite media coverage unthinkable a century ago, has not been sufficiently in evidence when and where it mattered.

Even broadcasting of Question Time in the Commons many would think of as too much resembling in Victorian terms a Punch and Judy Show and in ours a TV soap. It shows party leaders permanently on the hustings; it lets us see the whites of their eyes. But it seldom explains, beyond mind-numbing generalities, why the government is doing what it does and why others disagree with it. That is done, if at all, by ministerial interviews on radio or television. Mostly, politicians leave politics to be argued out between journalists.

For when Parliament is visible, it is no longer sufficiently responsive. What was appropriate reserve for Queen Victoria and Gladstone is no longer appropriate today. It should however be easier for the monarchy than it is for Parliament or politicians to combine sufficient responsiveness with visibility. For few welcome royal views, much less royal decisions; so the monarchy is not normally called upon to explain what it does. The aggressive public demand on the royal family to be public in its grief for Princess Diana was in truth mainly inspired by a desire to be reassured that the royal family felt bereaved as the public did and to the degree that the public felt appropriate.

This is not the place to discuss the different feelings that characterise public as opposed to private grief. It is only to be noted that both, however different from each other, are genuine and powerful emotions. It is by now essential for Parliamentarians, politicians, the royal family – all in public life – to be approachable, and to be open and articulate about their feelings.

But politicians have to go further than the monarchy. Politicians must engage in open debate. They are required not just to be human but to be right; and not just right, but seen to be right, by presenting to the public and arguing over the facts and feelings that form their views. They must keep neither facts nor feelings to themselves. So much the public now assumes the right to demand.

This book maintains that Parliament, in a developed democracy, is the only appropriate forum for this, that Parliament has been failing in providing that forum; and it proposes in detail ways in which Parliament's performance might be improved, primarily by reforms legitimising and extending the function of the House of Lords. To these proposals for reform we now come.

2. A PARLIAMENT
AMONG THE PEOPLE

"A popular instead of an hereditary basis" – those are the prophetic words from the 1911 Parliament Act that ring so true today. A popular basis for the House of Lords must in short order be constructed if the people in impatience is not to annihilate it.

The underlying principle of reform can only be to bring the people nearer to Parliament and the House of Lords in particular. That is what is meant by bringing Parliament up to date.

There is nothing paradoxical in this. Even the caricature earl in his castle and lands had his popular beginnings: he spoke for the men and women in his domains, as the monarch did for the realm as a whole. This function of representation was the lord's justification; but his position long outlived his usefulness. The nearest the hereditary peerage has ever got, under the remorseless hammer of economic and social change, to parallel the constitutional monarchy has been to assist during the week the government's legislation in the House of Lords and to open a stately home to the public at week-ends.

This kind of proximity the public will no longer settle for. In fact the lord on show in his drawing room on Saturday and in the Chamber on Monday were two sides of the same penny that the 1911 Act sought to consign to history.

But the time it has taken for some such reform to come to the top of the political agenda shows that constitutional reform is a proceeding that the public is profoundly suspicious of: we know that it is, like any other policy, something governments do to maintain their own standing at a particular time, and the form it takes will for sure be moulded to their agenda of the day. It is for this reason that we prefer evolution to revolution. Nevertheless there are moments in history when we feel as if by instinct that the time for radical change has come. Ours not to kill, nor, however, officiously to keep alive. We do have a right to insist upon this, though: that constitutional reform should, so far as humanly possible, be carried out above the political battles of day-to-day and above all should not merely serve the government's expediencies.

What makes radical reform so hard to carry through for the people's rather than the government's convenience is the obvious fact that only a strong government can attempt it, and nothing is harder for the people to control than a strong government, especially in the matter of how it is governed.

For major reform is only soberly to be attempted. It is built, like a marriage,

146

to last a full generation; and out of it is to come only in due course the reforms to succeed it. But a strong government – and especially this government – will tell us that what it has put in a manifesto and/or confirmed by a referendum can and should be adopted, and there is an end. The limitations of manifestos and referendums have already been discussed. They apply in bold and with underlining on the page of constitutional change.

A manifesto is a snap-shot of a party's intentions at a general election. The more detailed it is, the more certain its provisions will not be ideally suited to circumstances after the lapse of time and and honing of vigorous debate. Besides a party is elected on a programme as a whole, often on a balance of unpalatables; and any pretence that the electorate choosing a party is signing a detailed compact with an incoming government on the legislation to be carried during a Parliament, as if a vote were a sort of contract, complete with fine print, is a government's self-serving propaganda.

It starts out as a paradox but is confirmed after a moment's thought that the more detailed and comprehensive over a vast range of topics that a manifesto is, the less likely it is that the proposals in a manifesto on any one topic will in fact correspond to appropriate legislation in its final form. In practice however any Bill originating in a manifesto will be subject to Parliamentary scrutiny: a manifesto is for the electorate only so good as the Parliamentary process to which it will be subjected.

A referendum is an attempt to reduce the shot-gun pattern of a manifesto's approval to a rifleshot that pins public opinion to a clearly discernible point. But it is often pointed out that referendums fail in this admirable aim – and for a whole range of reasons.

The first is the familiar and unanswerable point that, almost invariably, the result of a referendum is unfairly influenced by its wording. Another way of making the point is that the government by implication and generally before full debate decides on its preferred way of handling a problem; other ways are suppressed unless the referendum becomes an unwieldy questionnaire. This can only be seen as a systematic objection to referendums, that is made the more damning when the results of a referendum are, as often, close.

The point is admirably illustrated by the contrasting results of the two recent referendums on the Scottish and Welsh assemblies. It was long clear to many with the political judgment that politicians, especially with all the modern psephological aids of polls and surveys, are supposed to be able to cultivate, that support for the Scottish assembly would be overwhelming, for its tax-raising powers underwhelming and for the Welsh assembly dubious in the extreme.

The Labour government could, in fact, have safely introduced at once a Scottish assembly without tax-raising powers, then have introduced tax-raising powers for Scotland later if support held up, and later still, if appropriate, introduced a Welsh assembly if appropriate, and so on – and all without any referendum whatever.

Instead however of taking the opportunity to gain by experience and to take Parliament along with it, the government is saddled with decisions of doubtful effect and which, incidentally, the British people as a whole has had no opportunity to influence or vote on.

In fact, despite its huge majority and a weakened Parliamentary system, the Labour government has virtually by-passed Parliament and Parliamentary accountability. For it has appealed over the head of Parliament (and ignoring what the English might feel about these assemblies) direct to the Scots and the Welsh and in the latter case got (wholly predictably) a very equivocal answer. It is obvious that the Blair government had no need to do this. It does what it likes. For Parliament is nowadays the dog that doesn't bark.

That leads to another big point. It is Parliament's duty to look at policy as a whole. But by isolation of individual issues – eg devolution in Wales or Scotland in isolation of the effects on England – government evades the need for a coherent policy. Another likely case in point is the government's eagerness to abolish the hereditaries' voting rights without having developed a coherent plan for the Second Chamber that would be left. If that policy meets determined Tory opposition, the government will, on current form, try an appeal to a referendum. But by going over the head of Parliament to the people, it will be the people that government is short-changing. For only Parliament can form a judgment on the coordination of government policies – and is indeed there for that very purpose.

It follows from all these reflections that neither manifestos nor referendums nor any combination of them are capable on their own of generating or arriving at a package of Parliamentary reforms that will command the consensus that both satisfies the public and assures the reforms themselves of the continuing acceptability that a constitutional reorganisation must command. Also, since Parliament is in fact both subject and object of whatever is to be done, Parliament on its own is also not competent to judge how it should be improved. No institution, particularly the supreme institution, should be sole judge in its own cause.

Nevertheless the case for a wide-ranging constitutional debate is unanswerable; but it must also be one in which Parliamentarians play the lead role by mediating between government and people.

Perhaps a natural approach to focussing public opinion in the way best calculated to achieve a consensus on House of Lords reform – which is what a commission would be for – is to set up a consultation process as near as possible to what one would hope that the reforms would themselves achieve.

The aim for the reform process itself is to set up a system of consultation between government, Parliament and people which leads to a Parliamentary settlement which will satisfy the public as fair in itself and best calculated to achieve representative popular government for the future.

The aim for the reformed House of Lords in the context of Parliament as an essential organ of government is for the reformed Second Chamber to slot into a system of government through Parliament which fairly represents and implements what the public wants.

So it should not be too hard to devise a system of consultation parallel to how one would hope government through Parliament might in future work – in fact to take constitutional reform as a case study and example of how government and Parliament should in future tackle (and has not in the past tackled) strategic issues of serious public concern. A constitutional settlement which, as led up to and implemented, does not achieve the widest and best-informed consensus possible cannot be one that achieves in future the wisest and most representative government.

By what method might a consultation process on a major public issue be set up by the present Labour government – or indeed by the outgoing Tories – before Parliamentary reform is seriously examined? And how might that method be improved? One would not have thought it difficult to devise a method of popular consultation about a popular Second Chamber.

Until recently the most likely route had been thought to be a White Paper on overall reform strategy to be published in the summer of 1998, before the passing of a simple Bill abolishing the sitting and voting rights of the hereditary at the end of of the year. It would be drafted by civil servants assisted by government-friendly academics, and would incorporate a draft referendum Bill in terms that suited the government for formal (and foregone) debate in the Commons. This second Bill would follow in the following session (ie in the autumn of 1999).

If either Bill was not passed without demur by the Lords, there would be murmurings from ministers and government-sympathisers to the effect that of course the Lords would not like what the government proffers to supersede them; and then the government would hope to ram both through despite opposition, using the Parliament Acts, before the end of the Parliament.

The aim of rubbishing comments from government would be to divert attention from anything intelligent or constructive that the Lords might actually say. They would be combined with threats of further bevies of government peers and the standard cry that only the people could decide in referendum anyhow; and so in a climate of mindless recriminations the Bills would be passed, and probably the referendum in their wake.

True, the government may not have been expecting quite such an easy passage as this for their legislation, much as they might desire it. But if they do seek to test and educate public opinion in a way that would result in a stable constitutional settlement which itself ensured more responsible and democratic government, an altogether more thoughtful approach to the electorate is required than what is offered. In fact the current threat from the government to the Lords (April '98) is that they will attempt to force through their first short Bill, to abolish the sitting and voting rights of the hereditary peers without even sketching their wider scheme beforehand.

Labour's current proposals constitute a fine object lesson on how not to carry through Parliamentary reform. For they evade any promise of an overall scheme for debate before implementing their simple manifesto pledge to remove the hereditaries.

Recently published proposals, though not in technically government publications, give a fair idea of Labour's intended methods. These sources are the Constitution Unit's January '98, *"Reforming the Lords, A Step by Step Guide"* (with separate explanatory papers) and Anthony Barnett's *"This Time"*, which explains the background thinking. Mr Barnett 'was the Founding Director of Charter 88, the influential movement for the constitutional reform of the United Kingdom'.

The CU rehearses (without question) the outline from Labour's election manifesto and proposes three stages of reform.

First, as Stage 1 and without more ado, as 'an initial and self-contained reform, not dependent on further reform in the future', the hereditaries' voting and attendance rights are to be abolished.

Next, as Stage 2, a Joint Committee of both Houses will develop a 'new set of conventions to govern appointments to an all-nominated House of Lords', a mighty quango, blessed by a mighty Joint Committee of both Houses, whose aim will be that 'over time party appointees as life peers should more accurately reflect the proportion of votes cast at the previous general election'. As a sop to the hereditaries, life peers should include a leavening from hereditaries with a record of established contributions to the House.

Finally (and perhaps) Stage 3 would 'take account of any change to the electoral system for the House of Commons, devolution, the growing influence of the EU and incorporation of the European Convention on Human Rights – with possible roles for the Lords in representing the nations and regions of the UK or as a human rights and constitutional watchdog'. Some 'independent non-Party body' – a quango piled on a quango – would explore in these contexts 'the role, functions and composition of the Lords'.

The CU Paper with addenda considers in detail the voting implications in a Second Chamber of appointees to track party proportions in the Commons.

But one has only to look at the suggested terms of reference of the Joint Committee of both Houses for Stage 3 to see how vague and 'iffy' the whole government scheme is to be. Functions, powers, relations with the Commons even whether or not the Second Chamber is to be elected at all – in short, all the genuine issues of Lords reform, are to be shelved until Labour have abolished the hereditaries to get a compliant second chamber of appointees. All this despite the writers' explicit recognition of outstanding issues, such as:

ways and speed of balancing (by consensus or imposed) party elements in the Chamber,

legitimacy of appointments and

the strong wish of both the Lib Dems and many Labour supporters for an elected or 'predominantly elected' Second Chamber.

Such a startling evasion of any need for a coherent policy can expect a startling idealogical base; and fortunately it is to hand with Mr Barnett's book.

Mr Barnett is fairminded after his fashion. On p. 176 he quotes Lord Carnarvon's 1995 Paper (*Second Chamber* 1994) pointing out that the hereditaries would 'vote themselves into history... in favour of a reformed House which was more effective'; but this is represented as 'hypocrisy and bluff' which, he says, have served the hereditaries well for centuries, 'so well that they are almost natural characteristics' – a ripe phrase indeed. But on the very next page he remarks on this approach: 'However hypocritical it may be coming from their Lordships, it is a good argument. Surely Labour should first decide how it will replace the Lords with a democratic chamber?' He then suggests how this yawning gap in Labour's policy might be filled – by reference to classical Athens 'a 201-strong governing jury drawn by lot'. Some such aleatoric assembly would – somehow – 'have the democratic authority to protect basic constitutional principles, if the government goes off the rails'.

One wonders if the Labour Government's birthday suit is better replaced by such a user-friendly, if old-fashioned, figleaf, blown out of the chaos of Athenian political life. I shall not adopt it, while joining Mr Barnett – and perhaps Lord Carnarvon – in euphoria that May Day '97 heralds reform at last and 'lasting emancipation from deference' (page 281) to shoddy thinking of all colours, in the hope that consensus may grow out of mutual respect.

Underlying Mr Barnett's more extravagant forays is a strategy of reform closer, perhaps, to the mainstream of neo-socialist reform. For his 'utopian realism' and 'incremental totalisation' – 'a careful step-by-step approach guided by a transforming overview' – he claims the European Union's founders as fore-runners. The difficulty is to find it in either Labour's policy or his book. 'One … reason,' he points out, 'for the government's reluctance to provide an overview of its plans is uncertainty where they will lead…' Then referring to Labour's Scottish White Paper with delight – as if it provided any such overview – he quotes, with possible approval, the *'good Conservative'* William Rees-Mogg's destination – 'a fully federal system… the final constitutional settlement'. We are left in doubt whether this is also Mr Barnett's destination or Labour's. One suspects that his principle of incremental totalisation does not *allow* for such a clear vision of any aim – and that Labour has none either.

It is here that any parallel between EU ideals and Labour's populism diverges. Not only did the EU founders grasp the transnational imperatives of economic cooperation: they had a stated ideal of European convergence. By contrast, Labour seems to have no aim but the boyish adventure of reform itself.

With step-by-step reforms we are on a slippery slope. Splendid, we are told – *'glissez'* and enjoy it! We are left no guiding star except the fireworks of 'the celebrated night of May 1st', when 'revenge… was the order of the day'. Pass…

Nevertheless it is possible – and I would urge both logical and helpful – to apply the notion of incremental reform in a wholly different way.

You look both at what you have and what you have not in the context of what you want, then you ask the shortest and simplest route from where you are to where you want to be.

Here is the step-by-step approach of Part II. It may only be another way of saying you decide what's wrong before you decide what to fix, except that it also indicates a method of moving from diagnosis to cure. It tells you to make the best of what you have and to use that as the basis of your improvements and modifications. It tells you to look for and then to make the minimum and simplest alterations to what you have that will allow you what you want. It requires you to define not just your destination but your way there in terms of what you have, want but have not, *and all in terms of your practical experience*. That cuts out also a large percentage of opportunities for human error, class prejudice and mistaken prognosis. And it spares the loss of the good with the bad.

If Lord Irvine, 'with emphasis', thinks it possible to undertake 'each reform… strictly on its own merits [so that] it need have no further consequences than the ones he has taken into account…[so that reforms] are not starting a process, but stopping the rot' (ibid p.255) then the Lord Chancellor lacks Mr Barnett's under-standing of the dynamic of constitutional change. At least Mr Barnett does not mind where he lands so long as he falls in faith. Lord Irvine is falling floor after floor and repeating as he accelerates downwards 'so far so good'.

Any constitutional change has a knock-on effect on all future possibilities and actualities. Thus to start from New Labour's first brave and unhesitating step – the Scottish and Welsh Referendums – not Lord Lord Irvine, not nobody, has the faintest idea how the new Parliaments will affect Scotland, Wales or the Union. There have been enthusiasts a) for UK federalism, b) for separate nationalities and c) for the Union's long-term health, among those who have welcomed the referendum results. One does not know which Lord Irvine favours, but some of them, and perhaps he, are sure to be disappointed. A government should agree with the electorate (or electorates) where they want to land before throwing them out of its window.

The alternative approach is to use what you have got and see what in it can be developed or adapted before deciding what to replace. It is the chess-player's strategy. A clear win, however undramatic, is always preferable to a speculative sacrifice. Whatever your playing strength, unclear sacrifice closes options (espe-cially longer strategic options) and too often leads to ever more desperate resources on the way to inevitable defeat.

We now use this rough exposee of what the Lords at present do to systema-tise their work into something approaching a job spec which can in turn be used to suggest ways of job development. For the 'working peers' do a regular job of work, often very well and professionally. But their work has grown in a self-pre-scribed and haphazard fashion. As Donald Shell has pointed out for example, it was never intended that the House of Lords should lead in Parliamentary scruti-ny of EU proposed legislation; and as we have seen Tory governments and some MPs made not inconsiderable efforts to clip their wings. Nevertheless their work goes on because there is a need for it that the Commons cannot satisfy.

But like any other professionals, peers' productivity can benefit from scruti-ny. Features of it for question are, for example:

a) is their work in those fields i) most productive and ii) best suited to their abilities?

b) if it is, are there other fields as productive and suitable or perhaps even also less productive but uncultivated into which their work could in principle be extended.

c) if so, what extra resources (or back-up, eg from the Commons) and train-ing would be needed to allow them to take the extra fields into their cultivation, in addition to those which they are already managing?

d) if not, what extra resources would allow them to do their current work more efficiently?

e) is their manpower suited i) to their current work ii) to more work that they might undertake?

f) are i) their working methods, ii) management systems, iii) their level of authority and support ideal for i) their current work and ii) any extra work?

g) what would be the financial implications of any recommended changes to a) to f), i) on their own and ii) plotted against productivity?

h) what would the effect on their productivity be a) to f) were put in another context and/or if they were replaced by altogether different personnel and/or management?

It will readily be seen that a) to g) are ways of looking at the peers to see how their performance measures up to its present context, so as to consider incremental changes and modifications to their current role and productivity.

h) on the other hand looks at a wholly different context and personnel for the necessary work. This might in principle include the House of Lords' abolition in favour of a remodelled House of Commons: I continue to argue against this approach on a variety of grounds. It also includes consideration of functions, powers and personnel which might (or might not) result in the election of a wholly different Second Chamber with a very different remit. It is the second alternative that I choose – but not until a) to g) have been looked at to see what improvements there could be to the Lords' performance (and to the performance of Parliament as a whole) without major reform. For only then, I believe, can the need for major reform be fairly assessed.

Would peers welcome a systematised scrutiny of their activities? I think so for two reasons. The Lords' electoral illegitimacy has especially since World War Two taught them a humility that governments and some MPs might well emulate; and as a result the Lords have already gone surprisingly far to adapt their ways to current needs.

Seen from the perspective of their work, as opposed to the lack of notice taken by governments of it, the Lords' performance has nothing to do with their absence of electoral legitimacy. Their work could be outstandingly performed (in many observers' view is often outstandingly performed) while achieving very little because no government is much concerned beyond the question whether it is bound for electoral reasons to take note of what they do.

If this were so (and many observers, again, think that it is so), it is government's obstinacy (and their creature's, the Commons majority of the day) that necessitates giving the Upper Chamber electoral legitimacy. This has profound implications for the substance of reforms to be proposed for the Lords. It sets that substance in stark contrast to the way to be found of getting them to the House and keeping them there.

If it were perceived that the Lords could perform their current work and all additional work that should be put their way with additional practical support, then the need for electoral legitimacy would be seen to stem from the determination of government and its Commons majority to take note of their work on no other basis. It will be clear that governments (Tory and Labour alike) have given the Lords a bad name to hang them.

An indication that government itself recognises this is to be found in the coy doubt expressed in the CU's January '98 document as to whether, once the hereditaries are removed, the Lords as appointees will need any electoral legitimacy. If government and the Commons treat the life peers on their merits the electorate will have no need of a say in who they are. The public, thinking hereditaries should no longer have a right to vote in Parliament by virtue of birth instead of election, supports their exclusion, only to find that government and Commons had no intention of providing an elected Upper Chamber in the first place.

So much cosier for government and Commons to fix themselves a non-elected majority. No fear of a second chamber that might show up the shortcomings of the first. Government and Commons can then build up their new subsidiary creature in the public mind to ensure its non-elected electoral respectability. Is that indeed Labour's strategy? The answer will depend on a fair assessment of the Lords' work and how it might be made more more broadly effective with reasonable support and without uprooting them.

Starting with the Lords' work in a), we travel happily down as far as f) ii) unconcerned with the their absence of electoral legitimacy. We do not hit that issue until we ask in f) iii) whether the House of Lords has the appropriate level of authority – that is, appropriate to the work the Lords do and to the work that with some but not extraordinary support and reorganisation they could do.

If we could answer f) in the affirmative, we should leave the Lords, with manageable changes, essentially as they are. We should never get to h) which conjures up the twin spectres of the abolition of the Upper Chamber and of its reformation.

However we shall find that f) must be answered in the negative. We have drawn morals from governments' treatment of the Lords. We shall be forced to agree that our democracy's health needs either the Lords' abolition (requiring in turn a reformation of the Commons) or a reformation of the Lords on the lines of h) conferring electoral legitimacy, controlling composition and attendance and ensuring adequate powers to interlock with the House of Commons. We reject the abolition of an Upper House; and accordingly we plump for its reformation.

But in arriving at that conclusion by this route we shall know a great deal more about what kind of reformation our democracy needs and about how to achieve it without losing the best of what we from our history we have built up.

a) How productive are the Lords and are they well suited to their work? Their functions can now be looked in the context of Parliament's working as a whole. For this purpose their contribution can best be divided into the legislative and debating work on one side and into their committee work on the other. For the first category depends on their link to the Commons: the second has developed largely on the Lords' initiative.

Legislation and debate, with the redress of grievances, are the traditional functions of Parliament. Redress of grievances, except in so far as it can (often) be generalised in debate, has up till recently fallen on the Commons because of the constituency system. The citizen's route into Parliament has been through his MP. In practice this is hardly so any longer. The MPs duty to a constituent has been largely handed over to the media. This fact has resulted in calls for fewer MPs and larger constituencies (which on grounds of value for money should be supported, so long as they too get the support of an adequate secretariat – with knock-on implications for the Lords).

Similarly because of the Commons' historical role as the people's representatives in matters requiring state finance the Commons has an exclusive role in Parliament's control of public finance and taxation. By contrast the Lords' traditional slant has been towards constitutional guardianship. The legislation nowadays introduced in the Lords reflects this bias.

Most – in fact I think almost all except some Liberal Democrats influenced by US procedures – would favour the continuation of this work split. Which is not of course at all to say that MPs have nothing to do with constitutional issues or that the Lords should have no views on policy issues with financial implications. But those who regard any increase of the Lords' influence as an infringement of the Commons have not sufficiently explored the possibility of beneficial developments in these trends, both for a work-split between the two Houses and for better cooperation between them.

As it is, the Lords have shown themselves highly competent legislators and debaters in all sorts of issues thrown at them. The competence of working peers (hereditaries and life peers) is generally admitted. Their composition is for many purposes superior to the Commons'. Below we shall consider why. Here however the breadth of their competence is to be underlined because it is so much wider than the fields covered in their committees.

Since in the Lords not only debates but also legislation (which occupies around twice as much time) is dealt with on the floor of the House, the active peers are kept very busy on Commons-related work. However their work in committee off the floor of the House is highly thought of, for examples, as we have seen, in science/technology and on EU affairs. Their committee work in fact is nowhere near as broadly based as their work in legislation and debate, which covers virtually all policy issues except finance and taxation. So – room for broadening of the Lords' committee work?

Meanwhile one can say fair and square that the Lords' contributions in terms of quantity and quality are both considerable and, as things are at present arranged, indispensable. The Commons could not do it without them. Since they do essential work well, the supplementary question whether the work they do is that best suited to their abilities cascades into b) – what else they might do.

b) The Lords' potential contribution, even within the House as now constituted, can be seen from logical extensions of their two main areas of activity – legislation and debate on one hand and committee work on the other – and from some combination of the two.

First except firmly from the Lords' remit public finance and taxation – though not strategic and medium-term issues arising out of them – and we see the Lords already participating in all other fields of legislative policy and debate. Their substantive contributions are more focussed. But where they shine they are bright. Shell and Beamish analyse with enthusiasm the work of their Science and Technology and of their European Affairs Committee. This contrast obviously invites inquiry whether the Lords' committee work could spread more widely over fields where they have demonstrated expertise in legislation and debate.

Over the last three decades in particular (after the failure of the all-party talks on Lords' reform in 1969), the Upper Chamber has wisely restricted itself in the main to those fields in which its members have acknowledged expertise and the Commons have little interest. For the Salisbury Doctrine had its origin in the Upper House's need to avoid where possible clashes with the Commons. And besides, the Lords are relieved, by virtue of the very non-elected status for which they are criticised, of the constituency burdens of MPs (tho' not of a steadily increasing burden of work).

The two committees mentioned are good examples of the Lords' self-restraint. It may seem strange that MPs are not fired by science or Europe (and other related topics). But 'a week is a long time in politics'; and not just prime ministers but MPs sometimes have difficulty in seeing further. Besides, the unbearable quantity of work laid upon MPs leave them little time to think beyond the morrow. They are the victims both of that well-meaning Treasury meanness that allows MPs grossly inadequate research and secretarial help and of the admirable but burdensome duty of personal attention to their constituents. They are squeezed at both ends with ever more to cram into their heads and ever more of the public on their heels.

The Lords chose well in their committees where to focus attention. For their experience of scientific affairs is unmatched in any European legislature (and of European affairs outside the EU Parliament itself). But these are but examples of what they could as well do.

The first thing to notice is their breadth of experience which combined with their immunity from the hurly-burly of daily politics fits them ideally to a continuing attention to medium-term policy issues. That such work need not lead to too many squabbles with the Commons is shown by the committee work they already do.

Later under section f) we shall examine their European work to see both how it needs to be modified as EU institutions have been growing and how the Lords' European Communities Committee could be a paradigm for committees on other subjects (since in particular the ECC does not encroach – directly at least – on Commons ground).

Here there is only the need to identify and then list areas of public interest which Parliament so far very inadequately covers and which the Lords could, with some outside help, effectively cope with.

One underlying objective under discussion is the reclaiming as a function for Parliament by the Lords of medium-term policy debate. There is an interesting guide in the contrast between the European Select Committees in the Commons and the Lords. For the Lords' ECC is set up to look at policy and does so, while the Commons committee does not.

This is but one example of the disadvantage under which the Commons' Select Committees labour. Another, which is also a pointer to an extended Lords' function, is this: briefly, their central function is to shadow government departments. Theirs has been a steady and unsung contribution since the Crossman reforms of the 'sixties were developed by Norman St John-Stevas and others at the end of the 'seventies. But their effectiveness is restricted by the irreconcilable antithesis between their membership which is party-political and their aim which is to bring to government's attention matters which the committees as a whole can agree on. That conflict nearly always rules out policy recommendations and has an inevitable tendency to limit attention to minor and non-contentious failings, waste and incompetence. Finding what political opponents can agree on is highly desirable so far as it goes; but it cannot possibly cover more than a small proportion of what a government department does.

Professor Tivey has pointed out, with modesty but also enthusiasm, that one possible territory for the Lords is administration. Scrutiny of quangos and of local government (and, later, of regional government) are but two heads that might come within this category. But scrutiny of departmental policy is at least as important a field for Parliament to reclaim.

There is really no good reason why Parliamentarians should not prepare and initiate policy in conjunction with government. There are just a number of good excuses why they do not.

The principle excuses are lack of information, time – and organisation. Whitehall has for many years jealously guarded a monopoly of policy preparation and the information essential to it. For as Lord Franks said – and he was one to know – 'information is power'. In principle provided government is not interfered with in its own confidential preparation of policy, the information upon which it is based should be equally available to Parliament. On no other basis can the Opposition in general or Parliamentarians in particular test the policy proposals which government turns into legislation to go through Parliament.

Civil servants are public servants, not government's creatures; and Parliament is no less a part of government than the government itself. Moreover the public has a right to know, subject only to government's duty to keep information secret to the extent needed to protect the public itself. If and to the extent that government cannot operate without a right of confidential discussion between ministers and civil servants and so on, the public's right to good government requires that discussion to be private. Similarly if information, made available to Parliamentarians and through them – or even directly – to the public, harms the public when falling into unfriendly or competitive hands, that information is to be protected. Finally – and this is especially true in administration and local government and most of all in taxation – information frequently belongs to individuals and is not for government to bandy around.

Beyond these three categories – government-privileged, secret for public protection and individually private – information that government uses for policy and administration should be available to Parliamentarians for the purposes of monitoring government policy and performance. Until recently there have been genuine reasons for a more draconian secrecy regime. First of all separation of what should and what should not be made available was difficult if not impossible. That is so no longer. Information-handling is the primary new skill of our civilisation. Secondly events and people once moved slower and the public were less inclined to a hands-on approach to their government. Election-time was their time to think.

Nowadays the public fall into the opposite trap. They feel they can decide difficult issues without the information essential to do so. They are encouraged in this by a lazy Parliament that does not sufficiently explain in debate and through the media the complexities behind decisions. And by self-serving media who sell themselves – newspapers, air-time and so forth – by advertising techniques which encourage the public to feel that feeling good and expressing opinions off the top of their heads makes for efficient democracy.

Second after information comes time. Parliamentarians have simply much too much to do, even if they had the information to hand, to scrutinise government policy and administration.

And that, thirdly, is because they are not organised to do the job. It is the subliminal reason for the demand for regional, devolved and more powerful local government that the public knows that Whitehall has not for many years been able to govern except by an ever tighter hold on the purse strings. But Parliamentarians themselves are not well organised, trained or supported so as to filter and apply even the essential information for developing policy, let alone for checking on the administration. That is why Parliament's third traditional role (after legislation and debate), the redress of grievances, is well on the way to being a dead letter. It has been taken over by the judges' development, dramatic over the past thirty years, of administrative law, on one hand. And, of course, by the media on the other.

A theme from now on will be to indicate how Parliament (and the Upper Chamber in particular) could without dramatic reform be better organised to participate in scrutiny of policy and administration.

It is crucial at this stage to indicate at this stage how this fundamental function of Parliament might be divided up between the two Houses. For the concept is for the two Houses to complement each other, to their mutual advantage – the very reverse to destructive rivalry. This applies to both ends of the governmental process (policy-making and executive/administrative scrutiny) which it is here proposed should be the Lords' domain) no less than for control of government legislation and day-to-day executive action in the Commons.

The line between theory and practice, both in policy-making and in administration, are fuzzy; and the fuzzy areas are the stuff of politics. Nevertheless, with goodwill, the two are generally distinguishable.

What the government does from day to day, especially in managing the country's finances and pushing through controversial legislation, is dictated by timing and prioritisation. This has been and should continue to be the Commons' preserve.

The preparation of options, however, and the review how government generally operates, are better kept for a different forum, where cool reflection is the order of the day – the Lords.

Moreover government action which has not been earlier the subject of such analysis is unlikely, when the moment of decision comes, to be the best-coordinated response to circumstances. Painstaking preparation is a hall-mark of good government no less than decisiveness.

Up till now policy-preparation has been almost exclusively the preserve of the civil service, in concert with ministers. This is out of date and anti-democratic. Parliamentarians should be trained and supported to contribute. In that way only can the public pulse be taken into account early enough to influence decision-making when it comes. The faster events and information move, the earlier inputs have to be made. It is a bathmat that the Commons gets consulted too late on EU matters. What is not recognised is that this weakness applies to Parliament across the spectrum of government action. The earlier the Lords can analyse and propose, the better the Commons can be prepared to scrutinise government decisions.

In short both Houses need to be quicker off the mark in order that Parliament can keep government in its place; and this speed of reaction will be much enhanced if the Houses recognise which is to do what to and with whom. Similarly at the other end so to speak of the digestive process, in administration, the civil service, together with non-governmental agencies to whom they delegate (the quangos and others) are given too free a hand. But there are two different types of question here – methodology and application. Nobody pretends that a clear line can always be drawn between the two, especially when circumstances dictate that one should follow almost immediately on the other. But how quangos in general are set up and work (in itself a complex question of sub-categories and stages and so on) is in principle a different question from how they work in particular cases. What is more, it is impossible to evaluate the second without having first examined the first. The Commons Departmental Select Committees would be better equipped to test departmental (and quasi-departmental) activities if some Lords' committee had done the necessary preparatory work. And many government messes would be forestalled. And open government would be better served. In an effective Parliamentary system the Upper House ought to prepare the principles upon which the Commons should scrutinise government action. Generally this requires the Lords to deal with principle beforehand and the Commons to enter the lists with government at the time for action.

The most telling illustration of the proposed work-split between Lords and Commons is the hardest to make work – in financial matters. It is clear that the Commons have the sole responsibility for Money Bills and the responsibility for current financial policy. How is this to work, for example in relation to Bank of England current brief of handling the economy? First of all, it seems a scandalous departure from principle (and an abdication of the Commons' responsibilities) that the Chancellor should hive off (I almost said 'privatise'!) his responsibility before Parliament to manage the day-to-day economy. That this corresponds to the brief of the European Central Bank is no extenuation: both the British government and the EU are set on taking financial policy outside democratic control. However, if we assume our government is set on this policy, the House where in principle this policy can be debated democratically – preferably well in advance of its implementation – is a Second Chamber, which is both seised, as the Commons is not, of European affairs and also able to take a view (if only as on a constitutional matter) – as the Commons also is not. Control of the economy is on the way to being off the Commons' agenda.

Meanwhile there are three general categories in which the Lords' knowhow could be better turned to effect. There are those fields indicated by extensions of their committee work. If for example they can cope with European affairs, they could equally well cope with foreign affairs, international aid and trade and the international environment. If they can cope with science and technology, they could equally well deal with education and health.

The next category is indicated by the peers' (and peeresses'!) legislative and debating prowess. Recently the House of Lords has made formidable contributions in the field of human rights, particularly press freedom versus individuals' privacy. Under the Tories they made equally influential contributions on penal policy.

This second category is an open class and is only offered here by way of examples. It is fact very broad and is best looked under e) and f), where working methods are discussed. For its breadth is determined by the way the Lords look at their work.

For this same reason, it leads into the third category, which in many ways is the most interesting. What of the numerous issues in our national life which never or only sporadically surface in Parliament? Government jealously guards the right of initiation, the right to fix the agenda. Mrs Thatcher used to brush unwelcome thoughts aside. New Labour hogs the stage by reference to its own manifesto, as if nothing else in mattered in our national life. Whitehall then hogs information and, more important, its systematisation and the Whips keep Parliamentarians' nose to the the government's choice of grindstone. Huge areas of the national interest are either ignored altogether (such as Parliamentary reform by the Thatcher government) or farmed out by government departments to quangos or left to the media to talk about, preferably when some spicy scandal or some loudmouth makes an issue 'popular'.

The central point is that legislation, which takes up a huge proportion of Parliamentary time and a disproportionate amount of Parliamentarians' energies, ensures that politicians only have time to think about what government wants them to think about. Government shackles MPs further by concentrating their spare time thoughts on their career prospects and ensuring that they have an absolute minimum of research help anyhow.

Now you cannot legislate on global warming or the farming of world resources or third world poverty or international arms sales or systematic oppression by one race of another. What you can do is to concentrate minds at home *and abroad* on coordinated international policies which then will have implications for government action and/or legislation here.

It is simply *assumed* that nobody but the government of the day has any interest or say in such matters. The independence of all branches and functions of the Foreign and Commonwealth Office not only of Parliament but even within government is a byword. The DTI, Home Office and MOD are likewise empires of their own in their foreign dealings, which are many and various.

What with quangos and Whitehall's general monopoly of policy info, prep and admin on one hand and Parliamentarians' limitations of time and resources on the other, Parliament hardly scratches the surface nowadays of our national life. The newspapers, TV and radio are a much more effective source of debate and redress of grievances that both Houses put together. Accordingly, appeals over the head of Parliament are natural for any government with a populist slant, whether Mrs Thatcher's before or Labour's neo-corporatism now.

An example of this for which Mr Meacher made a fine show of contrition in the Commons (on February 25th '98) was Labour's sending (in advance of Parliament's opportunity to comment) to various consultative groups its paper on access to the countryside. As protest beacons are lit all over Britain, Labour's unpopulist treatment of country groups is for the moment a sensitive issue, so a mouthful of humble pie was ritually taken in the House. But the government is not in truth much to blame for consulting (its chosen) representatives of (some of) those most intimately affected. What is wrong is a Parliamentary system which is not properly geared to Parliament's knowing what is going on anyway.

It does not require much imagination to see how a combination of the Lords' scope of input into legislation and debate with their tried methods of committee procedure on European and scientific affairs could much increase Parliament's effectiveness in monitoring the outreach of government policy and administration.

If this new function was limited to a continuing and general review, it would much increase the Lords' effectiveness when from time to time government legislation popped up. In fact it could be slotted into the prelegislation and special standing committees that many are at present advocating for both Houses.

But here we trespass, as is inevitable, on f) below. It is only necessary to add that general policy committees in the Lords need not encroach on the Commons' first claim on contentious issues and day-to-day government scrutiny, much as the Commons would swiftly follow suit for their own purposes, claiming general priority, if the Lords introduced appropriate resources for theirs. There is nothing like fraternal rivalry to inspire improved efficiency. Nor is there any reason why the Upper Chamber should not show the way independently, if it can do so, without reform that goes further than internal reorganisation.

So – the list within the three categories of fields into which the Lords' proven general skills might allow their activities to expand without restructuring of the Upper Chamber:

i) Parallels to the Select Committees on the European Communities and on Science and Technology – medium-term review of *trends* in policy and admin (including the monitoring of quangos and government/quasi government agencies) relating to:

foreign affairs: international defence, policing, arms control and arms trade, aid and agriculture; international agreements of all kinds (even including finance and economic cooperation)

home affairs: economic industrial, commercial and employment development; information technology, dissemination and control; education and health – planning both for the future; trends in agriculture and land use (including housing, planning, transport).

Notable omissions here – beside responsibility for day-to-day scrutiny of departments and their agencies) are current policies on: national finance, employment, commerce and trade (both their development and regulation), transport, UK agriculture and land management, housing and planning – all of which should perhaps be the subjects of similar developments in the Commons with joint consultations between the two Houses, where, as frequently territories overlap). In parallel the Lords should keep the Commons regularly informed (and not just on paper) on the Lords' activities.

ii) Parallels to the Lords' legislative and debating skills – policy and admin relating to: human rights and freedoms, privacy and press freedom (and regulation), social and racial harmony, administration of justice, penal reform and law and order; the constitution and good government (national regional and local);

iii) Matters generally beyond legislation: the world environment and resources; world poverty and technology transfer; the ageing population; leisure and activity; spiritual and artistic development (eg the Millennium Dome!)

Parliament's (and in particular the Lords') involvement in these large issues would of course require a huge additional work-load on Parliamentarians. Nobody would think for a moment that any or all this could be undertaken without help. But the point of principle is that our government, is already concerned with all of these issues, though from want of information nobody knows much of what government is doing about them. From this it follows government should share some of the resources used on them with Parliament and the public should through Parliament have its input into them.

c) and d) Both for what the Lords do and for what they could do, if it was decided to be their function that they should, the same resources and back-up, beyond what they already have, are desirable. Of course however the more they do the more help they need.

We have already referred to most of them. Leaving aside (until f) the major question how best they might be organised to use their skills and facilities, we can see already all Parliamentarians (and the Lords in particular) need much greater secretarial and research assistance and less restricted access to government information and civil service help. Each House (and its members) should expect to cooperate better with the other in fields of common interest. The aim should be for the Houses to complement each other to the point where Parliamentarians can argue on equal terms with government in both the formulation and the carrying through and administration of policy.

Possible extra areas of responsibility for the Upper Chamber have been discussed; but the issue of the Lords' functions and the powers to go with them has not been discussed. However in view of Parliament's weakness in the face of the expansion of governmental powers it can already be assumed that the Upper Chamber's areas of responsibility should not at any rate be less than what they at present cover. These areas cover not just their committee work but a huge range of legislation and debate also. If it were decided that Parliament (and the Lords in particular) should extend their areas of authority the provision of back-up would be, simply, more of the same. So – what price an efficient democracy?

For if information is power, equality of information is essential for its control. Party control of the Commons and the Commons' ascendancy of the Lords has relieved government of the pressures required to assure Parliament these facilities necessary for a healthy democracy. Moreover the tendency of the press to jump in where Parliamentarians fear from lack of information to tread is a haphazard and unreliable alternative to a working Parliament. Media sales and ratings, not the public interest, are their first concern. The media are no more elected than are hereditary peers and exert a much greater, if uneven, influence. Press barons wield a power not constitutionally controlled. Freedom of the media is not the issue – but their equality with Parliament in debating power.

e) Has the people the peers it needs? Parliament is at a low ebb after the prime ministerial encroachments of the Thatcher years. The BBC has decided to relegate that long-running and well-presented programme, 'Yesterday in Parliament' to Radio 4 long-wave as a specialist interest, along with Test Matches – and the characteristic comment that if they can find the Test Match they can find Parliament too. The Speaker has herself complained with her characteristic forthrightness that, on the BBC's own figures, listeners to 'Yesterday In Parliament' will be thereby halved. But the blame cannot all be laid on prime ministers, nor even on the MPs whose fears of their Whips and of dissolutions and hopes of preferment left governments a clear run. Certainly a weak Parliamentary system of government controls has contributed, and its mean support for Parliamentarians also. But are their Lordships totally blameless?

We remember the MORI poll of spring '95 which found that the public felt by 3 to 1 that Parliament's scrutiny of government is inadequate. Let us assume that Parliament in general and the Lords in particular has been at last granted the staff it needs – Bernard Crick's first priority for an increase in Parliamentary efficiency. Let us assume also that Sir Douglas Wass's idea of a Department of the Opposition has been adopted. Forget for the moment questions of organisation. Even forget for a moment the low political credibility of a non-elected assembly well over half of whom do not regularly attend. Just looking at those who do attend (both regularly and on issues of special interest to them) should we say we have the right people in the Lords?

Their Lordships are a varied and distinguished bunch. But nobody could call them ideally representative of our society. Obviously there are too few women and younger members. This is far from a detail. It severely restricts the efficiency of the Chamber. But this defect could easily be cured over time by appointment (or in theory still by the creation of young women peers). And if male primogeniture is to be abandoned for the monarchy (as Lord Archer prescribes), why should not equality of the sexes (in some form) be extended to the succession of hereditary peers? Lord Diamond has campaigned for this for years. (See eg his Hereditary peerages Bill [H.L] 1992-3)

But there are other ways of being unrepresentative. Britain is a pluralistic society subject to an 'elective dictatorship'. For "where Bills have been carefully scrutinised in their entirety in the Commons and appropriately amended there, there is still a case for those Bills to be scrutinised from a different point of view – the point of view of the special interests primarily affected by them and able to express their views without slavish adherence to strict party discipline". (Lord Crowther-Hunt, *Abolishing the House of Lords*, The Listener, 4th December 1980.)

Membership of the House of Lords has built up, if not in a haphazard way, certainly in historical strata. More than half the hereditaries and 15% or so of life peers have landed interests. The country heritage is therefore over-represented. That is not to say that countryside interests have a specially good airing. In our overcrowded islands the electorate is primarily urban and suburban and accordingly unsympathetic to a House that harks back to an era demographically quite different. Country people are over-represented in the Lords but often feel themselves clubs of the elective majority (which they are not).

Similarly, by reason of Establishment, the Anglican Church is heavily over-represented but weak. In a pluralist state where support for the state religion is anyway in decline, plainly the sitting bishops are too many and even with a Rabbi together with a Cardinal or two (if the Pope allowed) would not be adequate. Many other cultural and ethnic groups should be represented as a matter of state policy. Many churchmen and most politicians would support this.

In other respects, however, the Upper Chamber is remarkably well constituted, as we have seen, to cover a broad canvas. Distinguished personages from all walks of life, many of them without firm party-political affiliations, end there, though as we also saw it would be better if more of them were women and arrived sooner. Besides those who man the strongest committees (scientific and European), there are those who contribute influentially to debate and legislation in most spheres of national life. The Lords' breadth of view and scope is a good deal wider than the Commons'.

Uneven attendance for this purpose is a plus. Regulars represent only 60% on most occasions. Hereditaries and life peers of distinction often attend on matters where they have something particular to contribute. Only something over one-third of life peers attend regularly (though about twice as many percent of Labour than Tory). But on a host of issues they are a valued occasional resource. Those wanting only regulars in Parliament have difficulty in finding a way for occasionals to make their contribution.

The Lords' very variety makes generalities almost meaningless; but one huge field, human rights, is a good representative example, bringing in such thorny topics as privacy, the freedom of the press, family rights, law and order and constitutional reform all under one banner headline.

At the time of writing the Human Rights Bill has completed its stages in the Lords (itself a tribute to their Lordships' prowess) and is about to go through the Commons. The European Convention on Human Rights was ratified by the UK long ago and affords British subjects rights of audience in the European Court of Human Rights in Strasbourg. But in my opinion the policy of its wholesale importation into our law was flawed by the government's failure to think through in advance the technical and legal consequences of so doing. Key questions, such as the conflict in Britain of freedom of expression (particularly for the press) with the right of privacy (both are written into the Convention), were never properly canvassed in advance in Parliament or anywhere else.

These conflicts will accordingly have to be sorted out *ad hoc* by the British courts. The result can only be great uncertainty as to the law until this is done; and it can only be done at great expense to the litigant. If there had been appropriate machinery in the Lords, many of these problems could have been tackled in an entirely different way. For there is no doubt that no better forum for such a study could be devised than the Lords as at present constituted.

In the event the government earned itself much merited embarrassment by having failed to think through in advance the effect of bringing in a law from abroad which conflicted with the Press Complaints Commission's voluntary code and enforcement procedures (such as they are). The confusion was added to by the uncertainty in British law about what constitutes the indigenous laws of privacy with which the Conventions' developed jurisprudence may or may not conflict. (See on this the excellent Research Paper 98/25 Privacy and the Press of February '98 and the 'lost' House of Lords' 1980 decision, *Morris v Beardmore* finally reported in *The Times* of 7th March '95).

Careful consideration in the Lords in advance of this legislation could have avoided half-cock government action; and the Lords might have come to other decisions even among themselves.

It so happens for example that the Convention gives a much more restricted right of audience to the Strasbourg Court than our domestic law would give for judicial review. The British remedy of judicial review is a recent development from old law and is geared to wrongdoing of government and its agencies, so that almost any with a 'sufficient interest' (almost any but busybodies) can bring such wrongdoing to the courts' attention. By contrast the Strasbourg Court long ago fixed the test of a right to a hearing at a personal wrong suffered by the complainant. In the February third reading debate their Lordships had to consider which of these two tests to go with. Ironically the amendment to the government's Bill to allow for our (better) indigenous test to apply was brought in by Lord Lester of Herne Hill whose personal efforts over years had been largely instrumental in the wholesale importation of the Convention – and unfortunately, despite the assembled weight of many law lords, the British test was voted down.

If as is not improbable a privacy law is waiting to be unveiled in our law, the net result in this case will be that the rule that the Convention where possible is read to override our law will result in a restriction on the right to a hearing in judicial review of privacy cases. It is most unlikely in my view that if this conflict between the domestic law and the Convention's jurisprudence had been picked up in good time that the government would have insisted on the Convention test. This government's impatience, not for the first time, resulted in a doubtful decision.

Meanwhile underlying the conflict, at any rate in British circumstances, between Articles 8 (privacy) and 10 (freedom of expression) of the Convention is a disarray in the media's treatment of personal rights. It seems wrong, and an abdication from the government's duty to guide the development of citizens' rights, that such an important matter should be left to *ad hoc* treatment in the courts.

Government's relations with the media, and their interdependence resulting from the weakness of Parliament, were shown in an unsavoury light in the dogfight over whether predatory pricing by newspaper magnates should be exempted from the simultaneous Competition Bill. The balance between low pricing of newspapers and the public's right to a broad press coverage should never have been left to a Parliamentary tug-of-war of press barons. It seems clear a Royal Commission should have preceded all this legislation, in parallel with generons Parliamentary debate in both Houses.

This is a section (primarily) about manpower and though as always questions of function and organisation obtrude, the subject of human rights raises in one way or another almost all questions about who does and who could and should do what in our Upper Chamber.

What stands out from our exposee is the broad competence of the peers in social and legal strategies, and the failure of organisation which should allow that competence to combine with government and the Commons. For government so far as it can seeks always to politicise the Lords and to make it if possible a pale reflection of the Commons. Where it cannot do this it seeks to avoid a structured investigation of issues or, failing in that, it breathes out threatenings and slaughter against the Lords regardless of the argument's merits.

That said, it is plain from the Lords' performance with their hands tied behind their back that no Parliamentary forum in Europe is better manned to cope with human and legal/constitutional issues.

There are a number of reasons for this. The first is of course the breadth of experience, much of it a-party-political, which the Lords can field. Among them are a goodly number of all political shades who do not give a damn for short-term party advantage. Often an ex-cabinet minister will feel free to oppose his or her own government's indiscretions. So now we have Lord Glenamara (Ted Short) opposing his own government's student loan scheme with the story of his own poverty resulting from having himself actually taken one out and paying it back.

Then there are the law lords, some of them retired but still active. One remembers their staunch contributions on penal law under the last Tory government – not as judges but debaters speaking from their own experience of justice administration. Now they should have before them the practical implications of the import of the Convention on Human Rights. For when the British judges cannot square British law with the ECHR, they are to say so and the government are to put matters right by subordinate legislation. Seldom can Parliament have so institutionalised the grand old political game of shutting the stable door after the departure of the horse – or so anticipated with such public equanimity miscarriages of justice (for the procedure only comes into play when the judges cannot enforce the Convention). But nobody could possibly be better placed than the law lords (past and present) to limit the pain.

A number of thoughts follow. So broad is the scope of peers that on any topic a number of different approaches are available to them. By tradition debates and legislative committees are taken on the floor of the House. But the Lords undoubtedly have the expertise to man specialist committees also, say, on human rights, to give just one example. Such committees might double as prelegislative and special standing committees (though not necessarily with all the same members if it were thought that legislative scrutineers should not be the same personnel as had earlier made the policy recommendations, to give a fresh look).

For in human rights issues there are detailed technical issues (as for example the threshold question mentioned above). These might better be discussed at committee level and brought to the House for decision when the technical arguments could with due notice be balanced against the political.

Again the law lords are to be considered in this context. They have both specialist and general expertise. An argument against relegating them to a constitutional court (even assuming the British wanted to present lawyers with a written constitution) would be the loss to Parliament of judges at the policy-making and legislative stages of the statutes that the judiciary would later have to rule on.

Committees will be discussed in the next section. The point here is the breadth of available talent among peers that allows for flexibility of approach. This wide scope is a prime reason for keeping so far as possible the membership as broad and multifarious as it already is. This very breadth is a palliative to Commons' fears of a look-alike competitor. There is no way that the Lords, as at present constituted, could split reliably on the party lines of the Commons.

Furthermore it is this variety that allows scope for expansion of territory. The ethos of the Lords is congenial to social debate. But the membership is too narrow. Ethnic groups and many minorities are badly under-represented. Other groups – trades unions, industry and so on – might be usefully included, more or less *ex officio*. Regional and national groups and interests should perhaps also be there; but their presence would require structural changes.

If the membership were yet further broadened it is not difficult to see how policy debate could extend the short-term tunnel vision of Commons' debate. The Lords would surely rise to the challenge.

f) The Lords' working methods and authority – do these suit both what they do and what they could do without structural reform? Upon the answer to this question will depend what kind of Parliamentary reform we go for.

It has been assumed so far that no rational decision on reform can be taken whether on the hereditaries' rights or on abolition versus structural reform without a fair assessment of what the Lords actually do and could do under the present dispensation. Labour (and in their train the Lib Dems) have so far sought to evade this elementary exercise on the ground that the decision on the hereditaries at least was decided in the general election. This is of course good politics and, maybe, poetic justice; but it is bad statesmanship. It is to use the Salisbury Doctrine against Lord Cranborne; but it is also to deny the public, for the sake of populist dogma, options before implications have been weighed.

In fact if we reconstruct the thought behind the 'referendal' theory which led in the last century to the Salisbury Doctrine in the first place, we see that it was just this kind of abuse of popular decisions that the Lords were seeking to combat. There are occasions when the public needs statesmen more than politicians. Those occasions occur when politicians stoop to demagogy, by which I mean when politicians wrest a quick decision out of the electorate and ram it through the Commons without allowing a fair weighing of implications. The Lords in the 'referendal theory' were claiming to represent the people better than the Commons did when the Lords had had time to think things out and the people hadn't.

Of course there was a heavy party bias in earlier days that led to the over-pressing of this line. For the Tory Lords were claiming a monopoly of wisdom in order to put the brakes on reform. But the fair-minded, those not professionally *partis pris*, will see the Tory Lords had a sharp and abiding point even when it was unfairly pressed. For then (not now) the Lords were packed with Tories against reform. Their 'superior wisdom' accordingly by invariable 'coincidence' always suited the Tory line. But none of this negates the principle that, whatever goes into a winning manifesto, constitutional reform without a fair evaluation is sloppy government and short-changes the electorate. It is just such sloppy government that rides rough-shod over minority interests – the elective dictatorship that only an effective Parliament can counteract. Here, if ever, the Lords are the constitution's guardians.

Mature consideration is the primary purpose of a Second Chamber. That is why as an interim reform the Lords' power of veto of legislation was substituted in 1911 with a delaying power. But to play that role well, the Lords need better organisation and support – and general acceptance of their role.

It is ironic that the Commons need the same for theirs. Instead of looking with jealous eyes at the Lords they would do better to demand from government very similar advantages to those which are advocated for the Lords in this section. Few would doubt that if the Lords got them, so too would the Commons.

For as MPs are under the hammer of their parties, so are the Lords under the hammer of the Commons. Hammers over Parliamentarians' heads do not make for effective scrutiny of government.

In the last section e) we chose the broad area of human rights as the leading example of what the current membership of the Lords is and might become capable of. That invited thoughts about the Lords' capabilities, present and perhaps to be developed, in social spheres. It also shone the light on the double function of the law lords, present and retired: they operate not only as the highest court but also as vigorous debaters and legislators.

Similarly in this section f) we look at the Lords in the context of the EU. There are equally good reasons for this choice in this context of organisation and support:

i) the field of European legislation is that in which the Lords have made a large and unforeseen contribution;

ii) what goes for Europe could easily be extended to the foreign brief which Lord Bryce supported for the Lords way back during the Great War. That in turn filters into influence on a host of long-running international issues – aid, arms sales and trade, the global environment and so on;

iii) earlier discussion has drawn attention to a need for structured prelegislative briefing of Parliamentarians. This applies above all to the Lords' European Communities Committee (and to the Commons' European Legislation Committee) because prelegislative influence on Euro-legislation is all that the

Westminster Parliament at present has;

iv) the Second Report from the Select Committee on Procedure, 1984-5 and some recent commentators (notably Ferdinand Mount in *T'he British Constitution'* Now at p.186) have advocated the development of Special Standing Committees during the legislative process (ie after second reading in the Commons) as a means of the self-briefing of committees on specialist subjects. What goes for the Commons would be as suitable for the Lords, especially if the notion is accepted that the Lords' membership profile is ideal for the continuing consideration of medium-term policy/admin issues. Something akin to SSCs might be used for the interplay of Westminster with the European Parliament whose influence is increasing to the point that it can no longer be ignored by Westminster as its point of entry into Euro-legislation;

v) the advent of Europe within British gates constitutes one of the two primary issues (beyond current political sentiment) defining the urgent need for the reform of Parliament. The other is the Scottish and Welsh Parliaments, together with other regional issues to follow. But plans for the co-ordination of the new Parliaments with Westminster plainly require structural reform in Westminster. The EU does not, as the Lords' performance has already shown, though it has been suggested that the Lords' influence could be even more effective with better organisation and support. Since we are still in logic at the stage of seeing what the Lords can and could do with minor internal and without major structural changes, their European function is a fine indicator of what those minor changes might be;

vi) and finally – constitutional change is a medium-term and continuing issue for which Parliamentary input and organisation so far just does not exist. The New Labour government has gone off at half cock – that is without a structured debate and policy – on national/regional reforms and has announced its intention to repeat the mistake with reforming the House of Lords. Parliament's handling of the EU is another huge issue. Handling of constitutional change by Parliament on one side and of Westminster's interface with EP on the other will each throw light on the other.

In short if with internal developmental changes the Lords can cope with home and foreign affairs (including Europe as it is now) we shall be left with a) Westminster's developing relationship with the European Parliament and the other EU institutions, b) devolution and c) the powers needed for some function yet to be clarified as guardians of the British Constitution, as the only substantive reasons for major change to the structure of Parliament.

That is not to forget the political imperative to reform the hereditaries' anomalous position; but this in my view has little to do with the House of Lords' effectiveness as a House of Parliament, despite the vague (and biassed) statement to the contrary in Labour's 1969 White Paper, except that an anomalous House, whatever else it can do, is in no position to act as our constitutional guardian. At least not if the work allowed them and done is the criterion of effectiveness. The need for that change has everything to do, however, with the public credibility of Parliament and the Lords in particular. But that purpose (and the country's democratic needs) will be best served by the substance of reform, that is, the recognition of the Lords' function within a strong Parliament. Electoral reform (inevitable anyhow) can follow on after that with little fuss.

The Lords have through their European Communities Committee and its Subcommittees been the only effective conduit for Parliamentary influence on European legislation. The Commons' brother Committee (with its narrower brief) has been defeated by the sheer weight of European paper for immediate attention, generally delivered anyway too late to influence events.

It is really no justification of this failure to point out (as others have) that Parliamentary influence in other EU states is no more effective. The success of the EU depends on acts of will. If the EU Council and Commission make no proper provision for Parliamentary input, it is up to the Mother of Parliaments to demand that the British Government demand it. Umpteen wrongs do not make a right; and our government makes other demands often enough.

If Labour wish to substantiate their claim to Euro-friendliness in the context of interdependent nation-states, then ensuring British Parliamentary input – and so others' – is the most far-sighted democratic contribution to the EU that Britain could make. The principle financial concessions (EMU and the rest) – in common with Mr Major whose policy Mr Blair is, I think, rightly imitating – Labour does not at present intend to make. It cannot safely do so, except within a firmly democratic political framework of Parliamentary government (national and European).

Meanwhile no one should think that the Lords' contribution has been enough. It just shows how much more they could do with appropriate resources and government support.

But we need to ask whether resources and support would be enough, even granted that the House of Lords as is has the members for the job. We shall find this question leads into significant reform in the Lords' working methods that is more widely applicable. But in isolation the Lords' reform will not work as it should.

What then could the Lords do, beyond what they do already, in EU affairs, with no more than internal organisational changes? And how does an answer to this give indications of how the Lords might better operate in other fields?

The essence of their ECC Select Committee is prelegislative work. It has to be, since Westminster has no direct input into the EU legislation process. Because of this the Lords have repeatedly concerned themselves with policy questions (including the impact of EU issues on UK domestic affairs – for which they have been castigated in the past by the Tory Government).

Prelegislative work is policy work. It is the UK government's monopoly of British input into EU policy via the Council of Ministers that lies at the root of Westminster's impotence in European affairs. Partly that is a result of the anti-democratic structure set up by the Rome Treaty itself which envisaged a cosy society of member-state governments working hugger-mugger with the Commission. In the early days (not now, as we shall see) the European Parliament was little better than a toothless talking-shop. And British governments have made no effort to cure it. That is because it suits governments (not just our own) to keep European affairs to themselves – and damn democracy.

And it has suited the Commons, overworked, unmotivated and unsupported by any reasonable secretariat, to leave its huge pile of Euro-documentation largely unread with the excuse that the government is in charge.

So it is that British ambivalence about EU membership and poor teamwork has so far robbed the EU of the distinctive contribution to European democracy that Westminster should be able to make. To be blunt, the Tory Governments never truly wanted the EU institutions to work as they might, for fear that an efficient coalition of nation-states might free-fall into federalism; and who is to call that fear for certain misplaced? But meanwhile Britain is an EU member and it is plain stupid not to make the best of it – and that includes making its institutions work as democratically as they can.

The Lords' brief encourages in its terms the scrutiny of EU policy issues. But governments have been able in a large degree to ignore and frustrate their contributions, mainly by exploiting the Lords' suspect constitutional position. In short governments have evaded Parliamentary scrutiny (and democratic input) by playing upon Parliament's weaknesses. That is shortchanging our people.

But strengthening Parliament – not least against government – should be the purpose of the reforms under way. The Lords' contributions, current and potential, are not to continue in frustration because governments like to avoid Parliamentary scrutiny. Contributions should first be attended to (even by governments) on their merits.

It is assumed that committee reorganisation, including reasonable demands for facilities to make them run efficiently, is an internal matter for Parliament. It follows that improvements, even wideranging, to the Lords' committee procedures could be done without structural reform of the Upper House. Could the current Lords' membership man a strengthened committee system? Their past form, certainly on EU affairs, indicates that they could. If so, then the low credibility accorded to them by government and Commons alike (who have their own convenience to fuel their prejudice) should not prevent them, if good government requires it. To ignore the Lords' European work and then demand 'reform' (by which so far the government means no more than the removal of the hereditaries) is no better than giving a dog a bad name.

What might such a new committee system look like and what might be its purpose and scope?

The House of Lords' Select Committee on the European Communities is a prelegislative committee, as we have said, set up "to consider Community proposals whether in draft or otherwise", to obtain all necessary information and make reports on proposals "which, in the opinion of the Committee raise important questions of policy or principle, and other questions to which the Committee consider that the special attention of the House should be drawn." A broad enough brief, in all conscience, that allows wideranging and proactive policy debate and influence. It is a whole lot broader than that of the Commons (representing of course the Commons' interest – or lack of it – as endorsed by government).

This Lords' Committee has the power to appoint sub-committees; and it has, defined by subject-matter. (Sub-c. A. Finance, Trade and Industry and External;

B. Energy, Transport and Technology; C. Social and Consumer Affairs; D. Agriculture; E. Law and Institutions; F. Environment; and there are occasional ad hoc committees). This structure could network a complete system for Westminster input into the EU. So far it is lines everywhere with a terminus nowhere.

Where should the Lords' EU terminus be? The European Parliament? If so, where do the Commons come in?

The Single European Act of 1986 and the Treaty of European Union of 1992 ('Maastricht') altered British Law in a fundamental way, at least so long as the UK is a member state of the EU. In technical terms, probably, sovereignty was probably unchanged. The Queen in Parliament (in the old definition) is still sovereign because (though this is not envisaged in the Treaties) the UK could no doubt find a way of leaving the EU. The Treaties are accordingly not fully derogations from British sovereignty; but that is a sterile argument of the type that gives lawyers a bad name among politicians. It amounts to saying little more than, 'Treaties can be broken'. As through history they have been and will again. But until that Day, European Law rules in the UK – OK.

This in not the place to examine the effects of this doctrine. But the political conclusion is obvious. Until that Day, Westminster cannot beat the EU and had better join it. One or other arm, the Lords or the Commons or both, had better take account of the European institutions, in the name of British democracy and in the interests of Britain.

The House of Lords is the Westminster institution which over a quarter of a century has shown an interest and built up expertise in European affairs. Just as the British Government is preparing (without being committed) for European Monetary Union, so the Lords would do well to be thinking how their European expertise could be released from its British straitjacket. For this requires no revamp of their House as an institution. Where then should they look?

Maastricht also altered the status of the European Parliament in EU decision-making. Article 189 provides that 'in order to carry out their tasks... The European Parliament acting jointly with the Council, the Council and the Commission shall make regulations and issue directives, take decisions, make recommendations or deliver opinions'. As D and KPE Lasok put it (in *Law and Institutions of the European Union*, 6th Ed'n 1994, at p. 198): "A kind of Byzantine system has emerged", which they explain in four variations. These are: a) the original consultation procedure; b) the '86 SEA 'co-operation procedure'; c) the '92 TEU procedure; and d) the '86 SEA 'assent procedure'.

Until the new procedures, the European Parliament (under a)) had only to be consulted, which even the European Court of Justice described as no more than 'an essential formality'. Now, under the new procedures, the EP has a kind of qualified veto. Byzantine machinations cannot be legibly transcribed on to a shirt cuff; but the effect of the EP's new status goes some way to convert a rubber-stamp into a potential printing-press of legislation.

For the Commission remains the main instigator of legislation, and the Council the main political authority; but the EP has at the least the power to delay EU legislation, and to propose amendments, before a 'common position' adopted (by qualified majority) in the Council can be proceeded upon. Out of powers to propose and debate amendments and to ensure those proposals are listened to an effective Parliamentary process can grow.

The new procedures are extraordinarily complex – the kind of complexity that results from the ingenuity of civil servants reconciling the practically irreconcilable. Such complexities do not make for expedition or efficiency. But the trend is clear: the EP is moving (by whatever slow degrees) towards a position of decision-making equality in an European triumvirate of Council, Commission and Euro-Parliament.

The political moral is also clear. If the EU is to develop as a confederation of nation-states unified by a convergence of economic interests (rather than a federated union imposed by a supposedly unified political will which makes covert use of economic manipulation) then it is to the mediation of a democratically sensitive Euro-Parliament that the achievement of this ambition will be attributable. For it is to the weakness of the European Parliament hitherto that the anti-democratic tendencies of the EU are to be attributed. The strategic example is in the field of economic policy. So those who object to the economic implosion of EU policies that threatens national identities should be developing political institutions to counteract them.

A combination of uncontrolled governments with bankers responsible to no political authority has resulted in a caucus of econocrats who feel no need to take electorates with them. A political decision is being taken to take economic management wholly out with the control of politicians.

And this political decision is itself being taken outside the democratic process.

EMU is being imposed on the publics of the member-states without their peoples' having explained to them the foreseeable consequences of economic uniformity that is imposed by an European Central Bank created for the express purpose of ignoring political pressures in the interest of low inflation and price stability.

If your government invites an economic computer to rule you, you should at least be warned that unemployment, industrial decline and standard of living falls will be the inevitable consequences of your economic failures. Not of course that it will turn out for you quite that way, or not for a goodly time to start with. Instead a complex, expensive, unworkable and unfair system of subsidies and featherbeds (like the Common Agricultural Policy) will be developed to conceal the initial conceptual fault.

The point here is not, of course, that a policy which sets out to ensure that the blind economic forces unleashed by European competition should systematically override European social policies is necessarily indefensible, perhaps indeed (as the failure of Russian Communism proved) inevitable. For it may be that in the end social policies that ignore economic imperatives germinate within them the seeds of their inevitable destruction.

What is wholly politically indefensible, however, is the placing of such a fundamental policy choice out with the political process. It may result in making the EU (or the most substantial parts of it) more competitive both in world markets and within the EU for the benefit of its consumers. But all this matters not to the democrat's argument. For using economic laws to preempt choice is to relieve politicians of their fundamental responsibilities and to erect barricades against public opinion.

For such manipulation of its peoples the EU has no mandate. It is dangerous to political and social stability; it is an arrogant take-over of its citizens' rights; and it is benevolent dictatorship by the back door. The hidden premises of taking economic policy out of the political process are that politicians are not to be trusted and that the public cannot – and cannot be educated to – take rational decisions. That way social chaos, if not madness, lies. The long-term result can only be suffering, disillusion and possibly the break-up of the European Union.

For there will always be losers who can justifiably complain that vast decisions were smugly taken over their heads – and indeed over the heads of all the EU's citizens.

There is an obvious parallel in this attitude to EU decision-making with New Labour's policy of removing the Bank of England from British Parliamentary control – presumably indeed an intended convergence with EU policy; and a less obvious parallel with the government's attempt to take constitutional reform (even before it has formulated its own overall scheme) out of the field of political debate. Neither policy would have been attempted had not the British Parliament not shown signs of terminal weakness, and if the government had not anyway considered itself beyond the restraints of public debate. It will be found that the Lords' possible contributions to both have themes in common.

Up to the present the Lords' European Communities Committee with its sub-committees has been dealing with European legislation ahead of its implementation by the EU institutions. Through the sub-committees it has covered EU legislation across the board by reference to general subject headings. This is a prelegislative function. It is also a policy-making function and forms the subject of Parliamentary debate. In fact debate is an essential prerequisite to prelegislative scrutiny and forms part of a seamless process of policy formation.

In the case of European legislation this process is the limit of Parliamentary involvement; for so far Westminster (like other Community-member parliaments) has no direct say in the EU legislative function. An anti-democratic feature, maybe – but there it is. But for those interested in extending the prelegislative function of Westminster, the House of Lords' treatment of EU legislation is the only show in town. And it is capable of extension into all the areas in which the Lords are competent to develop a prelegislative function. The examination by subject-matter rather than by reference to government departments (as in Commons' Select Committees) gives more freedom to prelegislative debate to cross departmental boundaries and is certainly appropriate to committees charged with medium-term policy discussion and sometimes formulation.

The key example selected of the European Central Bank raises immediately a question for the Lords' functions recommended here.

It has been stated that the Commons should retain long-established and hard-won control of government finance and taxation and of day-to-day policy. Should this mean that discussion of EU financial policy – for example the anti-

174

democratic position of the European Central Bank – be outside the Lords' brief? Not in the scenario being considered here, for two reasons.

First: the Lords have accumulated expertise in European Affairs. Their current sub-committees already cover finance among the whole range of Euroaffairs. Second the difference in scope of the two Houses is seen as the immediate (for the Commons) versus the medium-term (for the Lords). Up till now preparatory policy work has been the jealously guarded prerogative of Whitehall. But there is no good reason for this Civil Service monopoly. There are just the two old excuses which now should be done away.

The first excuse has been governments' (and Whitehall's) anti-democratic liking to keep information to themselves, often by abusing for their purpose the names of national security and the public interest and so forth. This the Freedom of Information legislation newly promised (for 1998/9) should largely make a thing of the past. But modernisation is now the government's figurehead. The key is the people's participation in opinion-forming. An essential prerequisite is fully informed Parliamentary debate at the prelegislative stage.

The second excuse has been the practical problem of making information – and only the proper information – available. Computer science has swept away this practical restriction.

So there is no longer a valid excuse for excluding Parliament from the policy-forming process. Moreover while the Commons should extend their committee system in the same prelegislative direction there is no reason for either House to have an exclusive on finance or any subject at that stage.

In fact, of course, the rivalry of the two Houses should also become a thing of the past (or at least something that can be handled on a basis of rational arguments on their merits instead of one House's credibility as against the other's) once the Lords are legitimised by a democratically acceptable route to membership. But credibility is a consideration that comes later on in our argument than the Lords' capabilities.

But the prelegislative stage is only the first hurdle (if the most significant new one) for the Lords' effective participation in government. The Lords should participate in the others too – including finance – from their special standpoint.

This is the second reason for including the Second Chamber in the process of government control as an integrated whole.

The Parliamentary function is (or should be) a single seamless process – from conception and debate, through advance publication of draft Bills (itself a procedure which Ann Taylor, as Leader of the Commons, has stated should be more used) to legislation and its consequences. Legislation itself is in need of some sprucing up. Special Standing Committees, which after a Bill's second reading allow committee members to brief themselves, is another procedure for development.

While the Lords' contribution can, necessarily, get no further in EU scrutiny than the prelegislation stage, that does not mean either that their approach cannot be applied in prelegislation to other fields or that this application cannot slot into the full legislative process in those fields. The reverse is the case. The Lords' method of considering EU issues has advantages, for the prelegislative stage, over Parliamentary procedures over a broad canvas; and to adopt it would prepare Parliamentarians for the full legislative process where it is to take place in Westminster (rather than only through EU institutions).

This is not the place to consider how such procedures might relate to the Commons' Departmental Select Committees. These are restricted in practical scope by adversarial politics, as we have seen. It is not easy to look beyond efficient use of allocated funds and administrative abuses when nearly all questions of policy are preempted by party politics. This practical limitation, indeed, is the overriding reason for reserving Parliament's input into medium-term policy and strategic planning mainly for the Upper Chamber.

The Commons is a party bear-garden. There is no way that its Select Committees can keep down the decibels when policy issues are under discussion. But that is no excuse for Parliament's not providing itself with a forum where policy can be discussed with continuity, good briefing, public participation and in a reasonable if not an altogether non-adversarial manner.

There are good reasons why the Lords might provide such a forum. By history, tradition and taste they have been insulated from the daily hurly-burly.

The Lords have a deep fund of experience and expertise. Their committees operate by subject matter. That means they cross (or could cross) departmental boundaries, to allow both for co-ordination and lateral thinking. And the ECC with its subcommittees covers the entire field of EU legislation.

This prompts two further thoughts, one lateral, the other vertical.

Under this subsection f) we have moved into this nexus of questions: whether the Lords' working methods, management, authority and support suit their current and possible extra work. We took their EU work as the key example for this section.

The conclusion so far is that their EU work covers with a very fair degree of success EU prelegislative work across the board. No doubt it could be improved with more resources, research help and so forth. Moreover the Lords' level of authority – their political clout needed to win them attention – is muffled by their electoral illegitimacy. But there is a workable system in being for all EU legislation. The question therefore is how it might be developed.

The answer is – both laterally and vertically, where the Lords have a legislative function, as in EU matters they do not. Not only is the Lords' EU example capable of extension laterally, at the prelegislative level, into other fields (for an obvious but not exclusive example, to human rights). It is capable of extension right on, in those other fields, through the legislative to the administrative scrutiny. Not only in fact to legislation but to departmental conduct (including departments' quangos).

It is in fact these two extensions that would give the Upper Chamber the medium-term policy-forming and monitoring role that is here envisaged for it.

It is worth noting that all this extra responsibility could, in theory, be taken on by the Lords without major structural changes to their composition. No doubt politically such an enhanced role would not be allowed them by either government or Commons (who have anyway their own axes to grind). But subject to weight of work divided among the most competent peers and to appropriate support, this work they could do and without major constitutional change. In fact it was by gradual and generally unperceived accretion – without fanfares and grand reforms – that the Lords won for themselves their EU prelegislative brief in the first place.

However we leave f) with three matters which the House of Lords could not solve by itself, even if it had the support of government and Commons.

The Lords cannot give themselves the electoral legitimacy necessary to accord public confidence to their functions, especially as constitutional guardians – whatever their scope and competence. Nor can they take any part in the restructure of Parliament required by devolution and the formation – however unclear its effects – of the Scottish and Welsh Parliaments. Nor can they arrange on their own for an acceptable Westminster input into the European Parliament; for it is not geared to interplay with national parliaments. Finally it is not clear whether their traditional function as constitutional guardians will be sufficiently bolstered by electoral legitimacy or whether a (minimum) increase in powers will also be advisable.

These unsolved problems far outstrip in importance the removal of the hereditary peers from the House (which is the sum total of New Labour's thinking to date on Lords' reform). It is these problems that justify structural changes to the House of Lords.

g) The financial implications of the issues raised in a) to f) bring into into play the vexed question of Whitehall's monopoly of expertise and information.

Two reasons have been suggested why the government should no longer retain so much public information in its bosom. First the public in general and particularly Parliament on its behalf have a right to it, except insofar as the public would genuinely be harmed by its disclosure and private rights are not infringed. Moreover the public is now in the mood to exercise its right. Second the modern methods of information-handling are now certainly sufficiently sophisticated to allow effective chinese walls between what should and what should not be disclosed.

Furthermore there have long been calls for a Department of the Opposition – that is to say, a department of civil servants whose duty is to keep the Opposition updated on government policy and affairs. In my opinion this idea is good – and its implementation long overdue – but insufficient. Parliamentarians should, in the public interest, have available what the government has. Otherwise equality of debate and fair scrutiny of government policy and administration is simply not possible. Besides there is no good reason why such information should not be publicly available. It is not properly government's preserve. The government has already promised a Freedom of Information Bill for the 1998/9 session. For the purpose of Parliamentarians that information should not only be made available but analysed, as for government, also.

These considerations invite the thought that government should share with Parliament and the public their public information and its handling, except insofar as circulation of that information outside government is harmful to the public. It is further suggested that Parliament should have the same assistance as government has in ordering that information for policy-making and policy-monitoring, so that Parliamentarians can debate with government on even terms.

The corollary of these suggestions is a great deal of hard work for civil servants during a transitional information-ordering phase. That would be a considerable public expense, and need not last long. Anyhow in the interest of good government it is long overdue. The continuing allocation of civil service time to Parliamentarians is likely to attract opposition on two fronts.

The Treasury on one hand will see this suggestion as causing unnecessary duplication (government has difficulty in seeing why the electorate cannot leave everything cosily to government). And parties on the other will complain about the relative allocations of time and facilities both between each other and between them together as against individual Parliamentarians and indeed members of the public, who will demand to be included in this information bonanza and the facilities that go with it. Moreover there will be rivalry at first between the Commons and Lords, particularly at the start when the scope of their responsibilities *vis-à-vis* each other is being settled. But these are little difficulties of reorganisation, though much fuss will be made about them.

The challenge is much less great than appears. Research and secretarial help (which all Parliamentarians could do with much more of) does mean their being relieved of the need to understand and use the new information-handling methods for themselves. When information is properly ordered and available, much of what civil servants could do for Parliamentarians, Parliamentarians can do as well for themselves.

In fact civil servants are finding an ever-decreasing need for their information-gathering services. One result of transfer of civil servants to Parliamentarians should be an up-grade of civil servants' work from gathering (and creating) information to the using of it. The conclusion is that there will be transitional expense during an operation essential to government anyway, whose marginal addition for Parliamentary and public facilities will turn out less than anticipated if the system is from the start set up to accommodate it.

Even duplication of civil servants can be limited by their flexible allocation between government on one hand and Parliamentarians on the other. For the same skills will be required for both.

Much will be made of the practical difficulties, which indeed will in the transition not be inconsiderable. If as probable government has been long engaged in developing systems for information-handling, but which do not accommodate the chinese walls (now easy enough to build in) that information shared between government, Parliament and the public will require, the expense of reorganisation will be exaggerated.

But the resistance to an information and research service for Parliament (and later probably the public) will not be from the practicalities or the expense but from a lack of political will. Government will not be quick to release funds to cut rods for its own back. The Commons, to start with, be may more afraid of an Upper House with a broad function than delighted with an information /research system in which the Commons will share. But in the long run if not in the short, the public will require it for the sake of efficient democracy; and the

Commons will profit thereby.

So we leave the subject with the thought: what the Lords need both for their present scope and for any broadening of it will come sometime anyhow. Moreover if the Lords demand it the Commons will support the proposal in order not to be second in the queue. So nobody should be put off by government's defence – the one that always greets any inconvenient change – that it is all too difficult, or failing that, too expensive. Parliament has only to demand the tools for the job, to get them. And practicalities shall not impede reform leading to a Parliament that can represent the people to government on equal terms.

h) 'A Parliament that can represent the people to government on equal terms' might be the bull's-eye for the crucial round of constitutional reforms under way. Earlier reasons were given against abolition of the Upper Chamber and against one based on wholly different principles from the one we have. Above all a new animal would be one that the public could not vote for with any genuine understanding of the new balance which such an innovation would introduce. Government is too powerful already, as it is. During the transition to a wholly new dispensation (even if finally it bedded down happily) government would be wholly out of control.

This consideration applies both to abolition and to a new Second Chamber based on a written constitution supported by a Supreme Court and which, presumably, divorced the executive from the legislature, on US lines. The first would soon lead to the other anyhow. The Commons would soon find it could not shoulder the Lords' work as well as its own.

There are many practical objections to 'the separation of powers' that was adopted as the guiding star by the Founding Fathers of the American Revolution. Such a constitution founds, in William Hague's words, 'a rule of lawyers in place of a rule of law'. It does not make for open government but for endless games of bluff between legislature and executive. It takes the most gifted and senior lawyers out of the legislative process. But above all to be remembered is the aim of the concept – to control the executive in the name of democracy and the law. For this purpose a balance was sought of executive, legislature and supreme court whose purpose was to keep the other two to a written document, the very interpretation of which, against new political backgrounds, includes a legislative function – and, in so far as executive action necessitates the formulation of policy and *vice versa*, an executive function also.

The US balance is based on the necessary antagonism of different functions and interests in a democracy; but it is artificial. For there is no true dividing line between the three functions. Good government is a seamless robe and best carried through in partnership. British judges, too, who maintain that they are not changing the law when they are 'developing' it are deceiving at least themselves.

The scope of judicial review and the law of negligence, together with the potential within the common law for a law of privacy (see the 'lost case', *Morris v Beardmore*) – all are major changes made by judges to the law since World War Two.

It is no argument against this conclusion that the legislature (almost entirely at the instigation of government) makes law also (and much more of it). But what is essential is that the executive should not make law on its own, uncontrolled by an effective legislature.

Nor is it practicable either in US or anywhere else to keep the executive away from legislation. For an executive has policies most of which require (outside dictatorships) legislation. Finally, by informed debate and party opposition, the legislature (here or in any other democracy) imposes limitations on the executive by forcing the executive to think through the practical and financial consequences of its policies.

The 'separation of powers' is a fiction that works through beneficial interaction of *partly* independent functions. Any attempt, however, to keep the three altogether apart impoverishes the system. At Question Time ministers meet the legislature regularly and face to face. The legislature needs the guidance of ministers and their supporting caste of public servants. And the legislature benefits in our system from the advice and influence of our senior judges.

Finally a written constitution creates a mini-legislature outside the democratic process when judges need to 'interpret ' it to bring it up to date with social and political needs. Otherwise a written constitution becomes a strait-jacket.

Accordingly this book has proceeded from what we have to what we might easily have before considering draconian reform. The underlying premise has been that the excessive strength of government requires a strengthening of Parliament through better use of an asset already in place – the House of Lords. This premise has led to a three-step investigation: what does it do, what as it is could it do – and what could it do with structural reform?

We have seen how current membership and procedures could be developed to cope with all the constitutional requirements of an Upper Chamber, *except* a) giving the Lords electoral legitimacy (the necessary but not necessarily sufficient counterweight to elected government), b) devolution and c) Westminster's interaction with the EU and its Parliament. And we left open whether electoral legitimacy would, on its own, together with the powers the Lords already have, allow them to exercise all the functions considered for them.

The changes to be considered then rule out both abolition and structural changes beyond those needed to satisfy those additional goals that internal reorganisation of the Lords cannot achieve.

It may seem late in the day to be considering electoral legitimacy, which has plainly been Labour's primary motive for Lords' reform. But ruling out bogus reasons based upon fashionable ignorance about what the Lords can and could do is a prerequisite to avoiding waste. The House of Lords is an asset, and an essential one, to be better used. The fact that successive governments and generations of MPs have chosen for their own greater glory to ignore it is no reason to deprive the people of it. For government is outwith Parliamentary control; and the House of Commons which could and should have been putting this right bears the blame – not the House of Lords which could not.

But the Lords lack of credibility is a compelling reason for electoral change, provided that is geared to enabling the Upper Chamber to do what otherwise it could not, but should, do and not geared to perpetuating successive governments' and Commons' failure out of self-interest to rebalance the wheels of our Parliamentary democracy.

Conversely focus on specific needs helps to indicate how electoral change should be carried through. In this case the overriding need is to find means of enabling the Upper Chamber to achieve its potential and then to add to it those functions which in its current state it could in no way carry out.

Thereby for the first time the issue of the Lords' powers is directly raised. It is not at once clear whether electoral legitimacy would be enough to enable the Upper House to achieve. From now on we shall be ever more in unknown territory. But a preliminary look at the powers of the Upper Chamber is now appropriate.

The approach to reform so far adopted would encourage as little change as necessary. In the case of the Lords' powers there is an additional need for conservative caution – the Commons' fears.

3. PASTURES NEW

Sovereignty does not belong to the Commons and never has. The confidence in their self-sufficient infallibility is a mirage. They are responsible to the people not only at elections but during their term as MPs. Their knee-jerk fear of losing authority if the Upper Chamber gains it is of very secondary importance to Parliament's duty of good government. Moreover their pretensions to power are refuted by their systematic subordination to government.

But in the proposals so far their fears would be unfounded. For the extended function suggested for the Second Chamber is one that Parliament has not exercised. It does not trespass either on the Commons' holds (such as they are) on the government purse strings and the scrutiny of current government policy. Besides, a more effective Upper Chamber redounds to the prestige of Parliament as a whole, especially if the Commons cooperate with their brother House and indeed share in the benefit of its new support system.

Nevertheless an increase in the Lords' powers simultaneous with the ensuring of their electoral legitimacy might be an obstacle to a settlement. Is it necessary?

The Lords can at the moment throw out subordinate legislation and hold up Commons' primary legislation for up to a year. Do they need extra powers?

With regard to current government policy the Lords' primary function is to ensure that Commons' legislation is properly thought through. If the Lords are not to have a power to throw it out, then their powers of argument backed by a threat of inconvenient delay has up to now often been enough to encourage government second thoughts. Negotiations such as this are the stuff of everyday politics. It is far from obvious that the Lords need a big stick; or that harmonious interplay between the two Houses would be furthered if they did.

The counter-argument stems from the length of a Parliament. Whatever the merits and demerits of government by manifesto, a manifesto gets increasingly stale as time goes by; and after mid-term (certainly, by the time of the fourth annual Queen's Speech) it is pretty well out of date.

But what in any case are the available alternatives? The present government favours referendums, which, together with an election manifesto, are being used virtually to bypass Parliament altogether. But referendums can be abused no less than manifestos. Both can preempt debate by fixing the formulation and evading practicalities and available alternatives. It was long ago settled under Gladstone (see in Part I) that the Upper House cannot force a general election. It was probably settled at the same time that after full debate (whenever that is deemed to have happened) the Upper House must eventually let through a Commons Bill, certainly unless a constitutional Bill (however that is to be defined). That is why the 1911 Parliament Act introduced the two-year delay rule.

Better debate earlier, better briefed Parliamentarians, maybe an independent Referendums Commission prescribing rules both for preliminary debate and for conduct of referendum campaigns – all these palliatives can and should be introduced. But the question remains whether the 1911 Parliament Act rather than the Act of 1949 got the balance right? The Home Report of 1978 proposed a return to the original two years. Others have supported this proposal. With the other improvements to Parliament's workings here proposed is an increase to two years imperative?

This is a matter of fine political judgment that will be better honed by experience. A right balance might well be found eventually to be this: to bring down the maximum length of a Parliament from five years to four and to keep the Lords' delaying power at one year, except perhaps for constitutional Bills when the power might be extended to two years.

Constitutional Bills abound and as devolution progresses will continue. But their definition will cause lawyers many head-aches and will lead to arcane debate. The effect on relations between the Houses of a 'legitimate' Upper House cannot be predicted. All might be sweetness and light. Or it might not. Better to defer considering the extension of the Lords' delaying power until we know.

There is another reason for this. Some Labour politicians are anxious to abolish the Lords' power (though seldom used) to throw out subordinate legislation. But the Parliamentary scrutiny of this huge volume of legislative paper (including of course EU legislation and annually increasing) which affects everybody's everyday lives is already overborne by Parliamentarians' overwork. Some of the suggestions made here are partly designed to reduce this backlog. It will be easier to leave the Upper House its powers on subordinate legislation if their delaying power is likewise left, at least generally, untouched.

There are other constitutional issues in the wings that this book seeks to avoid or at least defer to some future date when the effects of the current round of constitutional changes (huge enough) can be seen. The most important (or, if only a codification is then intended the only,) issue is that of a written constitution.

The notion of a written constitution seems best kept in reserve. Otherwise until the current round of constitutionalising has died down, the danger is that writing it down would provoke unnecessary dog-fights about what it is. Its composition should be merely a codification – an elucidation of what is. But in practice the drafting would throw up thorny political issues without a practical context to test them against. Uncertainty would then invite the raising of fresh issues generally thought settled. So the last time to try for a written constitution is a period of substantive reform such as is at present under way. Stability first, drafting after – if in fact a written constitution is even thought generally desirable.

In fact the practical results of trying for one would probably be an increase in factious and dogmatic arguments and the loss of the most senior judges to the

Parliamentary process by their being hived off to some kind of special constitutional court.

Similar arguments apply against artificial entrenchment of whatever reforms are now agreed upon (or forced through). Entrenchment is probably impossible anyway. The one axiom of Parliamentary government that is generally not impugned is the principle that no Parliament can bind its successor. An argument is fashionable at present however that Parliament might be able to prescribe how a successor might change a law of this Parliament. But in logic this seems fallacious. If a subsequent Parliament can change the substance of a predecessor's legislation this must include the formalities under which such legislation can be changed.

More to the point, however, is the doubt whether entrenchment is even desirable. Public boredom with constitutinalising lawyers and dogmatic politicians is quite as strong a muzzle on unnecessary change as dubious legal safeguards. On the other hand an artificial block on constitutional change seen by a good majority as necessary – where eg only a required two-thirds Commons' majority would achieve it – a block such as this could easily become a harmful impediment to the normal democratic process. In this case it would amount to the current government's attempt to preempt improvements by any subsequent government.

By contrast the Lords should not swallow the suggestion that what goes into a manifesto cannot be challenged for practicability and as the best solution of any known problem. Governments, especially towards the end of a Parliament can and will justify new legislation on grounds of changed circumstances.

A corollary is that a manifesto commitment (not in a Money Bill), that is drafted before a party is in government and before it is worked through in detail and the circumstances known, is as such subject to challenge, at a Bill's second reading or at any other time, by a revising chamber with the requisite electoral authority. The Salisbury Doctrine should be seen as a transitional compromise (as the 1911 Parliament Act was itself intended to be) pending the initiation of an Upper House with the requisite authority and committee structures to do its job.

In sketching a scenario that could give the Upper House electoral legitimacy and allow for interaction with both devolved Parliaments and the EU institutions, we have made fair progress by proceeding by elimination. That has indeed been a guiding principle – to change only what needs it. We have found that much improvement to the Lords' output could be made simply by wholly revamping their Committee structures to make a broadbased policymaking and monitoring organ, with much overdue technical support.

On top of that we have eliminated, for this round of reforms at any rate, a written constitution and a constitutional (or 'Supreme') court. We have recommended that the Lords' powers in general (but in particular both of delaying legislation and of throwing out subordinate legislation) be left mainly unchanged, at least until the impact of more urgent reforms can be assessed.

But we have added riders which might be taken into account in a later round of reforms – and which indeed would not require any further changes to the structure of the Lords. If later on the one year delaying power is thought to give the Upper Chamber insufficient control towards the end of a Parliament, a better balance between the two Houses may be found to reside in 4-year Parliaments rather than returning to a two-year delaying power in 5-year Parliaments. This might leave open the possibility of two-year delay even in 4-year Parliaments in Bills substantially changing the constitution. That issue might depend on the extent to which more effective debate combines with better managed referendums.

If subsequently a distinction were to be made, in a Bill's delay between constitutional Bills and others, the House of Lords Appellate Committee would of course have the final say on whether a particular Bill was or was not a 'Constitutional Bill' within the meaning of the ruling statute. But this question should be handled exclusively as interpretation of statute – the *effect* of the Bill in the light of the definition in statute of a 'Constitutional Bill'. Such an issue can easily be handled without turning the Appellate Committee into a Constitutional ('Supreme') Court.

'Interpreting' a written constitution is an altogether different exercise, in which the creation of judge-made law is inevitable – and out with Parliament – as social conditions change.

This point is emphasised because an important consideration in retaining the Lords' structure as near as may be to what it now is is to retain the senior judges in Parliament at the policy-making stages of discussion.

For by contrast with their ruling as an Appellate Committee about the 'Constitutional' status of a particular Bill, the law lords should retain a wholly different function during the the legislative process during which the ruling statute is itself made into law. For this statute is the one that says what should constitute a Constitutional Bill. That question, in Parliament, is something on which the senior judges plainly should have a say, before they end up as an Appellate Court applying the ruling statute to particular Bills.

Elsewhere we criticise the US notion of 'separation of powers' as artificial and misleading, and as keeping the best legal minds out of the (formal) legislative procedure. More practical is a separation of functions – legislative and judicial – in both of which the senior judges should have their roles. Much better that than have the judges legislate (out with Parliament and the democratic process) in a 'Supreme Court' later, under the guise of 'interpretation'.

Fully informed debate, on the lines suggested here, especially if supported by judicious use of referendums properly supervised under agreed rules monitored by an independent authority, will take much of the heat out of arguments between the two Houses in any event. What goes in election manifestos, in Bills (in either House), and in referendums will be seen as part of the single process of Parliamentary government, which itself it is the joint duty of the two Houses to keep in working order.

After these eliminations it is easier to see a path ahead for the current reforms. The scope of the Upper Chamber is to be broadened by extension from pockets of activity (the European Communities Committee, the Science and Technology Committee, various *ad hoc* committees) into general policy scrutiny over the whole field of government business. In particular the prelegislative function of the ECC is to be applied that widely (as indeed it is already through subcommittees of the ECC right across EU policy and legislation). The purpose of this reform is to be the strengthening of an arm of Parliament to joust with government on policy issues as an equally informed partner in government. Its effect should be to bring public influence to bear at early stages of government thinking and continually (not just in election campaigns).

But the scope of the Upper House should not be confined to prelegislation. In keeping with its current legislative function it should continue in the lawmaking process from conception through legislation to administration.

Avoidance of duplication with the Commons' functions can be assured by a medium-term perspective for its main efforts (except as a revising Chamber) and by the Second Chamber's sidestepping current issues of finance and central government programmes.

The current membership of the Lords has been found suitable for this wide-ranging function. But membership could be profitably broadened to take account of our increasingly pluralistic society. And the Lords would need support staff and a share in government's information machine for this extended function.

Nevertheless thus far the Lords' track record and the normal discretion of Parliament to order its own affairs, together with necessary government support for the improving of government, would have allowed progress without institutional reform.

But this plan was found to be incomplete for three reasons. It takes no account of the Lords' longstanding electoral illegitimacy, which weakens most of all the Second Chamber's traditional function as constitutional guardian. To add to that are two new and urgent fields of endeavour for Westminster to take possession of – devolution and the EU. Westminster is in danger of being bypassed both below and above – by the new national and regional Parliaments and by EU institutions as well.

For these three key issues of our Parliamentary democracy (and only these three), structural reform of the Upper Chamber seems imperative and urgent. The next question is how best to secure it.

At this point we may be said to at the border between Step 3 and Step 4 of our argument. Some light has been shone on what is wrong and we have some ideas of how to fix it. But the best (and most economical) way is still to find.

The deepest analysis – in truth the only one that looks at Parliament in the round – is the Bryce Report (Cd 9038: HL Accounts and Papers, vol X, 1918). Part II of this book was intended to explain the almost unbelievable enigma why neither it nor anything like it has ever been in any way applied in the ensuing 80 years.

Bryce puts the issue fair and square. There could be no question of the Second Chamber reasserting its 'coequal rights' with the Commons that had been the basis of the 1688 settlement. The Second Chamber must be no rival of the Commons, 'in particular it should not have the power of making or unmaking Ministries or enjoy equal rights in dealing with finance'. Its function must be to 'seek the mind and views of the nation as a whole' and in so doing 'recognise its full responsibility to the people, not setting itself to oppose the people's will but only to comprehend and give effect to that will when adequately expressed… [and] to enlighten and influence the people through its debates… [being] recognised [by them] as qualified to require the reconsideration of important measures on which their opinion had not been fully ascertained'.

Hidden within this is the extreme difficulty of defining a useful identity for the Lords as the Commons junior partner, on one hand, but as the Commons minder on the other. For once history (for Lord Bryce and for us) was in the way. We are seeking to systematise a true half-revolution – a standing of history on its head. For the junior partner has become the senior partner; and not even the granting of electoral legitimacy to the Upper Chamber must be seen to try to turn the wheel back full circle. To quote Bryce again: 'The Great Council of the Nation from which the House of Lords directly descends, the House of Commons having been added to it in the thirteenth century, is the oldest and most venerable of all British institutions, reaching back beyond the Norman Conquest and beyond King Alfred into the shadowy realms of Teutonic antiquity.' Now, not just the Lords but Parliament faces a crisis of identity.

In 1998, over three hundred years after the last Glorious Revolution, we are at the point of drawing a marker at the end of this slow turn, in time for the new millennium.

This book could be said to be one attempt to update the Bryce Report in the modern context. Maybe some sketch has already emerged. Before stepping out from Bryce into the final stretch, we remember his instructions.

The Second Chamber was to have a fourfold remit:

a) the examination and revision of Commons' Bills, especially when the Commons is forced to legislate under time pressure;

b) the initiation of (comparatively) non-controversial Bills (which makes the Commons' job the easier if what comes to them from the Lords comes fully discussed and put into a well-considered shape);

c) so much delaying power (and no more) … as may be needed [for] the opinion of the nation to be adequately expressed;

d) full and free discussion of large and important questions (such as those of foreign policy)… especially useful, Bryce thought, in an Assembly whose debate and divisions do not involve the fate of the Executive Government.

Elsewhere, in discussing composition, Bryce expanded on d). The Second Chamber must be competent in a whole string of policy and governmental areas – in public work (Parliamentary and local government and in the Civil Service and the Forces), in judicial work, in agriculture, commerce and industry, in finance and education, and in foreign affairs. We have taken the European Union as a sub-set of foreign affairs; then shown how the Lords over the last quarter-century have developed in sub-committees of its European Communities Committee an overview in EU affairs that surveys Bryce's whole canvas. As a logical extension of the Lords' EU overview, we have also sketched how a similar concept could apply to their Parliamentary functions, not just in EU matters but in all British government affairs from policy-making right through legislation to implementation and administration.

One motive for this approach has been the search for an economical solution, as Step 4 requires. But 'economy' means more than keeping costs down. The very word means 'governing the House'. It means finding a way for it to work smoothly with the minimum of waste, fuss and upheaval. Above all it means prescribing a workable and stable system of operation. House of Lords reform has traditionally been expressed in terms of composition, function and powers. But in truth there is a fourth requirement greater than these – the system of their interlocking.

We have seen how the Lords as they are could, with reasonable assistance and the logical development of what they already do, cope with all but three issues, none of their making – electoral illegitimacy, devolution and Europe. In fact these have a crucial factor in common – the Second's Chamber's interlock with three other sets of Chambers, with the Commons, with the devolved Parliaments and with the European Union institutions (in particular the European Parliament). It is fashionable fallacy (especially among MPs) to think of electoral legitimacy solely in terms of public election. If that was all there was to it, MPs would be in generally greater esteem (and also less touchy about a new Second Chamber which might act with greater authority and effectiveness).

Lord Bryce (as usual) had it right: a Parliamentary Chamber wins its legitimacy by doing well a job seen by the people as necessary. That requires consensus on a number of matters. Probably no such consensus is possible without a fair electoral start. But after that the Second Chamber must be seen to have the people, the brief and the powers to do the job, and then to be doing it.

On that analysis the Lords as we have them have been disqualified before the starter's pistol. But assuming a true new start (and a fair elective process) their performance in the race is what will fulfil their promise. They have already shown how well they can run, disqualified or not. But it is for that very reason that just electing them fairly will not help them run better. Apart from necessary help and logical development, what they need, after a sensible elective system, is a credible scheme within which to fit.

Crucial as all have seen is their relationship with the Commons. Any scheme which threatens the Commons' primary responsibility in managing the nation's current finances and the making and unmaking of ministries (in Bryce's formulation) is and should be consigned to the waste-paper basket. Enshrined in section 6 of the 1911 Parliament Act, is this noble catch-all: 'Nothing in this Act shall diminish or qualify the existing rights and privileges of the House of Commons.' Moreover the Commons Resolutions of 1671 and 1678 (ie even before the Glorious Revolution) specify: 'In all aids given to the King by the Commons, the rate or tax ought not to be altered by the Lords'; and 'All aid and supplies, and aids to his Majesty in Parliament, are the sole gift of the Commons…ought to begin in the Commons and ought not to be changed or altered by the House of Lords.'

The attempt by the Lords to throw out Lloyd-George's budget was disastrous for the Lords. By the same token any attempt to bring a government to a standstill or eject it would bring a swift and annihilating nemesis. But any suggestion of interference with the Commons' rights in these two regards, would, I believe, be worse than merely futile: it would rob the people of a Second Chamber with other functions in their way no less crucial to good government than the Commons'. We have now seen what those functions might be (perhaps have been evolving on the paradigm of the Lords' European Committees).

On the other hand the Commons' fears that electoral respectability would lead the Lords into impasse with the Commons are equally misplaced. No reasonable proposal would elect the Second Chamber for that purpose. The Lords could not and should not contemplate interference with the Commons' core functions. Any suggestion that they might would not survive five minutes of the public's fiery breath.

A corollary of this is the irrelevance to British politics of some versions of the 'senatorial' function of a renewed Second Chamber. The prospect of a government's finance being hamstrung by an Upper Chamber revolt on some Capitol-on-Thames is a mirage.

Perhaps the elaborate mediation proposals in both Bryce and among others the 1978 Home Report have tended unwittingly to foster this misconception in some Parliamentarians. Proposals for elaborate Joint Committees of Both Houses to cope with deadlock, by suggesting that the Lords might try to wrest governmental control from the Commons, draw attention away from what Joint Committees have often done and should do more, that is, to nurture cooperation between the Houses and to preeempt damaging wrangles that lead to inefficiencies. Joint Committees of the Houses should be geared to interlock, not deadlock, between the Houses.

The two-year delaying power for the Lords written into the 1911 Parliament Act certainly should always give enough time for the nation to think. But Parliament has to lead and respond to the nation's thinking – and be set up to do so. Perhaps the partisan spirit of the 1949 Act is to be deplored and reversed for an authoritative Second Chamber (in constitutional Bills at least). Maybe it might have a right to demand a referendum, properly combined with independently supervised public debate, on defined types of issue (maybe constitutional issues). But any suggestion of a return to the 'co-equality' (such as it ever was) of Lords and Commons of 1688 is best rubbished from the start of any argument for the sake of more constructive discussions of reform.

We are now ready to summarise this long discussion which has looked at the peers in operation with a view to what they do, could do and without structural reform cannot do.

The Lords' resources are impressive and capable of development. This would entail an extended committee system to treat Parliamentary scrutiny of government as a single organic process from policy formulation right through legislation to execution and administration. It would also entail a much improved support system for Parliamentarians in terms of research, secretarial and civil service help, to enable Parliament to argue on equal terms with government.

But such a reorganisation would not afford the Second Chamber the requisite electoral legitimacy; and it would be insufficient to cope with Parliament's interlock with new institutions that are already becoming part of our constitution, in the EU and in consequence of devolution. These three problems remain before us.

But if we can develop the Lords' own proven skills and extend their use, and if we can implement a scheme which covers these three outlying areas, no draconian changes to the Second Chamber are either necessary or desirable.

A useful corollary of this conclusion is a further conclusion that the Lords' powers can be left pretty much as they are and can be used to define the Second Chamber's role as 'constitutional guardians'. Their right to prevent extension of a Parliament beyond five years (or beyond four years if this were later found advisable), their delaying powers (unless perhaps extended to two years for 'Constitutional Bills') and their right to throw out subsidiary legislation can and should be left unchanged.

A more practical approach to the Lords' 'guardianship' is to draw them into an extended legislative partnership with the Commons, by maturing a committee system already present in embryo. This leaves the Commons' traditional functions equally undisturbed but results in balance restored of Parliament as a whole with government. This way conflict with the Commons is avoided in the interest of more thorough influence by the public on government.

The British are comfortable with organic development of what they have to fit new circumstances, most of all because it leads to predictability and stability.

The difficulties of achieving a stable settlement have always been formidable. Technical ways of 'entrenching' constitutional legislation are probably ineffective, since no Parliament can be debarred from undoing the work of its predecessor. Nevertheless once a new settlement is in place public opinion is likely to refuse for a good while to reconsider it whatever it is, and even if it is generally unpopular or unsatisfactory.

Consequently change should be attempted only after the most sober attempts to weigh competing solutions and getting the people both to understand and choose. The worst solution (and the most unfair one) would be likely to be one ridden through by a popular government on snap votes of whatever kind, whether in an obedient Parliament and/or a simplistic referendum. Moreover such a solution would be in practice irreversible for a generation.

So what is to be arrived at is a consensus arising out of a fair balance of the imperatives of government, Parliamentary and specialist scrutiny and the public's right to decide *when the issues have been genuinely canvassed and defined.*

That cannot be achieved by a combination of slogans and slick media policy. Any attempt by government to reform Parliament without ensuring improved democratic control of government itself by Parliament would be a cynical abuse of popular power.

For it is just Parliament's failure to control over-mighty governments that is the underlying constitutional issue. The House of Lords' illegitimacy is both the direct result of its undemocratic composition and a major cause of Parliament's ineffectual control of government. If Parliament had been doing its job and governments had been properly answerable to it, there would be no sufficient reason for reform anyhow. If for the sake of momentary popular appeal the Labour Government were to abolish the hereditary peers, replace them with party nominees and leave the House of Commons unchanged, the public would have every reason to feel abused by government and once more let down by a weak Parliament.

The essence of the task is to find a structure for the revised Second Chamber that gives it legitimacy within an effective Parliament. But legitimacy walks on two legs, the functions of the Second Chamber and its composition.

In the current climate there is a mild paradox about: the House of Lords is more criticised for its composition than for its function or for the way it is carried out. There are two very different reasons for this, the simple one and the hidden one.

The simple reason was best expressed by Gilbert and Sullivan long ago: "The House of Lords did nothing in particular, and did it very well."

Its composition, mainly of hereditary peers with no special qualifications or mandate to govern, is plainly out of date; and it has been so (and awaiting reform) for a long time. The House of Lords has accordingly cut a low profile, except on a few carefully chosen occasions; and it has done dutifully and with becoming modesty what its interim status left it to do.

The hidden reason is that it has long suited very well not only governments of all complexions but also the House of Commons that the Lords' composition is suspect and its function modest. Governments do not like powerful criticism whether constructive or not, and the Commons dislike the thought of a Second Chamber which might control the government better than the Commons has been able to do.

The more the Commons have harboured a sneaking suspicion that they have carried out their function no better than indifferently well, and the more governments have enjoyed freewheeling through the Commons, the more it has suited them both to have a weak partner in government. A weak partner whom they could slight or ignore on apparently respectable democratic grounds has been even more desirable.

Accordingly it has been easier to think of ways to give the House of Lords a composition which would command respect than to define a function for it that would be attractive either to government or to the House of Commons. But it is neither the convenience of government nor of the House of Commons that is primarily in issue when the subject is democratic reform of Parliament. It is the people's interest in stable, effective and representative government that Parliamentary reform is meant to serve.

It is assumed – anything else would be beyond the range of political possibilities – that a renewed House of Lords must not inhibit or be in competition with the core functions of the House of Commons. What are these?

They are twofold, interrelated and central to the function of government.

The House of Commons is the organ to which the government of the day is answerable in respect of both major policy issues and sudden or day-to-day issues. This is regularly reflected by Questions, especially Prime Minister's Questions, and formalised in the convention that a minister can be censured formally by the House of Commons but not in the House of Lords (other than in its special judicial function). The House of Commons also has the monopoly of Money Bills. These twin powers are the taproot of the House of Commons' authority. They are also intended to ensure that the government of the day is answerable to the people.

If it is thought that the Commons is not in fact satisfactorily fulfilling its Parliamentary duties, it is probably by freeing these powers from the excessive government control through Whips' and party discipline that the Commons' proper influence is to be restored. It would not be right or practicable that House of Lords reform should have more than peripheral influence on the control of ministers or of Money Bills. It is probably an unarticulated fear that a Second Chamber with teeth might seek to encroach on the Commons' prerogative in these two functions that lies behind the Commons' preference (and tolerance) for a Second Chamber that resembles more a poodle than an alsatian.

There is no intention here of proposing for the Lords the right to censure ministers or to take part in Money Bills; but that does not mean that a Second Chamber should not be able in one way or another both to criticise what ministers do or invite them to explain it and to influence economic or financial policy. For that would result in denying it any effective constitutional role, and in leaving the House of Lords (and Parliament as a whole) pretty well where it is. Those who would deny a Second Chamber influence on ministers or their financial policies should prefer to have a reformed House of Commons and no Second Chamber at all.

Apart from its residual constitutional ('guardian') functions – principally in the judiciary, the prorogation of Parliament and the delay of some legislation – the House of Lords has by tradition been primarily concerned in debate of public issues and in non- (or less-) contentious legislation. Those concerned, in constitutional reform, to build on what we already have will look here first to find and develop its role.

The parallel with the Commons' role with the Lords' is obvious. But the Commons is more concerned with day-to-day issues and grievances – and, because of ministers answerable to it, with core issues of current government policy; and the Lords has been limited to the Commons' leavings. It is in rectifying this unsatisfactory interplay between the two Houses that some at least of the improvements in the performance of Parliament can and should be realised.

In the overheated House of Commons a day can seem a long time; in the sedate and gentlemanly Lords a year or more can seem but as yesterday. Much that Parliament should be concerned with and influencing falls between these two extremes of focal length. The Commons, with an eye on re-election in their constituencies, tend to be parochial, and the Lords, having no constituency some might say, out of date. Yet the Lords, because they are subject to continuing criticism, do seem to have made more effort to modernise their view than the Commons to broaden theirs; and hereditary peers have much benefited since 1958 from rubbing shoulders with life peers of varied distinction and experience.

We have seen how it is possible to find a way of bridging the gap between the immediate and the old-fashioned. Parliament in fact has no effective mechanism of continuing policy review. It leaves most of the thinking to the Civil Service and academics, to the newspaper heavies and to the writers of manifestos at election-time. Because politicians, especially in the Commons, are insufficiently interested, briefed and acquainted with major policy issues, they are unable to argue on equal terms with government on the public's behalf but the world is now too big a place to be seen from a kitchen window.

Whole regions of policy that seem squeezed out of serious and continuing Parliamentary review include: (first and foremost) Europe and foreign affairs generally; the environment, at home and abroad; education and health (again at home and abroad).

We were struck that already in the Bryce report of 1917 a role for the Lords in monitoring British interests in foreign affairs was being recommended. Within that brief the European Union would naturally find a place, and probably environmental affairs which is now well recognised as a global matter.

Parliament has never been very effective in foreign affairs. The main reason for this is historical. Foreign affairs in Europe have been traditionally the concern of princes; and in the UK they still fall primarily under the royal prerogative exercised on the Crown's behalf by the government. Governments like to keep things to themselves when they can. So history, convenience and security have hitherto conspired to keep foreign affairs out of the reach of Parliament. This partly explains the hash which particularly the Commons have made of European affairs in recent times. The Commons' regular job has been the day-to-day concerns of our citizens. This must ever remain the bread-and-butter of politics. But the world is now too small a place to be left exclusively to government.

Moreover whether we like it or not we are no longer 'a nice little, tight little island'. Until quite recently the government could, by treaties and other agreements, bind the UK at international law in relations with other countries while leaving the effects of such agreements ineffective in relation to individual citizens unless covered by statute.

This neat split no longer applies now that the UK's most regular and pressing international relations are governed by EU law. Parliament can no longer stand aside from European affairs. Many European provisions are directly applicable in the UK after signature by British government representatives. Many MPs and many of the public dislike this arrangement, not least because they rightly feel they often do not know what is going on soon enough to influence it. To be blunt: if Parliament does not know what is going on in Europe, it is Parliament's fault – and the fault of Tory MPs in particular. Britain has now been an EU member for a quarter of a century. In EU affairs more than any other subject, what MPs do not know is what they do not want to know.

One thing the Commons choose not to recognise about our relations with Europe is the active role the Lords have been taking in European affairs.

We have considered the competing briefs of the Commons' and Lords' Select Committees on European Affairs. The scope of the Lords' Committee is wider, allowing for debate on policy. The work of the Lords' committees on EU policy has been the one unsung Parliamentary achievement of recent years.

What is also noteworthy is that these committees swing into action before the legislating phase of implementing policy. This is of course because the legislation is carried through not by Westminster but by the EU institutions.

Just because these committees operate before legislation is undertaken, they are a useful paradigm for how an amalgam of Standing and Select Committees might work to allow for Parliamentary influence on, and scrutiny of, issues both at the policy-making and the legislating stages. In the Lords EU policy debate allows for influence before legislation is set in stone. It is notorious how few of backbenchers' amendments in Standing Committee are accepted: so few that for many MPs committee work is a tiresome chore rather than a core function.

As Mr Mount puts it in relation to European legislation [BCN p262], "Parliament is facing a choice which it has not, as yet, fully defined...: either to become a dim and trivial chamber spluttering its pique at a series of *faits accomplis* or to become an effective forum operating in advance of the European Council and the European Parliament, shaping and exercising its veto over the national input into the European system".

Parliament (and the Commons in particular) is fast becoming as ineffective at influencing and revising *vis-à-vis* the British government as it is already recognised to be *vis-à-vis* EU legislation. Accordingly Parliamentary committees to be set up for EU policy and legislation could be used as paradigms for many other areas of policy and legislation.

There seems a strong argument for suggesting that the same committees that shadow government departments as Select Committees should also people at least in part the Standing Committees when departmental policy arrives at the legislating stage. Concerns that Parliamentarians too deeply concerned at the prelegislation stage might not be the most effective scrutineers of Bills could best be met by preleg committees being supplemented by say a third of new members at the legislative stages of a Bill.

But it is hardly consistent with Parliamentary dignity (or effective democracy) that government Whips, in particular, should nominate the majority members of committees monitoring the government's legislation. It is hardly surprising that non-government amendments are so seldom adopted in committee.

Accordingly it is for consideration that the functions of the two types of committees should be combined not just for EU matters but more generally for the purpose of Parliament's control of government. This is no less true of the Commons than the Lords. For, whatever Parliamentary structure we end up with, the House of Commons must remain the primary scrutineer of government policy.

It is also suggested that these amalgamated select/standing committees should be further strengthened on the lines of the rarely-used Special Standing Committees, endorsed by the Second Report of the Select Committee on Procedure of 1984/5. For these committees were empowered to summon expert witnesses and to commission reports and research. But such a Parliamentary structure would have serious implications for government expenditure and would in practice break the civil service's virtual monopoly of creating policy.

A strong Parliament would tread on other toes than just the government's – in the interest of bringing the people nearer to the government machine.

This discussion was billed as looking for ways to bridge the gap between the immediacy of Commons' responses and the over-gentlemanly Lords. It was also suggested that whatever was settled on as the best way to steer towards a stabilising consensus on House of Lords reform could also be used more generally as a way of ensuring Parliamentary control of and the people's representation in government.

It can now be seen that a strong link in the chain of communication between people and government can be forged by strengthening Parliament's current committee system on lines that have been already suggested but so far only sparingly and timidly used. This should be no surprise to those who are persuaded that the key to House of Lords reform is not tinkering with its composition but the refreshing of the Parliamentary process as a whole.

It should not be necessary to take measures to ensure that Parliament is at the centre of the consultation process of policy debate in general or constitutional reform in particular. For Parliament should still be there already. But it plainly isn't. So putting it back where Parliament belongs, at the centre of the democratic process, should be the primary aim any Parliamentary reform, of which House of Lords reform must be an essential part.

The House of Commons is the primary organ for the control of government, especially on day-to-day and current financial/economic policy. No change to that status and function is either desirable or practicable. But the Commons undoubtedly need to be more conscientious in their roles as sounding-boards and opinion-formers for the public, and more independent-minded in relation to party and government policy. MPs need both to be better informed and to communicate more effectively both with government and public.

One expedient to help MPs carry out their traditional role in the new climate of popular self-confidence and populist government would be to strengthen their monitoring committees on the lines suggested. These changes, however, would considerably increase both MPs' responsibilities and their workload – their functions would be closer to those of Whitehall and sometimes even of ministers – and so would bring in their wake demands for extra expertise, research and secretarial assistance.

This extra public expense would be worth spending, both to ensure better-informed communication between public and government and to increase public awareness and trust of our constitutional machine. Parliamentarians would soon find themselves back at the centre of public debate if they rivalled ministers in the persuasiveness of what they had to say and how they said it.

Reforms proposed here to the Lords are also designed to assist the Commons by ensuring co-operation between the two Houses and a pooling of their strengths and resources.

It follows from Parliament's central position between people and government that Parliament should take a leading role as facilitator of the required new constitutional settlement. But so far as possible people, Parliament and government should be equal partners in arriving at it. For the constitution is supposed to allow the government through Parliament to fulfil the will of the people. So much might be generally be agreed. What is hard is to see how this trinity should operate.

The argument so far, together with the detailed proposals for House of Lords reform which follow, are intended to restore Parliament in its rightful place in the centre of the picture. But this is an unconvincing programme unless it can be seen how democratic government can be practically improved by doing so. How would strengthening Parliamentary committees in the way proposed, for a key example, improve the consultation and decision-making stages of the reform process under way?

There are two good reasons for choosing the Parliamentary reform process itself as the test example for how the reformed Parliament could be made to improve our democracy.

The first is the present weakened position of Parliament which, taken as it is, can only result in Parliament's voice being muted, perhaps even drowned, by an over-confident government and a noisy public. This would clearly be the case if the government, later on in this Parliament after hugger-mugger consultations, used its huge majority to ram its own White Paper proposals in a Bill through the Commons and promptly resorted to a referendum to ensure its acceptance. This would be a hideous travesty of opinion-testing and opinion-forming; but it would be a rash constitutionalist that discounted the likelihood of such a course of events: the Tory Opposition is shell-shocked and unclear of its own reform policy; and the third party is too busy ensuring its own increased Parliamentary presence by a deal on proportional representation with a strong government to look carefully at any other issues of Parliamentary reform.

This first reason gives added force to the second, the inevitable conflicts of interest within a Parliament itself the subject of reforms it is charged with scrutinising and carrying through. Parliament weak as it now is has almost no hope of resolving its internal disharmonies in the interests of better control of government and more active support of the public will.

The purpose of strengthening the Parliamentary committee procedure is to put Parliament back where it belongs in the consultation and decision-making process of government.

Finally, for the purpose of this discussion, this committee structure is being examined as an essential part of a recommended procedure for arriving at consensus on the overall constitutional settlement that a reform of Parliament requires; and this settlement would include both reform of the House of Lords and the permanent setting up of such committees themselves.

It is crucial therefore to see how such a structure might work, first in the process leading to constitutional resettlement and then in other functions.

The role of Parliament has always been to mediate between the demands of government and the wishes and needs of the people. Since the Second World War, in particular, this function has been taken over – first insensibly and then at an accelerated rate – by radio and television, newspapers, opinion polls, referendums, and soon no doubt the internet. Parliament has been starved of the resources, in terms of structure, essential research and secretarial help and, it must be added, sometimes (especially in the Tory party) calibre of manpower.

As a result the public expects increasingly to interact direct with government; and this is an extremely unequal relationship, which increasingly allows government to do what it likes. For government fixes the agenda and has the resources to control it. Government has the informed and centralised will that the people cannot possibly match *whatever information is generally available.* In fact the more information that is available and the more individuals who access it and wish their opinions on it to be heard, the less control the public has of government, which can manipulate policy questions, their timing and the ways in which they are put. Examination of government through its Parliamentary representatives is at least as necessary now as it ever has been. But what is now also necessary is greater accessibility for the public to those representatives.

This is how the proposed new kind of Parliamentary committee might work for Parliamentary reform.

From the start each House would appoint its own Prelegislative Special Select/Standing Committee on Parliamentary Reform. In the Commons the proportions on members should be fixed on party lines. In the Lords members should be selected from regular attendees. It is suggested that the Committees should sit during the consultation process sometimes separately, sometimes together, as the Committees think fit.

In the first instance each Committee should sit to consider procedural and other improvements to its own House. Each Committee and its members should have adequate research and secretarial facilities and have the right to commission expert reports and summon witnesses, including other Parliamentarians, civil servants, academics, journalists and representatives of the public.

Each Committee should also be fully aware of consultations in the other House and should consider how proposals in one House might interlock and/or interfere with proposals in the other. For the Committees' joint aim should be the strengthening of Parliament's democratic role. Each Committee would be expected to issue one or more interim reports and a final report. Ideally a final joint report from the two Houses might be possible. It is to be expected, however, that strong minorities would appear in both Houses' Committees and these should also record their opinions. These reports should be published and debated in at least one interim and one final debate in each House. Before final debates the government would have been expected to issue a White Paper on constitutional reform, which in turn should be debated.

The idea behind such a procedure is of course that the public would have ample opportunity to consider proposals as they came along. Suggestions would be well aired in the press. The public would be heard on chatshows, in the letter columns and in political forums of all shades of opinion. Committee members and government alike would have their views tested before any number of audiences. If after all of that the government wanted a referendum as well, at least the questions and their implications would be before the public before the public voted upon them; and the questions could be more subtle than agreement or not with government proposals. Moreover if there was to be a referendum process, it should be monitored by a professional and independent body to ensure fairness – the least misleading questions, timescale and forums for debate and so on.

Legislation would then follow, passing through both Houses in turn in the normal way, with the same Committees officiating at the usual stage, unless it was thought appropriate to take the Committee stage on the floor of either House. But after all the prior discussion in Committee, probably detailed amendment at the Committee legislation stage is all that would be required; and for that function a well-briefed Committee of modest size has been found to be ideal.

And the government would be anxious to get on with other legislation. In fact the Committees might be found to have been sparing of standard Parliamentary time, although the burden on the Committee members would have been heavy.

It is hard to disagree with the desirability of Parliamentary involvement in public debate on these lines, both as a counterweight to government monopoly of policy-making and as a means of drawing the people into debate on how they want to be governed. If consensus on such a crucial public issue is at all achievable, then Parliament is more likely than any other arm of government to lead debate towards it.

This procedure has been a paradigm for more effective Parliamentary involvement in other continuing and major policy subjects. The same Committees would operate both at the policy-making and the legislation stages of debate, to guide government and involve the public in government as it goes along.

At the pre-legislation stage, where on this view Whitehall (government and civil service) has had an outdated and anti-democratic monopoly of policy debate and policy-making, new Parliamentary Committees could act as sounding-boards of public opinion and debate with government on something approaching equal terms.

For certain kinds of issue, mainly those on the world stage where Britain is but one though a major player, the pre-legislation stage is often the only point at which Parliament has any opportunity to exercise influence. Historically the government, exercising the royal prerogative, has had a clear run on international relations. This was already of concern to Bryce in 1917. Now it is a dangerous absurdity. Matters of crucial importance and also of burning interest to many, such as the world's economy and environment, international trade and aid, have bypassed Parliament altogether. Worse, Brussels has left Westminster Palace stranded like a whale by the Thames.

Parliament's failure to assert itself as the people's representative controlling the government is certainly the result of its lack of vigilance to adapt to changing political imperatives – in particular the EU and quicker popular awareness. But the remedy is equally in Parliament's hands.

In the past Parliament's failure to be proactive has mattered less because of the comparative slowness of change and isolation from world events. The advent of the EU is only the most immediately visible and inescapable indicator of a basic change, the ever-increasing interdependence of nations. The British Isles are no longer entire of themselves; economics, the demands of poorer nations, the threat of environmental change – the oeconomia of our world and how we live in it – in short, the whole world, is crowding in upon us.

Outside our shores Parliament's timidity is even more serious than within them. For even if Parliament is slow to call government to account on home affairs, at least Parliament has a say, and a big one, for all government's bullying – guillotines in the interest of forcing its programme through, and so on and on. But in foreign affairs Parliament has almost no say at all unless the government or sudden torrents of public opinion bring matters to its attention. Next after the Parliamentary reform programme, which in some form is recognised as inescapable, those reforms should be used to assert Parliamentary control of EU legislation, and after that of international affairs in the broadest perspective.

Indeed in deciding what reforms to make, EU and world affairs, and how Parliament should deal with them, is a crucial concern.

The proposals made here for a much-strengthened Parliamentary committee system are broadly extendable over both foreign and home affairs and equally applicable to prelegislative and legislative debate. Moreover they are equally applicable to both Houses of Parliament. But just as we used the constitutional reform debate as an example of how the new committees might work, so now we consider how the House of Lords might use them and be modified to use them better, without forgetting that analogous changes in House of Commons practice and composition might be right for the Commons later. There is no persuasion like the power of example.

We are ready to look at the proposed new committee system in the round. It is a flexible system: different committees will operate differently in order to carry out their different liaison functions. But the ruling idea is Parliamentary involvement in government scrutiny from policymaking through legislation to implementation. The study here is tailored to the Lords' medium-term/continuity approach. But elements in the scheme would fit the reforms already under discussion in the House of Commons under the guiding hand of the Leader of the House. It is essential that this should be so. For the interlocking of Chambers is a prerequisite for a workable system.

The general way of proceeding has been explained as a combination of the Lords' actual approach to the European Union in their ECC with a recommended approach to the procedure for the current round of constitutional reforms. The ECC example is the best available paradigm from either House on prelegislative scrutiny. But that stage is where it stops because of the overarching nature of European legislation. By contrast the reform procedure is a pragmatic suggestion to ensure public involvement in the Parliamentary process from start to finish.

There should accordingly be two Lords committees (one as is and one to be formed) on the European Committees and on Constitutional Affairs, though in the scheme that follows, Constitutional Affairs is to be a sub-committee of Law Committee, along with sub-committees on Legislation (preparation and vetting), on Law Reform and on Law and Order/Penal Affairs.

The ECC is to interlock both with the Commons Select Committee on European Legislation and with the European Parliament. Cooperation between the two Houses' Committees is at once an area where the Lords can help the

Commons. Members of the Commons Committee are for ever complaining that papers are thrown at them in huge bundles too late for intelligent comment. It is proposed that since the two Houses are already set up to be complementary, this relation should be built on.

The prelegislative stage (which is all Westminster is allowed by the EU) is itself logically split into the conceptual and the draft legislative stages. The first suits the pictures both of the Lords' main stance that we have sketched and of their ECC as it actually operates. The second could suit the Commons' role if time allowed.

In fact the Leader of the House of Commons, Ann Taylor, has already expressed approval of the idea that draft legislation should be published earlier to facilitate public and Parliamentary debate.

It cannot be beyond the bounds of human ingenuity to ensure that what comes to the Commons' European Legislation Committee has already been through the Lords' ECC at an earlier stage (hopefully in summary and in principle) and discussed by them in outline with their brother committee. This is a matter of coordination, no doubt regularly attempted but irregularly achieved, if only because EU institutions (including the Council of Ministers in which the British government has a central role) do not make inter-parliamentary liaison a crucial criterion (as it should be) of EU efficiency.

It is suggested that a similar split in the prelegislative function of Parliament between the Lords and Commons should be extended from EU affairs to government scrutiny as a whole. The Lords debates and proposes in outline, maintains a medium-term and continuity function. Then when the time comes for legislation a Commons prelegislative committee swings into action, discussing tricky legal issues not only with civil servants but the Lords' Law Committee also. Legislation would then proceed in the normal way (contentious legislation first through the Commons, the less contentious introduced in the Lords).

Once legislation is on the Statute Book there should be a similar interaction between the Commons Select Committees (which operate department by department) and a new Lords Administrative Affairs and Local Government Committee (probably working in subcommittees) whose principal function will be to ensure regular Parliamentary input (as Professor Tivey has suggested) into administration. This committee should pay special attention to quangos and government agencies generally.

The AALGC would be a welcome Parliamentary supplement to the newly developed function of judicial review. Hitherto the Commons Select Committees have had difficulty (because of their sharp party interests) in getting deeply involved until things go wrong. Redress of wrongs is the essence too of the judicial function. The criterion of success or failure of the AALGC will be its effectiveness in forestalling unnecessary government messes. This and other committees will be expected to liaise with other Lords committees also – for example the Foreign Affairs Committee (as we think of Arms to Iraq).

The Foreign Affairs Committee might be a promise to Lord Bryce kept. The historical fault line between Parliamentary scrutiny and the Foreign and Commonwealth Office has been earlier noted. This, of all the areas of government, will be the one most resistant to the notion that the public has a right to know what goes on. The concept of democracy is in truth inimical to that of Realpolitik which since Macchiavelli (and Henry VIII) has governed British Foreign Affairs. Said Henry, "If my cap knew my thoughts, I'd throw it off!" His notion of the overriding national interest, concealed in the bosom of an all-knowing ruler, is out of date. It no longer suits a shrinking and interdependant world where the flutter of a butterfly can trigger Armageddon.

It is true that few governments have learnt the lesson – the Chinese, perhaps least of all. But history will support Mr Patten's view of Hong Kong, not the FCOs – or at least its uncharacteristically public stance. In the open air it was seen blinking like a mole. The public has no reverence now for mystification. Government's claim to secrecy in the public interest is being increasingly circumscribed, if only because secrets are increasingly difficult to keep. No foreign power keeps secrets unless it suits it; and British civil servants have on occasion seemed to take the same view. This should in no way be taken to condone leaks from government which harm the public interest.

But it is a criticism of public servants who feel that public information is their exclusive province. 'Information is (their) power.' The use of it, even unconscious, for self-aggrandisement is a form of sleaze, in Lord Nolan's sense of what is publicly owned being used for private advantage by holders of public office. As a corollary to this approach to the availability of public knowledge, a clear line should be drawn between information which is to be and which is not to be available to Parliament and its committees. Parliament (and eventually the public) should have available for its deliberations all information whose availability neither harms the public nor infringes private rights. 'Private rights' however should be broad enough to include government working papers (as it would include a committee member's preparatory work in his brief-case). But once secrecy puts Parliament at a disadvantage in arguing with government, something is wrong. But the line is difficult to draw. In Parliament that should be, in doubt, a job for the Law Committee.

The FAC should have a wide brief – as wide as the FCOs – with appropriate sub-committees. Perhaps Environment and Aid should be one. Even Europe is but part of a global system. The interlock of environmental and human geography is nowadays adamantine; so much the better. Saving the rainforests together with rare creatures and medicinal plants, for example, is above all a problem of teaching their inhabitants an acceptable way of adapting to a shrinking world. That and the need to apply analogous self-restraint to the developed nations.

Trade and Defence is another nexus beyond our shores that might enjoy its own sub-committee. In the past one has often felt that these overlapping territories of government are at pains to give a false impression that neither knows nor wishes to know what the other is about. This is damaging to Britain's good name abroad and an unacceptable abdication of government responsibility. But this is a field of nuances and subtleties. Sub-committees should be overseen by a strong committee of old hands, such as abound among our distinguished peers.

Another Lords' committee of crucial importance should be the Law Committee. Senior judges, in order to preserve their seats of independence, are often anxious to disclaim not just a political role but, by implication, political wisdom also. But distinguished judges are and always have been legislators. Their role, in preserving the rule of law, is at the heart of any democratic structure. Their look-out however is above party politics or should be. This is a plea for the public to profit from their wisdom in advance of things going wrong (which is what litigation is all about). The Appellate Committee's function as the final court of appeal in litigation is in no way inconsistent with law lords' contribution to the legislative process as here widely defined from concept through to administration.

On law reform, on constitutional matters, on the drafting of Bills, on civil administration and penal reform their contributions have been consistent and valued. The only change proposed here is to systematise it as a regular part of Parliament's role in the process of government. It is admitted that this could draw senior judges into difficult political questions. My response is that elevating them on to a separate pinnacle as some kind of Supreme Court is wantonly to restrict their usefulness.

A case in point could be what is a 'constitutional Bill'. If, that is, my idea were to be adopted that there should be a return to a two-year delaying power, preferably within four-year Parliaments, but restored to the Second Chamber for constitutional Bills only. That notion would depend on a decision on what is and what is not a constitutional Bill. This procedure might allay, for example, the concerns of Lord Scarman, among the most distinguished of all constitutional lawyers living and himself long a law lord, that led him to recommend some years ago that constitutional Bills should require the consent of both Houses.

A possible solution canvassed here is for a constitutional Bill to be subject to a two-year delay, when in a particular case the Lords so insist, at the end of which a referendum could be held, itself the object of supervision by an independent referendums commission to ensure the minimum possible governmental manipulation of the process. Undoubtedly, in my estimation, the Common Market Referendum would have much profited by such a deliberative process. The public would have had a much better idea of what they were voting for; and subsequent damaging (and seemingly endless) recriminations would have been avoided. The delaying power has always been billed as the means of giving the public time for difficult decisions. In retrospect whether one wishes to be in the EU or out, it is hard to resist the conclusion that the decision of British entry was not taken with sufficient care.

This solution might be thought thematic with what of value underlay the 19th century Salisbury 'referendal theory' and the present Lord Cranborne's revival of it. But now the public is given not only time to think but the Parliamentary leadership in the doing of its thinking.

Such a system would however demand a most subtle balancing act by the Second Chamber to determine when and how to bring such powers into operation. That is and must always be a political decision – and subject unfortunately to occasional human error in application, as was the Salisbury Doctrine before it.

A case that could all too soon require some such deliberative procedure is the fate of the hereditary peers, whose electoral illegitimacy seems to have been virtually the only issue triggering New Labour's Parliamentary reforms.

Suppose that the House of Lords were to throw out the proposed short Bill to abolish their sitting and voting rights on the ground that no replacing overall scheme for the reform of Parliament is included in it.

Suppose further the House of Lords' Appellate Committee (and/or the Judicial Committee of the Privy Council) were to rule such a Bill illegal (and/or no Bill at all) on one or more of the following grounds:

1. that the Parliament Acts of 1911 and 1949 were never intended to sanction the dismantling of one House of Parliament by the other without its consent;

2. that even if they were intended to do so, the intention is a nullity because Parliament is not empowered to dismantle itself or a substantial part of itself (with or without the consent of all its parts);

3. that even if Parliament can do so, with the consent of all its parts, nevertheless one House cannot (under the Parliament Acts or not) dismantle the other without both its consent and putting in its place a Parliamentary system as democratic or better as that which has been dismantled.

The central argument on these lines would be that the one thing Parliament cannot do is to nullify or frustrate itself since its very *raison d'etre* is to represent the people to the government.

This is not an argument that a modern government (especially one with populist leanings) can easily brush aside. If a scrap like this broke out, we should be thrown wholly unprepared into an insoluble constitutional *impasse.* The very worst moment to put together a Parliamentary scheme commanding consensus and winning stability is one where Parliament (run down one has to say by an impulsive government) is seen to have failed in its basic duty to the public. Parliamentarians should already be considering how to cope, before the onset of turbulent times.

We are seeking a new and flexible committee system in the Lords to take over a large and neglected part of Parliamentary work, primarily at the start and towards the end of Parliament's function, as the overseer of government. Principle decision-making, in controversial legislation and finance, is left to the Commons, where it belongs. Besides a new focus on Parliament's policy-making and monitoring of the end-product of legislation, a third feature is the interplay among the committees themselves.

An obvious example is the interface between the Law Committee and the proposed Committee on Community Affairs and Human Rights. The hurried and wholesale import of the European Convention of Human Rights without serious study of its conflicts with British Law threatens both to confuse the public on what its rights are and to overload the judges with insoluble conundrums. The notion is to assume that the Convention law and the domestic are the same and then, when they are not, for judges to ask Parliament to change the domestic law.

This is plainly untidy and calculated to cause injustice in those individual cases where conflict is found. But no doubt it was not just the overconfidence of a triumphant new government but the absence of any workable Parliamentary system to cope in advance with such special complexities that led to such a non-

sense. Once these two committees are set up as proposed, conflicts can be identified in advance and some of these injustices forestalled.

Community Affairs seems a most profitable area for the Lords to take up,
suitable both to their membership and their continuity role. Education and
Employment (another of the dozen or so suggested committees) also. Another
subject, Health, might fit best with Technology under a head of Community
Science. These three would obviously interdine, at least.

But it is worth considering whether there should be a nexus of communication inbuilt into the committees by a more general rule that every committee
member should expect to be a member of one or at most two others – and should
even have liaison roles with Commons' committees also. Crossing of frontiers in
government scrutiny is one essential requirement of policy and administrative
continuity. There is no doubt that cross-fertilisation helps. Other examples are
Law with Community Affairs/Human Rights as above; Community Science
with ditto; Community Science with Administrative Affairs and Local
Government; AALGC both with Education and Employment and with National
and Regional Affairs; European with Foreign Affairs – and many others.

One particular thought is to adapt to the Lords an idea Lord Higgins had for
the Commons (when he was Liaison Committee Chairman in the Commons).
This idea was rejected by the last government as being too imaginative and perhaps Europhile: it is more likely to find favour with the new government. His
proposal was this: that members of European sub-committees (here we should
say Lords' ECC subcommittees) should be attached to the Commons
Departmental Select Committees (and here we would add, to the other Lords
Committees also), to ensure interlock of domestic with EU policies. Another
instance of constructive symbiosis for the two Houses would be intercursus
between Commons Departmental Select Committees and the AALGC, one of
whose prime functions would be to keep a watchful eye on government's use of
quangos and its relation with local government authorities.

This kind of 'interdining' could be used as a general paradigm for a new and
beneficial intercursus between the two Houses. Even if both Houses were ideally reformed, any continued failure to cooperate and interact within a single
scheme of government scrutiny would defeat the democratic aims of those
reforms.

Adapted to our scheme for the Lords (where Lord Higgins now is) this proposal would in particular require each of the other eleven Lords' committees to
include at least one member of the European Communities Committee (or of its
sub-committees).

So far we have mentioned these seven committees to illustrate the flexibility
of the system proposed. Probably there should be around five others – i.
Environment (roughly covering the territory of the current mammoth government department), ii. Finance and Industry, iii. National and Regional Affairs, iv
an Ad Hoc Committee (as at present) for sudden issues which fit no prescribed
scheme; and v, overall, a Coordinating Committee, chaired by an overall
Chairman of Lords' Committees and his Deputy.

The Coordinating Committee is the keystone of the system. Its primary job would be to act as liaison with the Commons and the government. One way of doing this is to foster intercursus between the Lords Committees and the Commons Select Committees. The ultimate aims of the reorganisation would be to encourage the working of Parliament as a single unit and the treatment of Parliament's scrutiny of government as a single coordinated function from policy-debate and policy-making right through legislation to executive and administrative action.

Another function of the Coordinating Committee would be to ensure the practicalities of the new system. The workload will be formidable; the research, admin and civil service support complex and at first bitterly complained of by government. For government is used to and will want to protect its monopoly of civil service support; and the Treasury will begrudge the expense of a new Parliamentary efficiency the need for which old habits of thought will make difficult to see.

One practical result of the reorganisation must be the adoption by the Lords of the Commons practice of taking Committees off the floor of the House. Committees will of course produce reports for general debate. Second Reading Debates would also be taken on the floor. Other major debates will be initiated there. Questions too, as now. But the sheer quantity and complexity of work must predominantly be undertaken back-stage.

Another issue thrown up at once is the attendance at the Committees of experts, civil servants – and, especially, Ministers.

It is to be hoped that the extended function for the Second Chamber will attract more Ministers into the Lords. The option chosen for membership is a two-thirds elected, one-third appointed mix (mainly to ensure the appropriate manning of the Committees).

It is not suggested that Ministers should be subject to formal censure in the Lords. As Lord Bryce pointed out the censure of Ministers is too close to the bone of governments to allow for reflective debate. But the Chairmanship of the Coordinating Committee should be seen as requiring senior ministerial rank and the Deputyship of his or her shadow. And Ministers from both Houses should expect to respond to all invitations, especially to that Committee. Such invitations need not always have any adversarial connotation. They should be more often seen as fostering the growth of cooperation between the two Houses and between the Second Chamber and the government. It should be a common matter for Lords' members to be invited to Commons Select Committees also.

None of the remaining Committees to be discussed has controversial connotations except, perhaps, the Finance and Industry Committee. Does this suggest a trespass contemplated on Commons territory? It should not.

The Commons is not to fear the Lords' encroachment on Money Bills, on current finance policies. Which is not, of course, to say that the Committee will not sometimes come to conclusions distasteful to government. It is a sad commentary both on the prestige of Parliament and on governments' views of the Second Chamber (as well as on the arrogance of governments), that opposition in the Lords to anything whatever that comes from government has up to now not been considered scrupulously on its merits but just an excuse for Lords reform, if not abolition. Once the Second Chamber is in fact reformed, such knee-jerk reactions will stand out as petty-minded and irresponsible (as often they have been).

Medium-term planning of the economy should not be the monopoly of government and its civil servants. Competition, at least, with our trading and financial neighbours (if coordination with the EU, for example, is unthinkable or practically impossible) requires open debate and clear thinking about EU and other arrangements. Parliament is the place for this. The recent hand-over of monetary policy to the Bank of England is an anti-democratic step, made the more unwise by its encouraging by implication the European Central Bank's ambitions to control of European economic policy. Implications of such demand sober, continuing reflection.

For just as Parliament has been sidelined by government in EU matters (not least by being pressured by governments, Tory and New Labour, towards the acceptance of currency control outwith democratic control), so at present the Chancellor has abdicated political responsibility for control of UK interest rates – and by necessary implication of interrelated issues, for control of economic policy as a whole also. Moreover by the same token he has distanced economic scrutiny from Parliament, and from the Commons, in particular, where it belongs.

It is hard to envisage how any Second Chamber faced with anti-democratic policies of this kind could keep silent. And who knows? Perhaps if the Lords took up the cry, the Commons might join the chorus?

The progression from policy-making to action leaves fuzzy lines – and should encourage constructive cooperation between the two Houses at the margins, if they accept their constitutional responsibility to scrutinise and criticise – but constructively – government policy in the interest of their electorates.

This cannot be achieved without continuity and patient coordination. Take the proposed Environment Committee for an example. Although most of the Lords' committees will be subject-based, in contrast to Commons' Select Committees which shadow departments, it happens that the Lords' Environment Committee's scope coincides with the Commons' brother committee. But that is only the start of consultation. The British environment in all its aspects from basic resources to transport, in planning the balance of town and country, the British environment is one with Europe and the world. We are no longer an island people.

So the Environment Committee is closely connected not just with the Commons but with the Lords' European and Foreign Affairs Committees.

Effectiveness in Parliament, as in government, depends largely on communication between interested groups. In the past the two Houses have largely gone their separate ways, to the detriment of each – and to the detriment of the public's right of representation.

This failure is a poor look-out for Parliament's relations with EU institutions and the new national and regional Parliaments. Indeed with the European Parliament it has already gone a fair way to being repeated. The cold reception of MEPs in Westminster and Parliament's poor record in controlling British participation in the Council of Ministers are just the two most startling symptoms of Westminster's diseased attitude to the world outside our shores.

Plainly some MEPs (at least) should be *ex officio* members of the Lords; and more peers should see the European Parliament as a fulfilling career. But these are but two timid steps along the way (but at least this time in the right direction).

What is required is the ECC's direct and regular input into the European Parliament, preferably in concert with equivalent committees from other European states. There is in fact no reason why the EP should not develop the kind of holistic scrutiny of the Commission and the Council of Ministers that is here recommended for Parliament (in particular the Lords) in relation to our government. As the EP's powers develop, that kind of interface will grow anyhow and the British might for once be in the van.

For as we have seen the EU institutions are profoundly undemocratic. At last the EP is developing a say in policy; but the rough interplay is still that the Commission proposes, the Council of Ministers disposes and the Parliament rubber-stamps.

To make matters worse the European Central bank is doing its best, under the banner of European Monetary Union, to remove economic policy from the sphere of politics altogether.

We have seen the wars that result when the forces are left in the uninhibited hands of generals. Economic wars can well be the end-result of the mechanistic policies of bankers who operate unchecked by democratic process and the compromises in timing and implementation that are the stuff of practical politics. First, of course, there will be the usual levies, subsidies and transfers, the artificial price and taxation structures, that bureaucrats always apply to conceal their false premises. But civil discomforts – unemployment, bankruptcies and the opportunistic profit-taking – are most likely to undermine the whole spirit of economic cooperation that inspired the European experiment.

The economic future of Europe depends on a sensitive democratic structure to underpin it; and this development is the more pressing when many peoples of various backgrounds are trying to learn to live together. A nexus of regional, national and European parliaments is the political infrastructure of any Europe whose peoples are to remain committed to convergent development.

At the European level intertwined parliamentary memberships should be a political goal. If in Britain national and regional parliaments are now a necessity for adequate public involvement in politics; and if, further, members of those parliaments and other local magnificos, like mayors, should have, as I suggest, a seat *ex officio* in the Lords, then similar arguments apply and will gather momentum elsewhere in Europe. It would be pleasantly ironic if a regionally orientated Second Chamber, such as is advocated here, were to become the paradigm for an European Upper Chamber, composed of regional representatives elected from throughout the EU. In fact Michael Heseltine proposed a sort of European House of Lords over a decade ago. But it is not just the EU that lacks a working system: we have to look to the integration of the national and regional Parliaments into our own Parliamentary system before it is too late.

For like it or not, the UK has three tiers of Parliament. The United Kingdom without that integration could just split apart.

It is to forestalling this wanton sadness that the Lords' new National and Regional Affairs Committee is targeted. The centrifugal forces operating on a nation without a strong national Parliament are now widely recognised.

But it all depends what is meant by 'nation'. We are a United Kingdom of historic diversity. Most of us want to keep it that way. Politicians are not generally so far-sighted. It is strange that Tories, in particular, should have been so generally carping at the prospect of a 'federal Europe' while failing to beware the break-up of our own Kingdom (Mr Major having been throughout the most distinguished and unfortunate exception).

We are still a unity of diversity; but it is imperative at once to develop the modern institutions needed to underpin it.

The NRAC should have this as one of its two chief aims. The other is to ensure, from Westminster, that new national/regional Parliaments/Assemblies ('NRPA's) give electorates the detailed and personal attention that is at the root of regionalism.

Our Second Chamber is to be regionally elected. It will therefore have regional contingents with eyes both on their constituencies and on the centre. It is also suggested that some appointees to it should also hold seats in NRPA's (or mayoralties) as well, as MEPs should be likewise represented *ex officio* in the Second Chamber.

Nobody knows how different versions of devolution are to work. Our inexperienced new government's failure to think such matters through has already been criticised. In is significant that their most serious effort has been for Northern Ireland which has its unique difficulties. In this Second Chamber the system is sufficiently flexible, while the groupings sufficiently specific, to accommodate liaison with NRPAs of any kind. Shared experience of members from different nations/regions will cross-fertilise.

The Parliament in this way will again take up again its burden of assisting the monarch both to unify and to represent the Kingdom.

4. TOWARDS A RENEWED HOUSE OF LORDS

The illness of the Lords' House has been found to be shared with the House of Commons: the two Houses separately and together have been too weak to hold the public's line against the tug of overmighty and unresponsive governments. A powerful medicine is ready to hand for both Houses through a more pro-active and developed committee system. But beyond that their needs diverge; and from here on we concentrate on the composition of the Lords – exclusively, except in so far as the needs of a better-integrated Parliament requires the renewed House of Lords to mesh in better with the Commons.

No-one doubts the Commons' authority to reform themselves in the interest of better public representation if the will were there. What remains doubtful is the power of the Commons (or of the government of the day) to reform the Lords without the public's, (the Monarch's) and their consent. For the House of Commons is directly elected by the people to represent them: governments owe their authority directly to the Commons.

Of the Lords the reverse is true. The Lords' role is ancillary to that of the Commons. No substantial reform of the House of Lords could be carried through without the blessing of the Commons, much less any reform by the Lords of the Commons; nor would there be any point in attempting such an operation.

For the Lords' job is to assist and complement the Commons; and any authority and credibility that the House of Lords retains in the process of government derives directly from that function.

This may seem too obvious to need re-stating; and so it might be if the Lords' weakness were not so often put down to the fact that the Lords (and particularly the hereditary peers) unlike the Commons are not directly elected. But this alternative diagnosis is wrong. For even if elected, the Second Chamber would remain ancillary to the Commons; and no reform requiring direct election to the Lords could or should ever be made except as part of a scheme to assist the Commons.

This common mistake is worth correcting for another reason: if it is not corrected the unspoken thought may direct reform that an elected Second Chamber might cure our Parliamentary 'M E'.

It is crucial to be clear what cause any proposal for direct election to the Lords might serve.

Direct election only gets you the job. It does nothing to sponsor your performance of it. Direct election of MPs, for example, has not in practice ensured their high public esteem. For many years the 'man-in-the-street' (a forgotten phrase now, by the way: for we are all out there together) has placed MPs among the professionals least worthy of esteem. Now – which is worse – Parliament is almost ignored.

A way in is to ask why election for the hereditary peers on the one hand is often seen as essential (if their continued presence in the House of Lords is to be allowed at all) and why election is not often prescribed for the life peers on the other.

Clearly there are hidden premises here of the kind that conceal resistance to open thinking. For if election is a prerequisite to representation of the public, it is at least as needed for life peers as for hereditary peers. For life peers are created on party lines and the government of the day creates more peerages for its own sympathisers than for those of other parties. Hereditary peers on the other hand are never government nominees. Their malady is their strong bias to the Tory party. The cry for their direct election comes from no deeper motive than a justifiable wish to counteract this bias – which would be more often satisfied by a (partisan) demand that the hereditary peers should be abolished altogether.

It follows that arguments for the election of hereditary peers are not to be heard unless they apply equally to life peers.

It is at this point that we bump into the central puzzle of how to govern a multicultural and pluralist country of growing egalitarian sympathies.

In the past radical egalitarians have sought equality of opportunity as a means to equal benefits and the eradication of privileged and entrenched elites as a road to a classless society. This programme has at different times been labelled as republicanism or Marxism; but its name is uninteresting to a pragmatic public.

What is now in plain view is the underlying fallacy of the programme. Equality of opportunity tends to systematise inequalities of benefits and the abolition of one elite makes way for its more organised and ruthless successor. Egalitarian governments end with truly Marxian inevitability as tax-manipulators and social engineers with a whole class of bureaucrats to implement (so far as they can) the adjustments that practicalities impose on ill-judged means to worthy ends. Republicans have their hearts in the right place but their heads in the air.

There has been a Copernican revolution (that curiously could well be ascribed to Marxism) in democratic thinking, which in their very different ways the failure of the Soviet Union and the Blairite landslide equally reflect. Economic policy does not revolve round social justice. Justice revolves round money. Governments have no alternative but first to manage the economy right, leaving people in their daily lives to fight out the distribution of benefits among themselves – and then to take care of the losers.

In short, government is too complicated to leave to governments. The interweaving of people's lives – and of countries' economies – is of a complexity far beyond any government to prescribe for by manifesto, let alone by slogan. People can only govern themselves and are increasingly demanding the freedom to do so.

Accordingly the discontinuity between peers' status and their function is to be explained by a new public self-consciousness and reflects concerns – but different concerns – about both.

Doubts about peers' functions derive from a lack of consensus about the Parliamentarian's role. It is at root as applicable to the MP as to the peer. At least, one may feel, the peer could be put on an equal footing with the MP by election of some kind; but it is generally recognised that this does not put the argument to bed.

In fact it is easily seen that even the manner of peers' election (or whether they should be elected or indeed be allowed to continue at all) depends on the function they are to perform. If that were agreed, no doubt an appropriate method of election could be devised; and then as a result of that method of election the peers' authority to perform their function would certainly be enhanced.

So what does our self-conscious new public think it wants of its peers?

No clear answer is to hand – for two reasons. We are talking of mood, though I believe a settled mood; and the public has not debated the issue or had a taste of what it might prefer to the *status quo*. But indications are not far to seek.

Common sense, for example, dictates that the Second Chamber should neither supersede nor duplicate the House of Commons. But so far as there is a perceived need which neither is satisfying, that is open ground for the peers to occupy.

However since the House of Commons by tradition is the only government organ that can directly summon ministers to give final account of themselves and that has controlled government finance and financial legislation, whatever the Commons' failings in these functions – and we have seen they are serious and systematic – the Lords cannot fulfil these functions for them.

What then is left for the Second Chamber to do?

Suggestions have been made in response to this when reform to the Parliamentary committee system was discussed. Broadly – the Commons deals best with government's handling of day-to-day affairs, and the Lords has tended to tackle longer- and wider-running issues. It is suggested that House of Lords reform should develop this tendency and that elections to the House of Lords should be geared to filling the Second Chamber with men and women suited to this function. But does this satisfy the new public aspirations we have identified?

Long gone are the days when the electorate was content to question government seriously only at election times. There are two main reasons for this – the speed of political change at home and abroad and the ever-expanding information about it in newspapers and, especially, on TV and now on the Internet. At the same time the public has recognised (what Westminster has wished not to know) that the world has shrunk in the communications revolution. Europe is now in our living-room and the world at our garden gate. People have found that they enjoy participating in chat shows or phoning in with their views. We have grown accustomed to being heard; but we have found that the media have been listening while the Parliamentarians have not.

This new awareness in the public has thrown down a challenge to Parliament that Parliament has ignored. Parliament has both failed to communicate with the public and to control and scrutinise government; and it has lost credibility in consequence with both. It is in fact difficult to predict how the public will react now to Parliamentary reform of whatever kind. For most political debate has bypassed Parliament and little is now expected of it. General elections are to elect a government; and the government will thereupon communicate with and through the media, justifying its actions by its election manifesto and, later, what it can claim to be thematic with it. If there is anything of special importance, government will go over the heads of Parliament to the public in a referendum the terms of which it will fix to suit itself.

There has been a constitutional landslide – and I do not mean the Tories' stupefying election defeat. Even though it crept up during the eighteen Tory years and the Labour government is now building on it. And even though the Tories were barking at the EU institutions (or just sulking) while their house was falling down around them. The other bigger landslide is also plain to see: Parliament has been smothered by government till government talks to the public only through the media.

But this profound change has gone unnoticed by Parliamentarians. The explanation for that lies in the British predilection for gradual change which makes signposts and clear criteria threatening and distasteful intrusions. But not even we feel that all surreptitious change is for the good just because it comes by degrees.

Profoundly anti-democratic as this change has been – since it leaves to government the monopoly of policy-making and even of implementation – it is very doubtful whether a written constitution would have brought the collapse of Parliament to public attention.

For a written constitution would now be intended merely to codify what we have (or whatever the government in its wisdom now decides to foist upon us). It is only at the moment of writing that the codifiers are forced to ask what the constitution actually is. That creates a temporary ferment. After that, as in the USA a chief justice once pronounced, 'the constitution is what the judges say it is'. But until they are asked they say nothing; and when they are asked they legislate outwith Parliament.

At one crucial faultline however – Westminster's meeting-point with Europe – questions even under a written constitution would have been unavoidable that we have evaded. For the Pro- and Anti-Europe groups within both major parties diverted attention from Parliament's urgent need to adapt to European institutions if (as the ruling caucuses in all the parties were insisting) the UK was to remain in the EU in one way or another. The Pro-Marketeers wanted to minimise the problems with a foreign system of law and government and the Anti-Marketeers tried to pretend that Europe did not exist. Both in fact let their public down.

Constitutional creep – which through the centuries has been the Britons' favourite mode of reform – was wholly inappropriate for the huge leap in attitudes and institutions that EU membership is demanding. If there had been a piece of paper, however rudimentary, on which 'British Constitution' had been written down, there is no way that Parliament's need to adapt could have been ignored, for all the shufflings of all governments determined to conceal from the public the plain fact that the British Channel has shrunk to a puddle.

But the snag with a written constitution is this: it would have been the judges – and the judges outside Parliament altogether – who would have pronounced upon Parliament's relations with Europe. That is not the British way. For lazy or no, the British do like to be consulted; and Parliament is the place for that. So the approach taken here is to leave written constitutions where they belong – on students' bookshelves – and to try to construct a lively forum for debate in which the public (and even senior judges) can participate.

But for the practical needs of reacting to outside international pressures, however, the eclipse of Parliament would not have shown up on any screen whether we had a written constitution or not. For it has always been Parliament's duty to represent the public and to control and scrutinise the government. Diversion over Europe was no more than a contributory cause of the last Parliament's weakness and lack of vigilance.

What has overmastered Parliament has been the swelling power of prime ministers and their governments which it has not been in the interests of MPs' career plans to challenge. And the last item on any PM's menu is the strengthening of Parliament's control of him (or in this case, of her and him). There are many active peers who will complain that Mrs. Thatcher treated the House of Lords with contempt; fewer MPs perhaps (though I know some) who will say the same – of themselves, if not of the Commons. It is poetic irony that the Labour Government is reaping not just the economic riches but the harvest of unconstitutional power that Mrs Thatcher sowed.

But such power, gilded by the government's flattery of media-land and, through it, of the public, is dangerously undemocratic. For the field is left open to the government to dictate policy with trivial pressure from debate or competitive initiation of policy. The public is fobbed off with photographic smiles and handshakes and little speeches. It is heart-warming (both for John Citizen and for Tony) for the public to be able to speak to the Prime Minister at some public appearance, on a chat-show, perhaps, or on a walk-about; but the effect on government policy is nil. Nothing is more conducive to a government's loss of rapport with the governed (as Mrs. Thatcher found) than to be bathed in the mutual flattery of admirers and admired.

At present the only serious locking of Parliamentary horns is during the Second Reading Debate on a Government Bill. Thereafter there is much sweat (especially among officials) in getting the Bill on to the Statute Book; but, with the rarest of exceptions, the conclusion is foregone. Quite invariably, however, since the mechanism for Parliamentary initiation and control of policy-making is rudimentary, two things will *not* have happened before the Queen's assent: neither Parliament nor the people through Parliament will have had the opportunity of influencing, on anything remotely like equal terms with government and its officialdom, the initiation, the moulding and the prioritising of policy, generally or within ministries. Without such an opportunity, current aspirations cannot be satisfied.

The public is a-fire with a thirst for news and a wish to comment on it. It is widely thought that a major factor in Labour's 1997 victory, at least in the size of the victory, was Labour's greatly enhanced presentation of their policies which showed up the Tories' worn-out public relations machine. Once more Labour is seen as building on a suspect aspect of Thatcherism. What is sauce for the goose is sauce for the gander: why should the constitutionalist be concerned, if all is evened out in the end? The response is of course that the public it is that loses, since policy is not tested and modified at its inception and good ideas, if introduced at all, are introduced unnecessarily late.

There is nothing anti-democratic about a government's aim to present its policies in the most attractive light – they will do it anyhow, and efficiency is never in itself a vice – *always provided* that presentation can be efficiently tested in itself and by reference to competing alternatives.

For one-sided presentation becomes quite unavoidably manipulation, not just of information but of the public to whom it is directed. In the first five months of the new/New Labour Government five senior officials of the Government Information Service were replaced (an unprecedented number in that time-frame).

Let us make all due allowance for a government's desire to sweep out eighteen years of what it would like to call cobwebs. But this reflects a serious acceleration of a tendency (which as usual was already much complained of in the Thatcher years) to politicise the Civil Service, whose guidelines, especially in the dissemination of public information to the public, are explicitly 'not party-political'. Mr. Alistair Campbell seeks to justify this with a diktat that 'media handling should be built into policy-making' – a formula that applied unchecked leads as day to night into the substitution of propaganda for policy.

Government cannot usefully be criticised for squatting in untenanted ground. For Parliament is asleep to manipulations of public debate and Oppositions hesitate to wake it for fear of disturbing their power to continue the manipulations when their turn comes. Therefore it is Parliament, not the government machine, that is to be reformed.

But until it is so, the public cannot be expected to recognise what they are missing – and government power increases at the expense of public debate and timely policy-making. It is to close the hole that he and his colleagues opened over the public control of government that the reforms suggested in this book are directed.

In logic, if the Lords, life peers and hereditaries (for the need for their election if it applies to any of them applies to all), were generally thought to be operating as the public would like, there would be no need to change the medication. Why elect those whom one would want where they are in any event? But if the public wants somebody else – then away with the unelected, and replace them with those to be elected in their place. For if it is the people who are dissatisfied, it is only by election of some kind that the representatives they want can be found – though it is perhaps for constitutionalists to suggest how appropriate elections might be devised.

The House of Lords has indeed won good opinions for their work in many fields, especially among practical and open-minded politicians and officials at Westminster. But the House of Lords in the country has born the brunt of confused dissatisfaction with the performance of Parliament as a whole – unfairly, since the Lord's hands have been tied by the Commons since 1911 and it is the Commons who have primary responsibility for ensuring the public is looked after in the way it wishes to be looked after.

Moreover the paraphernalia of Parliament no longer amuses the public and most of it is with good reason associated with the Lords. Pomp and circumstance have gone finally out of fashion. Down-sizing the monarchy is a-buzz. Ermine is moth-eaten. (Though where it is not, it has always been too new to be respectable.) Hereditary peers are no longer to be tolerated, whatever their individual contributions and no matter that their expertise cannot be easily replaced in Westminster.

Many of the hereditaries have only to gain by the overt discipline of election, since they will have little difficulty in showing themselves worthy of getting elected; and until they are given the opportunity to submit to election they are sitting ducks for the sporting instincts of the uninformed.

Justice must be seen to be done; and representing the people must be restricted to those whom the people have put there. Very well, the hereditaries shall henceforth be elected.

But if some kind of election is required for hereditaries as a matter of democratic faith, so then also is election of the life peers. For it is prime ministers, not the public, who have elevated them; and it is primarily prime ministers' power which is to be scrutinised in Parliament on behalf of the people. A prime minister's packing of the Lords with life peers in place of hereditaries will swiftly attact the suspicion of anti-democratic sympathies that it deserves. The public wants the replacement of hereditaries with elected; but it wants this for the purpose of better representative government.

And so we come to membership of the Second Chamber, the procedures for its selection, election and appointment.

The requirements can now be simply and quickly stated. We are looking for a Second Chamber whose members complement the House of Commons by concentrating on neglected fields of Parliamentary participation in government.

Those fields are i) general policy-making, especially the conceptual and prelegislative phases in the context of medium-term requirements;

ii) local government and administration (including government appendages, such as quangos);

iii) devolution;

iv) European Union;

v) cultural pluralism (including more younger people and more women).

In addition the Lords must include not only the committee structures but also the members, elected in so far as desirable, to continue their function as the constitution's guardians.

In all of these fields, in fact, the Lords have in the past made continual if unstructured and haphazard contributions, through their debating and revising functions. It would be irresponsible to lose their accumulated expertise and most economical to use it better.

So the intent here is, through an horizontal and vertical extension of the Lords committee system built on to the principles of their European Communities Committee, to systematise the Lords' contributions in these fields. Since they are largely untenanted ground, head-on conflict with the Commons will be avoidable; but co-operation (perhaps through a gathering momentum of joint committees) between the two Houses will be encouraged, even fostered. And the people will be better represented and enabled to influence the legislative process right through from conception to implementation. Where to begin?

We cannot do better, I think, than remind ourselves, in summary, of the three schemes which have come nearest to implementation – a) Lord Bryce's in 1918, b) Labour's in 1968 and c) Lord Home's in 1978. For we should build in reform on the accumulated wisdom of past generations (and our own). That way we are likely in our governmental system to reflect the subtle but creative combinations and tensions that make up our varied people.

The proposals advocated here will, in fact, be an attempted amalgam of all three schemes, updated for current conditions.

a) Lord Bryce (1918, Cd 9038) suggested a two-part Upper Chamber. Some 246 members would be elected by MPs regionally grouped. A further 81 should be appointed by a Joint Standing Committee of both Houses but this number would be supplemented by *ex officios* (law lords and bishops);

b) Labour's White Paper (Cmd 3799 of 1968) proposed an entirely appointed Upper Chamber. There would be 230 voting members composed mainly of all current life-peers (provided they attended at least a third of sittings and retired at the end of a Parliament in which they became 72). But these would be supplemented by about 80 new appointments (many of them hereditaries) to give the government an overall 10% majority of party-committed peers (so as to exclude an overall majority of peers including cross-benchers and *ex officios*). But a key proposal, in order to allow for continued varied influence from established peers and other hereditaries, was for a two-tier House. Peers who did not meet the voting criteria could attend, speak and propose motions, even though they could not vote. This scheme came close to cross-party agreement;

c) Lord Home's committee report of 1978 recognised, towards the end of a Labour government, that the *status quo* was indefensible and harmful to good government. His report proposed a two-thirds elected, one-third appointed House, that was plainly intended to combine advantages of both predecessors – election to give legitimacy, and appointment to include members with special contributions. There would be around 400 members. Elections would be by proportional representation (STV) for staggered 6 or 9 year terms, based on Euro-constituencies. But the two-tier proposals of Labour were not adopted, largely under the influence of Lord Hailsham who was convinced both that the Lords would never accept it and that, anyway, non-voting peers would have little braking effect on the 'elected dictatorship'.

But Lord Hailsham himself (as Lord Chancellor in 1982) urged "a predominantly or completely elected assembly elected from constituencies geographically different from those in the lower House and by a method of voting also different to the voting system in operation for the lower House".

The puzzle has been to combine independent-mindedness (that comes from expertise weightier than party influences) with electoral legitimacy. For in the words of Lord Carrington, "No elected body will ever be prepared to accept either a hereditary basis or a nominated basis as giving authority to challenge the elected House."

But elected and appointed members have tendencies to become party creatures – and to mimic the weaknesses of the Commons.

Accordingly, here is proposed a predominantly elected Second Chamber with both appointees and non-voting peers to keep the balance between party pressures and a more general and particular wisdom. Among appointees will be VPs *ex officio*, for example law lords, some bishops, some MEPs and others.

Lord Richard, the Leader of the Lords, is thought to be in favour, like Lord Home, of a two-thirds elected and one-third appointed House. This general balance seems very practical and it is adopted as combining electoral legitimacy with variety of view and expertise. It also happens to be particularly well-suited to the broadened committee system here proposed for the Upper House.

Lord Home's recommendation of staggered elections is also adopted, but for six-year, rather than nine-year terms. Elections every two years (preferably simultaneous with local elections) of one third of the elected VPs would keep government on its toes and encourage sensitivity to changes of opinion in the country.

To achieve this, however, initial terms at the first election need to be of different lengths. One solution would be, first time around, terms, in thirds, of 10, 8 and 6 years – with preference, perhaps, given to youth for the longer terms.

For it would weigh against the stability of the Chamber – and against the independence of elected VPs getting a new kind of calling under way – to start them off with terms shorter that 6 years.

This way after 6 years one third would come up for re-election, a second third after 8 and the third after 10.

The other obvious alternative is for shorter initial terms, from 2 – 6 years, say, in order to ensure quicker response from the electorate – preferably with extra rights to stand for re-election for the short-termers. Another possibility, the comfortable compromise – thirds of 4, 6 and 8 year terms. But any which way a rolling election system gets going.

At the initial stage availability of NVPs for selection would need to be coordinated with the alternative selected. In principle it would seem best for NVPs not to stay beyond 6 years if they were unwilling to stand for election in due course. In the first (preferred) case they could be topped up after 6 years as demands of the new system became clearer.

Too much party control of appointees also needs counteraction; and the current breadth of experience and personality is to be preserved and fostered. (This variety Lord Bryce himself referred to, especially in foreign affairs, education and the countryside.)

Here both clear criteria for the appointment of non-elected voting members and the continuing influence of non-voting peers will encourage independent-mindedness. They will also contribute hugely to the committee system that is advocated here – and generally help to enliven the House.

If combined with an elected majority, appointees judiciously selected for particular functions (an extension of the principle of appointment of law lords – noble 'horses for courses') will increase rather than decrease the authority of the House – and certainly increase its representational usefulness.

Perhaps we may here pay a parting tribute to Lord Bryce whose proposals eighty years ago contained the germs of all these ideas – a part-elected, part appointed Second Chamber with a broad policy function and with both a regional and a foreign slant that can now be taken up in the names of devolution and the European Union. The further we look even now into our democratic needs and available solutions the more often his far-sightedness looks eerie and other-worldly – as well as intensely practical and up-to-date.

We shall now try to sketch the composition of a Second Chamber suitable for the purposes outlined.

If elected members are to outnumber appointees by two to one, the first question is whether such a Chamber will command public respect – not as a rival to the Commons, but on its own terms.

My own judgment is that it will, provided its members are well balanced for the duties assigned to them. Elected members will, anyhow, as we shall see, go through a rigorous selection process before election and their contingent (through STV in regional groupings) will represent party feeling in the country much more accurately, in fact, than general elections have done in the past. The appointees will be there for non-party purposes to extend and systematise, so far as possible, the cross-bench tradition of a large section of the House. If to this combined voting House non-voting peers are to be added with seats in the House, numbers must be carefully controlled.

Lord Home, as we have seen, advocated an elected Chamber of around 400. 500 voting members seems an upper limit (especially if those who wish to reduce the numbers of MPs have their way later). The suggestion here is a voting Chamber of around 420. This allows 3 VPs per Euro-constituency (4 in the largest ones), say 280 in all, plus 140 appointees.

Elected members will carry party flags, almost all of them. Appointees accordingly should be selected on other principles, even though most will, like most of us, have their party sympathies. The way round the all-pervading party ethos seems to be a form of selection for appointees that is determined by specific function.

I suggest 5 contingents of twenty-four plus 20 senior party nominees (hopefully ministers or their shadows, some from all Opposition parties). Some such balance as this might fit the Chamber outlined: 24 law lords, 24 chairmen and deputies, 24 cultural leaders, 24 mayors and regional representatives, 24 MEPs plus the 20 politicos. The law lords are most worthily undisturbed. The intent would for chairmen to have deputies from other parties. The regionals would form the backbone of regional and local government committees. The MEPs would do the same for European Committees. The politicos would include the Lord Chancellor and his shadow, the Leader of the House and his and ministerial (and Opposition) party spokesmen in main areas – foreign, environmental, home, trade, health, employment and education and others.

Since it is important not to undermine the electoral credibility of the Chamber as a whole with the inclusion of the appointees, the way around is to show the need for them.

The crucial point is the difference in function of the Second Chamber from the Commons. Special and varied and individual skills are needed (and have long been available) in the Lords. The best illustration of this is the law lords, whose key role is still undoubted. What is not required is a reflection of the Commons' membership who represent, because they are typical of, the electorate, not because of any special skills. To construct a Second Chamber like the first would be futile and self-defeating. It could do no more than invite animus from the Commons, attacking their own image like a budgie with a mirror. It will be recognised by the public that for a Second Chamber to complement the Commons it will need to be different both in function and membership.

It follows from the new extended function of the Lords here proposed that special skills (and knowledge) will be required. Nobody who is not a distinguished lawyer – or a surgeon or an engineer or a banker – whatever his or her human qualities can double for the distinguished professional in his own field.

The same goes for Anglican bishops. Nor can Anglican bishops speak for those of other religions or even, sometimes, for other Christian churches. Britain is a multi-cultural society. What the Anglican bishops did for Parliament in past generations can now be done by a bench representative of our more open society. Since 1970 the Anglican church has regarded favourably the inclusion of other Christian churches. Perhaps the time has come (and Anglicans will accept) the notion of other religions and cultural groups as well. Once this principle is conceded the problem will at once be exclusion rather than the reverse.

There seems to be a groundswell in the Church of England (see eg the Archbishop of York's comments in *The Times* of Good Friday '98) towards loosening Establishment ties (if only to limit prime ministerial vetos of bishops). Simultaneously, Labour is thought anxious to include wider cultural and religious representation in the Lords. On these issues there may be growing up a consensus without tears.

I am not aware that the question of proportionate allocations between denominations and religions has yet been seriously addressed. Perhaps the Anglican bishops might be reduced to six, with six other Christian representatives and a dozen representing other religions and cultural groups. But this is a very tentative suggestion for a sensitive topic which can only properly addressed, if the principle is agreed, by religious and cultural groups among themselves. Perhaps it should be added here, though, that the idea of more varied representation need not concern those anxious to retain the Established Church (and the same applied anyway to some Anglican suggestions made in 1970).

The appointees are there primarily to strengthen the policy committees in which they would take part, besides their continuing duties as members of a revising and debating Chamber (of which their committees are seen as an organic part). Some (as at present bishops) should be appointees up to a retiring age-limit; others (such as MEPs and regionals sitting ex-officio) should sit only for the length of their qualifying qualifications.

This raises the awkward matter of attendance, which applies in varying degrees with most of the proposed appointees. Law lords and bishops, not to mention MEPs and regional magnificos, have full-time occupations into which their Parliamentary duties have somehow to be fitted. The problem is at its most acute with the law lords, since all of them are to retain their seats, whereas the sitting bishops and culturals, the MEPs and the regionals are only representatives of their fraternities. By contrast the chairmen and deputies would be expected to be full-time Parliamentarians, with an additional salary. The answer can only be one of practical flexibility. All except the law lords and the chairmen/deputies should be appointed from fraternities to represent them, on the understanding that they wish to give enough time to Parliament.

The law lords will in practice be supplemented from retired members (as they often are already) – though that raises another awkwardness inseparable from a Chamber largely composed of the established and distinguished, age attendance-limits. Lawyers are proverbial for retaining their mental agility in old age. Perhaps for ex-law lords and ex-Lord Chancellors age-exceptions should be made. For the other categories of appointees (but for chairmen/deputies only in cases of illness or incapacity), a system of occasional alternates from among the elected VPs should in practice be workable.

A word about the politicos. The new legitimacy of the Second Chamber should attract more attendance from ministers. Besides, it should be seen not only as legitimate but complementary to the Commons. One underlying aim of reform should be to foster friendly co-operation rather than the traditional rivalry of the two Houses. The Upper House will retain its more tranquil approach and use it as a context for quieter and more lasting thoughts, for a more leisurely approach to policy-making and monitoring.

The appointees will win ample respect from their key roles in the new Committee system. We have discussed this as a system. The appointees flesh out the picture. As a tentative picture and for illustration only, it was suggested that the Committees might look something like this:

1. Coordinating Committee, chaired by the overall Chairman or his Deputy;
2. Community Affairs and Human Rights;
3. Finance and Industry;
4. Education and Employment;
5. Foreign Affairs (subcs. A. Environment and Aid; B. Trade and Defence Sales;
6. Environment (subcs. A. Planning and Transport; B. Countryside and Agriculture; C. Natural and Man-made Resources);
7. Health, Community Science and Technology (3 subcs.);
8. European Communities Committee (subcs. as at present);
9. National and Regional Affairs;

10. Law (subcs. A. Constitutional Affairs; B. Legislation (preparation and vetting); C. Law Reform; D. Law and Order and Penal Affairs;

11. Administrative Affairs and Local Government;

12. Ad Hoc.

All Committees would have, and no doubt use, the power to set up sub-committees, which would also have to be satisfactorily manned.

The picture is, I hope, self-explanatory; and it is fairly clear into which Committees the appointees would mostly fit. The politicos should be represented in the coordinating Committee with the Lord Chancellor, the Leaders of the House and of the Opposition.

It is hard to pick out any for special mention. But Committee 9 on National and Regional Affairs will be deeply involved in a continuing (and it is hoped none too precipitate) process of integration of Britain into a new entity – hopefully a revitalised Union – that will affect the lives of all our citizens. This development will proceed in step with Britain's in Europe. The interplay of Committees 8 and 9 should be an example of interplay of all of them. For the policy-making process generates overlaps in both agendas and subjects.

Committees 11 and 12 are last but not least. Professor Tivey sees the expansion of the Second Chamber into the field of 'executive affairs' – quangos and local government finance to name but two. We see this as an extension at the bottom, just as prelegislative influence extends at the top the single organic process of government. Ad Hoc has covered (and will) anything that suddenly worries the public.

Now for the appointees' selection. There are strong arguments for avoiding direct prime ministerial or party nomination. Perhaps a rational compromise is for such nominations to be vetted by a joint standing committee of both Houses, who would have special responsibility to be satisfied of the candidates' suitability for their very particular jobs.

Such a system of selection gains in effectiveness by having clear slots for candidates; and by drawing both Houses into the selection process. Moreover the standing reproach of prime ministerial and party appointments is the political abuse of patronage. Clear choice of horses for courses short-circuits that complaint.

If the appointee Voting Peers act as the skeleton of the revitalised House, the elected Voting Peers gave it weight and muscle.

Since they are to constitute two-thirds of the Chamber it is their presence and energies that will determine its success or failure. They must accordingly be suited both to the functions and demands of the House. These are not quite the same as those of MPs with whom unnecessary conflict is so far as possible to be guarded against. The special requirement of their mode of election is accordingly to ensure i) their suitability for the Lords' new holistic approach to government scrutiny and legislation; ii) their electoral legitimacy; and iii) their interconnections with EU institutions and new devolved assemblies.

Lord Bryce long ago proposed their indirect election by MPs regionally grouped. This would have the effect of ensuring members of the Upper Chamber who commanded the respect of the Commons (thereby – besides other safeguards – minimising the prospect of unnecessary clashes). But it may be that direct input from the Commons is now more appropriate for the selection of those appointee Voting Peers whose seats are not a direct function of their status (such as law lords). That anyway is the approach adopted here. For independence from the Commons of elected VPs is as crucial a conception as avoidance of frictions; and the public is more insistent than it was in Bryce's day in deciding who shall represent it.

Moreover there is a structure waiting that was not available in Bryce's day (as the Home Report among others recognised) – the Euro-constituency. Election by regional groupings of these is ready to hand and satisfies democratic aspirations.

Regional grouping within an European context will also concentrate the electorate's mind on the two substantive, new and continuing issues – devolution and Europe – that have primarily necessitated the elections in the first place. Among the appointees will be MEPs from some of the same constituencies, as well as senior representatives from devolved assemblies.

All Euro-constituencies will elect at least 3 VPs (and the few biggest 4). So all should get at least their first two choices in the STV system proposed in the Home Report. (The larger the groupings the more mathematically correct will the proportions be.) But in practice the groupings will probably reflect the regional divisions as now soon to be proposed. It is simple to suggest one grouping each for Scotland, Wales and Northern Ireland – assuming that the new constitutional arrangements allow for it (as presumably the Unionist majority would think it should). Maybe around six groupings would suit England, so far the empty seat at the devolution banquet.

A proportional advantage for the nations over the English regions may be appropriate. Since the national/regional slant of the Upper House is aimed at countering the centrifugal forces of nationalism enshrined in Parliaments before an overall constitutional scheme is in place, a weighting in favour of the nations over the English regions may ensure that the national interests are clearly heard at the centre.

So nine regions are suggested with candidates grouped within them. Many have suggested staggered elections, perhaps of a proportion only of VPs, to allow for changes in political sentiment during Parliaments; and that is adopted here. Six-year terms (perhaps not renewable more than twice) would seem appropriate eventually, with elections of a third every two years to coincide with local elections in May. Those who had served more than three terms, if they have still fire in their bellies, would be strong candidates for appointment. But VP candidates should not be eligible to stand if they will attain the age of 75 during their term.

If these renewable six-year terms are thought appropriate for elected VPs, then the same terms should suit appointees, except those whose seats depend directly on eligibility through other appointments (law lords, bishops, MEPs, national/regional representatives, mayors and the like), who will be replaced as their functions lapse. Probably most should retire at 75, however, except perhaps such law lords as retire from the Appeals Committee but wish to continue to sit as VPs for a further five years (when some addition to the law lords' sitting allocation should be allowed).

Top-ups by by-election and appointments should go on the basis that replacements stand in the shoes – except for age – of the members placed.

We come to NVPs and the closely related subject of selection of VP candidates.

Elections are to find suitable peers to man powerful new committees set up to debate and scrutinise in an authoritative way government policy (and especially omissions from it) from a wider and longer perspective than that regularly taken by the House of Commons. Fears of conflict with the Commons' functions will be further curtailed by an explicit understanding that the Lords do not intervene in matters of current government policy and finance – though wide-ranging policy recommendations cannot avoid future expenditure implications. Elections must satisfy two different criteria: they must by their openness satisfy the public that the Lords is peopled by their representatives; and elections must be geared to identifying those best suited to carrying out the newly defined functions of the House of Lords. There need be no conflict between these criteria. The nub of these proposals is to proceed through the elections in two phases – first selection, then election.

In different ways both Parliamentarians (both MPs and Lords) current and in future – and through them of course their parties – and also government would have a say in selecting, out of willing candidates, the Lists of possible members of the Lords – not 'papabiles', but 'lordables'. And then the lordable should submit to public election.

By this means the two criteria of membership would be satisfied at different stages of the election process. The first stage would be geared at the functional requirement of identifying as big a pool as possible of those able and willing to do the job. In elections for the Lords (as opposed to Commons' elections) reliance cannot be put on just letting the ambitious and party-minded put themselves forward and get elected. At the second stage the public will have the chance to say which of the lordables they do and which they do not want to represent them. So only those who can do the job will have the chance to get elected; but of those only those will get elected that the public finds acceptable.

There is nothing in fact particularly startling in this concept. The vast majority of MPs go through a rigorous vetting process at the hands of their parties before they have any real chance of being adopted as constituency candidates. Sometimes one wonders at the parties' criteria and consequently the candidates who get through their screening process. But a measure of randomness contributes no doubt to the tapestry of the Commons. Anyhow no selection process is perfect; but the principle of MPs' selection would not be far different from the proposals here for the Lords – provided the different functions of the two Houses are taken into account.

Qualification to be an MP should be recognised as significantly different from qualification to be a member of the House of Lords. The hoops the two sets of Parliamentarians need to have gone through differ as do their Parliamentary functions.

At the same time, a spell in the Commons will be a powerful aid, other accomplishments being equal, to effectiveness in the Lords. It is far from being only the convenience and personal debts of governments that has led to the elevation of so many ex-MPs to the Lords in the past. Experience of the Commons has long been recognised as a huge advantage for Lords members who are to be ministers; and it is intended that this opportunity should continue in their House as reformed. An understanding of the pressures on MPs should be generally well-represented in the memory-bank of the Lords; for though, as will appear, their selection will depend on some share of specialist or professional skills, they will need also, if they are to do their job in a statesmanlike fashion, to be practical politicians also.

It is intended that henceforward the two Houses of Parliament regard it as a virtue, instead of a covert tribute to practical necessity, to work together. For analysis of policy options for the future leads to action then – what the Lords say in 2000 will come up for the decision in the Commons in say 2002 or 2004. Integration of the two Houses and of their membership is as crucial as the separation of their functions.

Part of the new urge towards downsizing, towards popularising, towards the eradication of stuffiness and historical mumbo-jumbo from the machinery of government, is an impatience with a slavish adherence to outmoded formulae, protocol, ceremonial.

For a long while quaintness was acceptable, if only as a tourist draw for kiddies and Americans. But that sentimental attachment to old forms for oldness' sake has vanished. The people has become more sophisticated. It no longer identifies the wisdom of tradition with games theory. It prefers football and efficiency. A pretense that neither House is aware of what is going on in the Other Place no longer amuses; and in so far as such pretense is an excuse for Parliament's failure to act as an effective constitutional unit, it is no better than a nuisance.

So the renewed House of Lords should be geared to complement the House of Commons, not to be in competition with it. It follows that the personnel for the new House should suit its special role; and we should accordingly expect it to be less than likely that selection methods found suitable for the Commons would also suit the Lords.

The concept of the interrelation recommended here between the Lords and Commons might be called strategic back-up for the tacticians in the front line of public representation and government control. Now strategists and tacticians are very different animals, different in experience as well as temperament – although some of each group occasionally develop into the other, generally under pressure of circumstance.

No doubt a kindred intention underlies the practice of elevating as life peers to the Lords men and women of established distinction in many professions besides politics. The strategy of this book is to build on and systematise the best of earlier practice. The requirement however to fill specific committees for the scrutiny of identified areas of policy may lead to a more focussed approach to deciding which of the great and the good should be thrown into the pool out of which election to the Lords is henceforth to be effected.

A similar perception explains the respect won throughout Whitehall by cross-bench Lords, many of whom are hereditaries. Preservation of the crossbench element in the Lords would be a natural consequence of the criteria here considered for inclusion in the renewed House. For what crossbenchers bring to this party is a broad and non-partisan approach to intractable and continuing political and social problems for which no definitive solution is in the short run even conceivable, let along practicable, since policy, good or bad, will inevitably grow by stages and generations, like Russian dolls.

Obvious examples are, implications at home and abroad of coordination of trade and economic policy, of race relations and minorities, of trade with technology transfer to the poorer South of the world, of environment and food production, of health and education, of European cooperation. None of these regions of policy should be left to the hugger-mugger studies of civil servants and the propagandist wheezes of spin-doctors or to populist governments, which neither separately nor together are always competent to build into their policy considerations the underlying aspirations, hopes and fears of the public.

To satisfy this requirement the only feasible method is to define the job and to fill it by election. A two-phase system is proposed for doing this – of selection and then election. The first is in two stages, preselection and selection proper. Selection is itself divided into two rounds.

For ail Voting Peers are there for a demanding and skilful job. This applies no less to those elected than to those appointed. There is a fashionable idea going the rounds among populists who pride themselves on some knowledge of antique Athenian institutions (but apparently less of their history) that VPs should be selected by lot. But being a Parliamentarian is a hard-won skill. Nothing is more firmly and immediately instilled into newly elected MPs (especially by the whips) than their need to learn. Since their function is to be more subtle even than MPs', it is advisable that some VPs should have learnt some of their skills before taking up their seats.

Since Voting Peers will be professionals (whether elected or appointed or *ex officios*), they should have salaries and allowances comparable with those of MPs. *Ex officios* already with salaries should have at least generous allowances (and preferably more-than-nominal supplements to their official salaries).

There is a vague notion associated with antique wool-gathering (appropriate more to be sat on than to stuff the sitter) that the Upper House should be some kind of popular jury. Which demonstrates a further misunderstanding, this time of how a court works also. Parliamentarians are required within their sphere of competence to be both judge and jury.

It seems even desirable that VPs should have some experience of Parliamentary life before they are elected. This is where the Non-Voting Peers come in.

For it is proposed that Non-Voting Peers should constitute the pool out of which the Parliamentary joint standing committee should select candidates for the VP elections. NVPs should continue to have the right to sit, speak and propose motions (subject to attendance rules – probably one third of sittings, which has often been adopted in the past as a fair criterion of commitment). But they should not be entitled to vote or be paid more than the going attendance rate.

Appointment of NVPs, especially by those parties under-represented in the current Lords, can be less stringent than either appointment of VPs or selection to stand in VP elections. Hereditaries will also get a chance to be selected as VP candidates. There is even an argument for VPs to have the option for a child (male or female – whether or not, perhaps, the eldest of either)) to inherit, on their death or retirement, the right to sit as a NVP. So a tradition would run on but with neither party nor gender bias – if we accept the assumption that children follow their parents' politics.

In the past there has been strong opposition among the hereditaries to the notion of non-voting peers. It is understandable that with the centuries behind them they would like the vote as well as the rights to sit speak and propose motions. But it is no longer politically possible for them to retain this right without some merit other than birth established (whether election or rigorous appointment); nor is it reasonable that in a modern democracy they should expect it.

There was however a second reason for the peers' anxiety to keep their vote in the unreformed House of Lords that deserves serious thought. Despite their Tory bias their Lordships have been conscientious opponents of the 'elective dictatorship' – the potential oppression of minorities from strong party government led by all-powerful prime ministers and unquestioning MPs. It was this consideration that inspired Lord Hailsham's entrenched opposition (especially before 1979) to the notion of a two-tier House.

Guardianship of the constitution – however imperfectly separated in any Parliamentarian's mind from party advantage – has been an abiding concern and function of the Second Chamber, and should continue to be so.

But the hereditary voting right of peers to block for a year oppressive legislation has been an impediment altogether too fragile to control overmighty prime ministers – and for many compelling reasons. The most obvious is that the democratic authority of hereditaries is so puny that when push comes to shove a prime minister with a comfortable Commons majority can and will ride roughshod over it, the more easily because the hereditaries will almost inevitably be accused of defending some interest of their own (however peripheral). Furthermore they will probably lose their voting right anyway as a Pyrrhic backlash to their opposition, and the constitution will end worse balanced than before their intervention.

With the exception of their right to veto prolongation of Parliaments beyond five years (which anyway is an absolute veto not subject to the delay limitation and which none – least of all in this book – are agitating to remove) the Lords' current constitutional rights are rightly seen (in the current balance between the two Houses) as both inadequate to control and ill-suited to forestall an 'elective dictatorship'. Even the five-year rule is protected more by political reality than the Lords' authority. Any government seeking without overwhelming national support (eg in time of war) to prolong its life invites summary punishment when a general election is finally held. Even for an unpopular government to go to its full term (as Mr Major's did in 1997) can be electorally damaging.

Moreover though it is the hard truth that as a result of their dubious legitimacy, the Upper House as a whole (life peers no less than hereditaries) has in practice already long since enjoyed little more sitting, speaking and moving rights. A vote which only delays for a while and invites only threatenings and slaughter is not much of an asset, and a wasting asset at that.

What sways opinions is a good speech, well-timed and well-publicised. Such speeches in the Lords have frequently over the years had clear political influence that far outweighs the weight of any single vote. A right for a non-voting peer (whether hereditary or a life peer) to speak in an authoritative Upper House might well be thought more valuable than such a right combined with a vote in the current House.

A resource altogether more effective against the elective dictatorships of prime ministers and their Parliamentary parties is an Upper House that can argue on equal terms with government, on the basis of the same information and with the requisite electoral authority; and that can even on occasion forestall oppressive governments before they are committed, in manifestos or anywhere else, to carve in stone laws of 'Medes and Persians that alter not'. For it is the predilection of populist governments (Tory and Labour) to commit themselves (whether in election campaigns or after) to ill-thought-through and undebated legislation that has led to undemocratic government and Parliamentary impotence.

It has therefore been the objective here to erect a comprehensive barrier of Parliamentary consultation and debate to power-hungry governments that both increases the authority of the Upper House and limits the need for the formal increase of its powers. By the same token participation in such a House, even without the vote, for non-voting peers (whether hereditary or life peers) might be thought by some, especially those who rate their power to persuade, to be worth their renewed attendance. For it there are peers of established ability who have been troubled both by the lack of credibility of the House and its treatment by the Commons whose contributions as NVPs in a revitalised Chamber might soon be valued.

But the chief arguments for retaining NVPs are the retention of variety of membership and expertise, together with a build-up of experience among those going on to stand for election as VPs. Breadth and depth of experience have been the Lords' strength. The party appointments of NVPs to make up pool numbers will have a side-effect – the continual introduction of new blood from all walks of public life, practical no less than cultural. There will be, let us say, representatives of TUC and CBI alongside those of ethnic minorities. That is a fine safeguard against the oppression of minorities.

The proposal accordingly is for a phased election of that two-thirds of the voting Upper Chamber which is to be elected. These members are to be professional legislators whose function, in partnership with the remaining of specialist appointees, is to ensure continuity of Parliamentary control of government policy and legislation from conception through to implementation.

Into this seamless robe will be woven scrutiny of government policy and prelegislation, debate and legislation, executive and administrative action.

But in relation to current central government programmes, the Upper House will, as now, have primarily a revising role. And the House will continue to have no say in money Bills – though this will not inhibit debate and discussion about financial and economic policies, especially in those committees concerned with related topics.

It is recognised that this line, between planning and implementation, will often be broad and fuzzy. For thinking leads to action (and generally the sooner the better). But disputed demarcation lines are the stuff of politics; and their fair resolution is a test of a healthy Parliament.

Finding and preparing elected members of the required calibre will be a serious and difficult process. So a phased process of qualification is proposed, based on a progression from non-voting to voting status.

The system proposed is this. First a preselection process from among existing peers (hereditary and life peers) to establish sitting and speaking rights; then a selection process (probably itself in two stages) to establish candidate lists; and finally public elections by STV for nationally/regionally grouped constituencies.

Preselection will narrow down Non-voting Peers to those who are willing to meet minimum attendance requirements. Regular attendance' has been thought of in the past as requiring attendance at a third of all sittings; but for this purpose a requirement of a quarter of sittings may be enough. NVPs will receive nothing more than an attendance allowance; and it is urgent to attract sitting members in the prime of life (men and women) who will be leading busy lives and willing later to stand as VPs.

To ensure a fair pool for national elections, political parties (except generally Tories, to counteract the current imbalance) will be encouraged to nominate additional candidates suitable and keen for this coming job (especially the youthful and women). However these nominees will not be required to undertake to stand, only to meet the minimum attendance requirements.

It is suggested that all eligible peers (including these nominees) who are prepared to undertake the attendance qualification should be welcomed for one 6-year term as NVPs (except those, say, 72 at the beginning of their term). This will allow most current life peers as well as distinguished hereditaries, to continue for a while; and also, subject to age, to decide whether to seek to stand next time around as VP candidates.

After their 6-year term if they are not willing to go through the selection process (perhaps also if they are not in fact selected, certainly after two attempts), they should stand down in favour other and fresh first-termers, to allow for fresh and younger blood.

There is another good reason for retaining a large contingent of first-termers – the cross-bench factor for which the Upper House has been so long respected. Any system of public election nowadays will unavoidably have a party bias. But those who do not intend to go on to election will have every incentive to retain a sturdy independent-mindedness, which will not, however, be subject to the standard moan that non-elected Parliamentarians are slowing the government's legislative progress. But, if persuasive, they will be heard.

The selection proper for VP candidature should be more rigorous – perhaps in two rounds.

First there could be a compilation of a List by and from among the peers themselves. Or in fact Lists. For it is unreasonable to suppose that members of one party would be the best to select lordables to represent another. But the objective at this point would be to ensure that all Lordables going further would have the endorsement of at least one body of Parliamentarians. Many recently have referred with approval to the old method of securing representative contingents of Scottish peers by selection from and among themselves. Such procedures encourage *esprit de corps* among the peers themselves.

Then maybe here should be a further scrutiny by a joint standing committee of both Houses. This is not unlike Bryce's suggestion, except that candidates would then be required to submit to public election. Involvement by MPs at this stage will foster cooperation between the Houses later. The emphasis in both rounds should however be suitability for the special job in hand. It is to be hoped that not too many NVPs will be created as political place-men-and-women. In the second round candidates would be expected to nominate at least three committees, on any two of which they would be willing to serve, and to defend their suitability for that function.

Nevertheless there are a number of ways in which NVP lists can be drawn up. So no attempt in detail is made to prescribe which should be adopted. That would be a matter for rules which the two Houses would draw up in consultation with the Government and Opposition parties. The probable solution is a system of committees which would be graced with the name of an Electoral College.

Lest it be thought however that NVPs will have no useful function unless selected for election or indeed elected, it is to said here that, although they cannot vote, NVPs can and should be encouraged to speak and move both in committees and on the floor of the House, in any procedural frame. Their influence, though naturally inferior to VPs', need not be less in practice than the contributions of many active peers now: it would depend on their persuasiveness and personal authority. Besides, NVPs should include subject to retiring age, all ex-VPs

Moreover NVPs would add to the variety of attitudes expressed, to the cross-bench elements and the creative youth of the Chamber. It is hoped that there will be an increasing number of women nominees also. But beside the vigour of youth – and quite as essential – the House of Lords will require participants with the ripeness to consider major policy issues in perspective.

Ageism (which means the young consigning their elders to oblivion before their time) is a wholesale robber of experience; and such losses, especially in a House whose function is to look beyond the political imperatives of the moment, the public can ill afford.

On the other hand there are undoubtedly too many Lords members who are over, say, 55 – and far too few women. Among hereditaries who wish to join the ranks of NVPs, a daughter, especially where there are no sons, might be made eligible when over 25. Furthermore it is of course a heresy (but one more will not hurt, so here goes…) to suggest that life peers and later all Voting Peers should have the option (perhaps on retirement, not just on death) to pass on eligibility to a Non-Voting Peerage to a son or daughter (over 25). For tradition and training counts in the formation of character and interests; and it is clear also that all NVPs of whatever provenance must go through a rigorous system of selection and then public election before getting the vote in Parliament.

The elections themselves will require some considerable wastage of candidates, though in a system of STV by large groupings, reasonable predictability of success and failure can be used to keep the disappointed candidates within manageable limits. It is suggested that unsuccessful candidates (or those who have served a term as VPs) should always be entitled to sit for a further 6-year term as NVPs, and, subject to age stand again for election, whether at the end or during that term.

So we have a programme to people our Second Chamber for new and greater purposes; but it is based, I hope, on the best experience and theory of the past.

But always to remember: the validity of this programme (and of all the competing programmes sure to be canvassed in the coming months and years) depends on whether the public feels, after it has had good time and opportunity to think things through, that this the best way to satisfy its, the electorate's, new-found confidence – the political confidence to take its part in government – the confidence which Parliament till now so woefully failed to give generous rein.

For our democracy is a troika of people, government and Parliament. Wish them *bon voyage*.

A Summary of Recommended Reforms

The Aim: a popular Second Chamber.

The bulls-eye: a House of Lords in a Parliament that represents the British People to their Government on equal terms.

Methodology:
examine the Lords' current activities;
decide how they could be thematically extended;
and only then:
decide on structural/institutional changes.

Principal conclusion: logical extension of the Lords' current activities could allow them without structural change to carry out all proposed functions, except a) interlocking with the European and devolved Parliaments/Assemblies, and b) the continuing – but with authority – their function as 'constitutional guardian'.

A Popular Second Chamber's Functions:
are those of a Second Chamber

i. taking the second part in a Parliament of two Houses which splits integrated scrutiny of government (from policy-making and prelegislative preparation through legislation to executive and administrative action) into complementary functions between them – that is, in a unified Parliament of diverse functions which reflects our diverse country;

ii. concentrating (with independentmindedness and expertise) on:

a) policy formulation in all fields, b) non-controversial legislation and revising Commons legislation, and c) scrutiny of government methods of executive and administrative action -

but leaving to the House of Commons:

a) prelegislative consideration of Bills as a first step to its dealing with all controversial and mainstream government legislation, b) scrutiny of current government policy (especially financial policy), and c) case by case issues through Commons Departmental Select Committees;

iii. interlocking with the European Parliament and the new devolved Parliaments/Assemblies to ensure integrated popular representation in government;

iv. enjoying the authority derived from clear functions and (mainly) public election, to act as 'guardian of the constitution';

v. securing the above by the development from current Lords' committees (particularly their European Communities Committee and their Science and Technology Committee) of a new comprehensive committee system – initially 12 plus sub-committees (together with its new secretariat with civil service backing, to be shared with the Commons); while

vi. retaining (and developing) its current functions.

The Second Chamber's Powers

An incremental approach to Lords' reform encourages the minimum of changes to the Second Chamber's powers. For example the Lords' right to veto prolongations of Parliaments would remain.

The proposal here is for the one-year delaying power to remain, except for constitutional Bills, when the 1911 Parliament Act's 2-year delay would be reactivated.

This extended delaying power could be reinforced, at the option of the Second Chamber, by a power to demand a referendum to be monitored by an independent authority.

But the above balance is predicated on a change (the only one suggested exclusively for the Commons) to four-year maximum instead of five-year Parliaments. For manifestos and mandates get progressively stale after two years of a Parliament.

The Lords' power to reject subsidiary legislation would remain.

Composition of Second Chamber

An amalgam is proposed of Lord Bryce (1918), Labour (1968) and Lord Home (1978); for the aim is at constructive consensus.

A two-tier Chamber is proposed of Voting and Non-voting Peers (VPs and NVPs).

VPs would be two-thirds elected by proportional representation (STV, regionally grouped – including Scotland, Wales and Northern Ireland – by Euro-constituencies); and one third appointed. Both election and appointment would target functions of the Second Chamber as above. VPs would number about 420.

All elections and appointments (after transitional provisions) would be initially for six years. Initially one third would be elected for ten years, one third for eight, one third for six (priority for longer initial terms being given to youth). Thereafter elections of one third of electeds every two years. By-elections and top-up appointments as required by vacancies.

Appointees would normally have the option of a second full six-year term; but *ex officios* would be replaced by their successors in office. (But age limits for all.)

VPs and appointees would have professional salaries (extra unless *ex officios* – who would be allowed at least generous attendance expenses). For NVPs, attendance allowance only.

NVPs would have speaking rights etc but no vote. NVPs would be allowed subject to age limits one initial six year term; but to continue thereafter they would have to go through a selection process aimed at public election. Ex-VPs subject to age could continue as NVPs..

Preselection for NVPs first six-year term – only – (but subject to age-limit) would depend exclusively on undertaking to attend at least one quarter (or perhaps one third) of all sittings. With those limitations, all current peers would be entitled to sit. Hereditary rights would continue as NVPs. VPs would have an option to nominate a child (male or female), if over 25, as NVP on retirement or death. NVPs would thereby provide a regular stock for VP selection.

Selection with a view to election would be in two rounds. First parties would draw up lists out of available NVPs, including additional appointments to allow for a sufficient pool of all main parties. Then a joint standing committee of both Houses would select from those with a rigorous view to the Chamber's functions. This JSC would also advise on appointee VPs.

Start date for elections and appointments – as soon as may be.

EPILOGUE

Parliament is Britain's most costly constitutional inheritance – costly in an ancient sense. But Parliament is sick, has been sickening for a very long time. Now is the time for healing, for the new millennium.

Two new treasures are even now being added to our heritage, first the European Union, not, foremost, as an economic force but as a 'new and precious model of liberal order in the European state system' (Mr Tim Garton Ash in this week's *Times*), and second a new devolved system of devolved government within the United Kingdom, so that our people may be more immediately represented.

In all these glories the House of Lords has an enduring part to play.

Curtain up.

May Day 1998

SELECT BIBLIOGRAPHY

Lord Alexander – The Voice of the People (Weidenfeld 1997)

W. Bagehot – The English Constitution (1867 – Fontana Ed'n '63)

A. Barnett – This Time (Vintage '97)

V. Bogdanor – The People and the Party System (CUP '81)

V. Bogdanor and Butler (ed) – Democracy and Elections (CUP '83)

K. Bradshaw and D. Pine – Parliament and Congress (Quartet Bks '72)

Viscount Bryce – Letter of Viscount Bryce to the Prime Minister (1918 Cd 9038)

The Constitution Unit – The Reform of the House of Lords (and other Papers, '96-98)

D. Butler and Kitzinger – The 1975 Referendum (2ed'n Macmillan '96)

The Earl of Carnarvon (and others) – Second Chamber ('95)

B. Crick – The Reform of Parliament (Weidenfeld '64)

A. V. Dicey – Law of the Constitution (1885-1915)

Erskine May (ed Boulton) – Parliamentary Practice (21ed'n '89)

S. Finer (and Others) – Comparing Constitutions (OUP '95)

S. Finer (ed) – Adversary Politics and Electoral Reform (Wigram '75)

B. George and Evans – Parliamentary Reform, the Internal View

Ph. Giddings and Drewry – Westminster and Europe (Macmillan '96)

B. Hadfield – Whether and Whither the House of Lords? (NI L Q '84)

I. Harden and Lewis – The Noble Lie (Hutchinson '88)

Lord Home – The House of Lords: Report (Cons Rev Ctee '78)

House of Lords Library – House of Lords Reform Proposals '68-'96

House of Lords Library – The Salisbury Doctrine ('97)

D. Judge (ed) – Politics of Parliamentary Reform (Heinemann '83)

D. Lasok – Law and Institutions of the EU (6ed'n Butterworths '94)

Lib Dems – Here We Stand (FWP6, '93)

I. Loveland – Constitutional Law (Butterworth '96)

J. Maltese – Spin Control (US)

J. Morgan – the House of Lords and Labour Government '64-70 (OUP'75)

F. Mount – The British Constitution Now (Heinemann '92)

Tom Nairn – The Enchanted Glass (Picador '88)

P. Riddell – Parliament Under Pressure (Gollancz '98)

S de Smith and Brazier – Constitutional and Administrative Law (7ed'n Penguin '94)

D. Shell and Beamish – The House of Lords at Work (OUP '93)

C. Turpin – British Government and Constitution (Weidenfeld '90)

White Paper – House of Lords Reform (Cmnd 3799 '68)

Index